The
8
ESSENTIAL SKILLS

FOR
SUPERVISORS
& MANAGERS

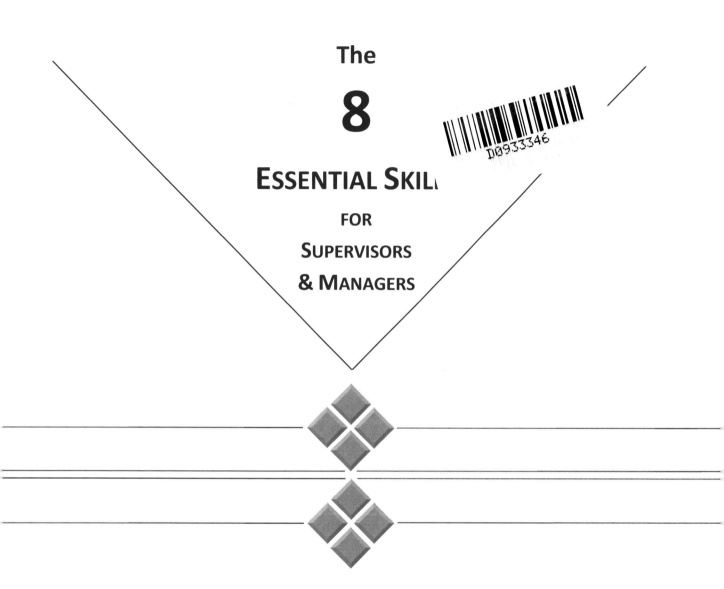

Paul Knudstrup

MCG Press
P.O. Box 61
Lawton, MI 49065

Manufactured in the United States of America

Cover Designed by: Carol Derks

Edited by: Jan Andersen

Library of Congress Cataloging-in-Publication Data
Knudstrup, Paul.

The 8 Essential Skills for Supervisors & Managers
Paul Knudstrup

1. Management. 2. Supervision. 3. Self Improvement. 4. Decision Making.
5. Performance Management. 6. Problem Solving. 7. Leadership.
8. Managing Change. 9. Work Relationships. 10. Personal Growth

ISBN# 978-0-9821817-0-6

Library of Congress Control Number: 2010902614

What Others Are Saying . . .

"A well-written, practical, and insightful book that should appear on the must-read list for everyone who wants to enhance their management and leadership effectiveness. "

Joan Gurvis   Managing Director   Center for Creative Leadership, Colorado Springs

"The 8 Essential Skills outlined in Paul's book provide an excellent road map for leaders at all levels."

Brent Butler   Director Human Resources   Parker Hannifin-Hydraulic Systems Division

"If you manage others, this book is a must for your toolkit! The 8 Essential Skills are outlined in a simple, smart, and useful way to help you become a better leader."

Mart Sedky   Director, Organizational Development   Kansas City Power & Light

"This book is a great tool for managers at every organizational level. It provides valuable insights and clear direction for enhancing your people management skills."

W. Ford Kieft III   President/CEO   Select Bank

"Paul brings a unique combination of insight, practical experience, and innovative thinking to managing people. This book is a valuable tool that a manager can pick up and use each and every day!"

Bill Ruud   President   Shippensburg University

"I have worked with Paul for a number of years and am delighted he has put his very useful concepts into this book. The 8 Essential Skills will give you the knowledge you need to build a winning team."

Christine Stasiw Lazarchuk   Director, Global Consumer Insights   Ford Motor Company

"This book represents Paul's depth and breadth of expertise, and it's a must read for anyone who manages and supervises people."

Rev. Dean Francis   Senior Pastor   First United Methodist Church of Evanston, Illinois

"A terrific guidebook for the journey into management. The 8 Essential Skills is thorough, understandable, to the point, and filled with easy-to-identify-with lessons that can readily be applied to everyday issues and challenges."

Al Vicere   Executive Education Professor of Strategic Leadership   Penn State University

"When building your team, The 8 Essential Skills charts a proven pathway for success."

Brent Reinke   Director   Idaho Department of Correction

"Paul has done a great job of presenting important, fundamental principles in a simple and easy-to-read manner that all of us can use every day in our careers and personal lives."

Tom Schlueter   President   Keystone Community Bank

"Very thoughtful and thought provoking. Paul's book is a valuable resource for any manager or supervisor who wishes to improve their skill set."

Pat DiGiovanni   Deputy City Manager   City of San Antonio, Texas

"Paul's 30+ years working with successful front-line leaders uniquely qualifies him to provide a combination of insight, practical experience, and innovative thinking for managing people. This book demonstrates that becoming a great leader and manager *is* within reach for all who strive for excellence."

Frank Hojnacki   VP Human Resources   Cooper Power Systems

"Paul's book is an essential read for anyone who leads people. The 8 Essential Skills is an important addition to the recommended reading list in my Leadership class. This is 'good stuff'!"

Craig McAllaster   Dean and Professor of Management   Rollins College

"An excellent resource for any manager!"

Susan Wallace Schmitt   Vice President, Human Resources   Rockwell Automation

Acknowledgments

The creation of this book has been supported by some wonderful people I've met during my life's journey. And this is the place where I get to tell you about a few of them. The challenge, of course, is that I can't thank everybody who has helped me along the way. So if you don't see your name here, it isn't because I don't remember you.

For nearly 30 years my friend and colleague Jan Andersen has taken the raw material of my writing and turned it into exactly what I meant to say. This book exists because of her encouragement, support, wise advice, and occasional prodding. She is an amazing editor, writer, and communication consultant.

Mary Jo Asmus asks better questions than anyone I know. I am proud to have her as a colleague and friend. Watching her become a first-class executive coach with a national clientele has been a real pleasure. Having her as my coach has been a privilege.

Gretchen Johnson has the best marketing mind I have ever found and her ideas, advice, and counsel are invaluable. She is another of those "neat to hang out with" people I've been fortunate to know, and a great colleague and friend.

No book ever sees the light of day without a thousand and one details being handled effectively and efficiently. That would be the province of Vicky Scherff, who has researched, recommended, created, adapted, and endured through all of those details. Thank you, Vicky!

In the 1980s, while I was running a university management development center, Jan Andersen recommended I take a look at a two-day program featuring a guy named David Allen. That was the beginning of a long, mutually supportive relationship with a remarkable teacher and thinker. Over the last 30 years David has become a major figure in personal productivity and organizational effectiveness. His California-based firm serves clients around the world, and his landmark book, "Getting Things Done," has been translated into 22+ languages and sold millions of copies. David continues to be a valued colleague and an inspiration.

Over the years I've worked with, advised, and helped develop some excellent managers and leaders. John Bernhard, Doreen Brinson, Dick Dunsing, Russ Gabier, Marge Guthrie, Deither Haenicke, Darrell Jones, Rick Lattimore, Matt Mace, Carl Sachtleben, Anne Thompson, Al Vicere, and others provided models and lessons along the way. Pat DiGiovanni, Bill Larson, Jane McLaughlin, Ron Melchiorre, Brent Reinke, Bill Ruud, Susan Schmitt, and Edie Trent are standouts as managers and leaders, and any organization they serve is a better place for their presence.

Daughter Kiersten and granddaughter Brynn continue to be delights in my life. They remind me that the future is indeed bright, and the next generations will find ways to make this world a better place.

Finally, for more than 30 years I have been married to Susan Shirkey Knudstrup, a talented educator and wonderful partner in life. She amazes me in so many positive ways. I can't wait to see what our next decades together will bring, and I dedicate this book to her.

Paul Knudstrup

Table of Contents

Forward: How to Use This Book   9

Introduction   11

The Job of the Manager

1 The Many Hats You Wear   17
2 What Managers *Really* Do   27
3 Why Managers Fail   35
4 Great Expectations   41
5 The First Step on the Ladder   53

Skill 1 – Managing Yourself

6 Your Personality Preferences   63
7 Your Remarkable Brain   75
8 Your Innate Talents   83
9 A Cluttered Mind   89
10 Choices, Choices, and More Choices   95
11 Managing Your Focus   101

Skill 2 – Communicating for Results

12 Communication 101   113
13 Choices in Verbal Communication   119
14 Nonverbals: The Silent Influencers   123
15 Writing: Communicating When You're Not There   127
16 E-Mail and Texting @ Work   133
17 The Active Art of Listening   139
18 Not *Another* Meeting   145

Skill 3 – Building Successful Relationships

19 Healthy Relationships   155
20 Managing Your Boss   165
21 Creating a Great Work Environment   169

Skill 4 – Managing Others

22 Creating Outstanding Performance   183
23 Improving Individual Performance   189
24 Managing Your Team's Performance   195
25 Feedback and Evaluation   203

Skill 5 – Managing Change

26 The Dynamics of Change   217
27 Creating Successful Change   225
28 Change: Large and Small   237

Skill 6 – Solving Problems and Making Decisions

29 What's the Problem with Problems?   249
30 Solving Real Problems, Every Day   259
31 Creativity: From Decision to Implementation   277

Skill 7 – Leading and Empowering

32 Leaders and Leadership   291
33 Leadership Traits, Skills, and Styles   297
34 Empowering Your Employees   307

Skill 8 – Growing Yourself

35 Setting Developmental Goals   327
36 Creating and Using Action Plans   333

Putting It All Together

37 Putting It All Together   349

Appendix   355

Forward

How to Use This Book

If you're a front-line supervisor or manager – or you supervise staff in those positions – you're busy. In fact, although this book is packed with ideas designed to make your life easier, you're probably way too busy to read it cover to cover.

So we've made it easy for you to use this as a sort of skimable reference book for professional success, offering practical advice regardless of the size or type of organization you're in.

Feel free to approach this book in whatever way makes sense to you, given who you are and where you are in your own professional journey. For example, you can:

- Quickly read the whole book once, then go back and choose the *Skill(s)* you want to review in depth.

- Start at the beginning and work your way through each of the *8 Essential Skills* over time.

- Look at the table of contents to select the *Skill(s)* you most want to learn about right now, then read those chapters.

- Look at *Chapter 37*, "Putting It All Together," for a quick overview of the main concept behind each *Skill*, then choose the one or two *Skill(s)* you want to read about first.

- Just pick up the book and randomly open to any chapter – *sort* of a managerial potluck. You're bound to find something of value.

Regardless of where you begin, we suggest you read the first section, "The Job of the Manager," before jumping into the individual *Skills*. This will help you understand the various roles played by supervisors and managers. It will also give you the foundation for the *8 Essential Skills*.

The *Appendix* contains a number of references, examples, and tools that will help you on your journey to success. For instance, if you're interested in reading more about managing, personal development, or leadership, take a look at the *Other Recommended Readings and Resources* list for some good ideas. And if you want to learn more about useful assessment or problem-solving tools, you'll find information about several great instruments.

Dip in. We hope this helps.
Enjoy your journey!

Introduction

The material in this book has been in development during the last 10 years, growing out of a 40-year career managing people, departments, budgets, facilities, programs, projects, and bottom lines. During all those years I read, listened, practiced, studied, and thought about how we manage ourselves and each other in organizations of all sizes and types. What has emerged is a book about the human realities of being a supervisor or manager.

If you're a new supervisor, a recently promoted manager, a team member who is now leading the team, a project professional who is responsible for managing projects with other independents, or you currently manage any of these types of people, then this book is for you. That's because it gives you the keys to success – *The 8 Essential Skills for Supervisors & Managers.*

Front-line supervisors and middle managers (the first and second rungs on the traditional management ladder) have the most difficult, challenging, and exciting positions in any organization. Their work frequently goes unrecognized, but they're absolutely essential to an organization's existence. They usually get grief of some kind coming from both directions – their direct reports and their bosses – but they're in the ideal position to have a positive effect on those same people. And they often don't have enough information about the organization's strategy, but senior management relies on them to manage the employees who must implement that strategy every day.

Having a brilliant and charismatic CEO is great, but that isn't the key to real success in any organization. If anything about organizations has become crystal-clear in the past decade it is this simple fact: the individual unit-level supervisor or manager is the biggest single factor in how engaged, committed, and involved employees are. And that translates into how successful the organization is. It's possible to have a great company without a brilliant CEO, but there's no way that a company can be great without successful front-line supervisors and managers.

The potential value of this book isn't dictated by where you work. The *8 Essential Skills* apply to all levels of management and all types of organizations. Some examples might not directly apply to your situation, but the fundamental concepts you learn will be useful. In fact, you might not actually be a *manager* in the formal sense of supervising employees at all; you might be leading a team of independent contributors and outside contractors who are working on one or more projects. If so, you're still supervising and managing and have responsibility for the success of the project, and you'll still find this book valuable.

The first step, the beginning of this particular road to your future, starts where anything starts . . . inside *you*. Becoming reasonably adept at *Skill 1 – Managing Yourself* may take a few months or a number of years. But regardless of when that self-management light bulb goes on, it's likely to be the driving force that gets you serious about developing your skills. And given the reality of life in the 2010s, all any of us can offer is our skill set, our experience, our reputation, and our track record.

This book is the initial work in a series that will help keep you thinking and growing for years to come. Your comments and suggestions are always welcome.

Paul M.C. Knudstrup   PaulK@MidwGroup.com
Kalamazoo, Michigan   www.MidwGroup.com
June 2010

THE JOB OF THE MANAGER

"Management is about human beings."

Peter Drucker

The Job of the Manager

You've probably heard the saying, "When you are up to your ass in alligators, it is difficult to remind yourself that your initial objective was to drain the swamp."

Most managers can easily relate to that statement. It often seems that really important things – initiatives, projects, and ideas that could make a major positive difference – drown under waves of problems to solve and details to handle. Most experienced managers agree that they sometimes feel overwhelmed and out of control when they try to deal with the challenges and changes they face. They describe what they do as something like herding cats or grasshoppers. It's a job that's complex, ever-changing, challenging, exhilarating, frustrating, satisfying, and never boring.

The traditional view of what it means to be a supervisor or manager has materially changed in the past decade. You may supervise a team or functional unit with a group of full-time employees reporting to you. But these days you're just as likely to manage a variety of people working on several different projects. Some of them might be employees. Others might be employees who officially report to someone else. They might be independent contractors. And then there are freelancers who work for several different organizations. In this era of rapid change, globalization, and contract workers, you need to look beyond past notions of what a supervisor or manager does.

When you're responsible for the results of other people, success means being able to fill a variety of roles at work. If you're like most of us, some parts of the job are easy for you. There are certain roles that you're good at, that just seem like a good fit. But there are other parts of your job that, well, could use a bit of improvement.

If you're new to supervising others or are about to move into that role, the whole thing can be more than a little scary. You may know current or previous managers who you think are positive or negative role models. You could develop your approach to managing based on the successful example of a supervisor you admire. Or you might say to yourself, "When I'm a manager, I'm *not* going to operate the way so-and-so does. What a jerk they are!" Either way, they serve as guides to the kind of manager you want to be.

Since you don't have the luxury of taking months to get up to speed, being successful means understanding what you need to do, learning what you need to learn quickly, and hitting the ground running from day one. In today's challenging economic environment there's little room for business as usual or a casual approach to managing successfully.

This section of the book describes the job of the manager in today's rapidly changing, globally interdependent world. Let's begin with a simple question: "What do managers *really* do?"

Chapter 1
The Many Hats You Wear

Before drilling down to the level of specific tasks and behaviors, it's helpful to get a handle on the bigger picture – the various roles a manager must take on.

A successful supervisor or manager is like a juggler trying to keep lots of balls in the air at the same time. The balls have different shapes and sizes and, to make it even more complicated, they often change in mid-air. I know from personal experience that sometimes it isn't the variety of balls you're juggling that makes things difficult. You just can't ignore any one ball for too long or it will fall to the floor.

> Your only job is talent development.
>
> *Tom Peters*

The Manager's Roles

So what are the manager's different roles? Typically, they include:

- Coordinator, planner, organizer

- Teacher

- Coach

- Technical expert

- Culture developer & keeper

- Interpreter

- Decision maker

- Communicator

- Quality guide & monitor

- Team member

- Team leader

- Relationship builder

> A company finds its destiny by answering three questions: "Who are we," "What do we stand for," and "How do we serve?"
>
> *Tom Chappell*

Coordinator, Planner, Organizer

Traditional business schools teach us that planning and coordinating the work of a team or unit is a core part of any manager's job. But the way that is handled today is very different compared to what was done 20 years ago. In the past the manager served as an expert in a narrow area who planned the work of the team, handed out assignments, and generally kept close tabs on the team. Supervision was often closer, more directive, and involved more "telling."

In today's organizations we see a constantly shifting mix of employees, independent contributors, professional consultants, and outside contractors working on any given project or team. As a manager you're likely to be responsible for a number of different projects. Each will have a somewhat different mix of participants, and you may formally supervise only some of them. The playing field is broader and it involves a wider mix of individual relationships.

In this age of globalization you might find yourself supervising remote workers – employees and independent contractors who work in other countries and time zones. That changes the basic equation of how managers and employees operate, communicate, and work. Planning and coordination will still be an important part of your job, but the look and feel of what that means in daily life will be new.

Teacher

Managers and supervisors work with employees who have a wide variety of skills and knowledge. This means you're frequently placed in the role of teacher with employees, particularly if they're new to your organization or team. You will, in effect, be teaching them how to do their job. At the very least you'll need to teach your employees about the expectations that will affect their success. Your expectations and those of the organization will be hot topics for conversation and instruction, particularly as part of each employee's orientation or "on-boarding" process.

Coach

The role of a coach is different from that of a teacher. As a coach you'll be a guide, motivator, encourager, and supporter in your interactions with employees. When you coach employees you're less focused on telling or showing and more focused on asking questions or involving them in figuring out what needs to be done and how to do it.

When you coach employees you're actively demonstrating your confidence and trust in them. If you don't trust your employees to do their jobs, then you either have the wrong people in the jobs or you haven't sufficiently trained them. In either case the problem isn't with your employees but with you as their manager.

Successful coaches focus attention on their employees' individual talents and strengths rather than their faults. Helping people grow and develop almost always leads to increased enthusiasm and better results. In the coaching role you don't ignore or overlook errors, but your focus will be on discovering the source of a problem and making sure the same error doesn't happen again. Ultimately, coaching involves being more of a "problem identifier" than a "problem solver."

The team with the best players wins.
Jack Welch

Technical Expert

In many organizations the manager of technical workers is a technical person as well. Of course, technical skills are different from managerial skills and the best technicians don't always make good managers. Still, all managers bring a certain technical expertise to their job. It may be skill in a major responsibility in a unit, such as sales or production. Or it may be advanced expertise in a professional area such as engineering or IT.

Whatever your technical skills, your level of expertise will tend to diminish in proportion to the amount of time you devote to nontechnical work. The more you manage, the less likely you are to keep up to date technically. But you need to keep up to speed at least enough to guide the work of your unit. This can be a two-edged sword. On the one hand, you need to have the technical "chops" necessary to be viewed as competent by your employees. On the other hand, if you spend too much time and energy on the technical side, you may be ineffective as a manager.

Culture Developer & Keeper

Every organization has a culture – the way it operates and its values, philosophy, history, and future aspirations. Organizations are like living organisms made up of many parts, with complex relationships, customs, unwritten rules, and patterns of communication.

> Great companies are defined by their discipline and their understanding of who they are and who they are not.
>
> *Howard Schultz*

You have a responsibility to understand the culture of your organization and how your team fits into it. Then you need to be able to pass on that understanding to your team. Where are we going? How will we get there? How does what we're doing fit into the bigger picture of the organization's culture? What norms and standards apply to us? A critical part of this role happens when you bring a new team member on board. This is a particularly important time because your team's cohesion and productivity may dip until the new member's talents and blind spots are fully integrated.

Interpreter

Every organization develops routines and standards. From the gas station or shoe shop on the corner to the biggest governmental agency . . . from the local storefront church to the billion-dollar worldwide nonprofit agency . . . all organizations have rules, policies, and procedures. They may be formal, written, printed in small pamphlets, or stored in loose-leaf notebooks taking up several feet (or yards!) of shelf space. Or they may be informal and unwritten.

Whatever those rules are, as a manager you're responsible for teaching, guiding, interpreting, and explaining the rules to each of your team members. What are the rules, policies, and procedures in our organization? How do we do the work and why do we do it that way? Merely handing down the rules and explaining how to carry them out isn't enough; people need to know *why* so they can truly understand "how we do things around here." Once they understand the what, how, and why, they'll be much more likely to do what needs to be done in the way it should be done.

Decision Maker

Managers make decisions all the time. Who to hire . . . what to have them do . . . what tasks take priority over others . . . which team members should attend a new training program first . . . when to start doing something new . . . when to stop doing something that has been done in the past. Making decisions is part of every manager's daily life.

Some of us enjoy making decisions, seek opportunities to make decisions, and make them quickly (sometimes based on very little information!). Others seem to struggle with making even the simplest decision. They postpone, waffle, beat around the bush, and change their mind a dozen times.

Over time and with practice, you're likely to get more comfortable with this role. You'll see that making decisions too quickly can lead to consequences you hadn't thought of. At other times the decision needs to be made quickly, before you miss an opportunity. Shoot from the hip? Sleep on it? Regardless of how you tend to handle

> What separates those who achieve from those who do not is in direct proportion to one's ability to ask for help.
>
> *Donald Keough*

them, as a manager you must make decisions. (For more about decision making, see *Chapters 29-31*.)

Communicator

No manager can be successful without learning how to be an effective communicator. Too often communication is seen as primarily about speaking, which overlooks other powerful methods. Being able to get your message across in writing (on paper or electronically) is critically important. Also, listening is frequently ignored as a communication skill. And finally, even when you're not saying anything, remember that your body language and nonverbal communication say a great deal. (For more about communication, see *Chapters 12-18*.)

Quality Guide & Monitor

Understanding, upholding, and improving the standards and results that define the quality of work is another basic role for managers. A manufacturing plant must pay attention to how well the goods produced meet the needs of its customers. After all, if what you make fails to meet your customers' needs, will they buy from you again? Likewise, a nonprofit organization must monitor the quality of the services it provides to its clientele. And a government agency must pay attention to how well it meets its legislative mandate and delivers services to the public.

Once you establish excellent customer service, you provide a safe harbor to which customers can always return.

Stanley Marcus

Many organizations have come to grief because of quality problems. Think of FEMA's response after Hurricane Katrina or the IRS in the 1990s – both examples of federal agencies that have had significant quality problems. When comedian Lily Tomlin's character, Ernestine, snorted, "We don't care; we don't have to; we're the phone company," millions of people laughed. Why was it funny? Because it was very real to people who had suffered through the 1-800-WeDon'tCare attitude of the regulated monopoly that used to be the telephone company.

Regardless of what your organization does, you're responsible for understanding and monitoring the quality standards and expectations that apply to your team's work – and for making sure your team understands them too.

Team Member

Managers lead and direct the work of teams in most organizations. However, all managers also play the role of team member. You need to know when to lead and when to let someone else on the team step into the leadership role. Think of it as temporarily setting aside your managerial ego for the good of the team – especially when this results in a more effective team, better decisions, or faster implementation.

When I directed a management development unit in a large organization, I enjoyed making decisions and made them quickly. My staff caught on fast and were happy to bring many decisions to me; they delegated upward very effectively. So I ended up making many decisions they should have been making. At first I thought I was helping them. But because I solved their problems for them, I robbed them of the opportunity to make their own decisions. Eventually, with the help of a key manager who reported to me, I learned that I was not using their skills effectively. Once the light bulb went on, I began to shift my approach. I started saying, "Sure, I'd be happy to discuss your problem with you, but you know the situation much better than I do. When you bring me a problem, please bring your suggested solution." In the long run, this made for a happier team and I had more time to focus on what I really needed to be doing.

Team Leader

Even managers who are adept at deferring to others on the team and leveraging their employees' talents and strengths need to assert leadership, make decisions, and move the team forward. This becomes particularly important when the team has been foundering for awhile, when it's facing an emergency, or when it's heading off in a direction you know will result in disaster.

You need patience to make sure your own push to gain closure and action doesn't get in the way of teamwork and collaboration. It can be a tricky balance. Remember the old saying, "There is no 'i' in 'team'"? It's still true. But there are times when strong leadership is needed. The wise manager learns how to spot those situations and act accordingly.

Over the years I've become especially fond of Perry Smith's statement, "Help me discipline my in-box; don't bring me issues you are competent to decide." Think about the implications of his statement and what it says to your employees. It works well on several levels:

- It says, "There are issues that are within the scope of your job and expertise, and I think you can figure out which issues those are and what needs to be done about them."

- It says, "I'm confident in your ability to make good decisions on those issues and implement them."

- It says, "When you face an issue that you think I can help with, let me know how I can best do that."

- It even says, "You decide what to keep me informed about and when to do so."

What an affirming, empowering viewpoint!

Relationship Builder

No manager, regardless of how brilliant they are, will be successful unless they're able to create and sustain successful relationships with others. Those relationships may be with their direct reports, boss, peers, customers, or other stakeholders. A key to success in building relationships is to invest your time and energy in those that are closest to you and have the potential to create real problems if they go sour. In his book, "The 7 Habits of Highly Effective People," Stephen Covey talks about the concept of an Emotional Bank Account. This makes a lot of sense to me. It's the idea of making regular "deposits" into our relationships with others. So which work relationships in your life could be better? (For more information about building successful relationships, see *Chapters 19-21.*)

Management Roles Self Assessment

Below is a list of the roles of a manager. On a scale from 1-5 (5 = very effective), rate yourself on how effective you feel you are in your current job.

Role	Rating 1 – 5
Coordinator, Planner, Organizer	_____
Teacher	_____
Coach	_____
Technical Expert	_____
Culture Developer & Keeper	_____
Interpreter	_____
Decision Maker	_____
Communicator	_____
Quality Guide & Monitor	_____
Team Member	_____
Team Leader	_____
Relationship Builder	_____

What roles are you really good at? What roles need improving? Keep this in mind as you continue reading.

Management Skills for Success

To become a successful manager you need to develop and refine your ability to play these and many other roles. As with any complex job, you'll be more skilled in some roles than others. To a great extent, your skills have to do with your previous experience, your education, and the role models you've had so far in your career. Your current skills also have to do with your natural talents and the strengths you've developed over time.

But ultimately, your effectiveness as a supervisor will depend on your own attitudes and beliefs. That's because each role requires a positive mindset that continually motivates you to learn new skills and practice them consistently.

This chapter describes the overall framework of being a manager – the different roles you play in leading a team of people. *Chapter 2* puts some meat on the bones of that framework. It lays out the kinds of tasks supervisors and managers do every day.

Chapter 2
What Managers *Really* Do

As you saw in *Chapter 1*, supervisors and managers perform a wide variety of tasks. Some of them are things that all managers need to do regardless of where they work. Other tasks might be unique or unusual managerial activities specific to an organization.

The following skills are typical of those needed by almost all supervisors and managers:

- *Skill 1* - Managing Yourself
- *Skill 2* - Communicating for Results
- *Skill 3* - Building Successful Relationships
- *Skill 4* - Managing Others
- *Skill 5* - Managing Change
- *Skill 6* - Solving Problems & Making Decisions
- *Skill 7* - Leading & Empowering
- *Skill 8* - Growing Yourself

We explore each of these in detail later, but here's a brief overview of each of them.

Skill 1 – Managing Yourself

To successfully supervise or manage others, you first need to successfully manage yourself. This seems obvious, but it's not as easy as it sounds. Specific behaviors are needed for effective self-management, and the good news is that they *can* be learned. Some of these include:

- How you use time

- Your approach to accomplishing the goals and objectives of your unit and organization

- How you recognize and deal with important issues

- How open and approachable you are to your employees and others

- Your willingness to keep up to date technically

- Your level of self-confidence and ego maturity

- Your willingness and ability to make decisions

While the other seven *Skills* are important to your success, *Skill 1* is the foundation for the rest of the *Skills*. Without the ability to effectively manage yourself, you'll constantly be playing catch-up, regardless of your abilities in the other *Skills*.

For more information about *Skill 1 – Managing Yourself*, turn to *Chapters 6-11.*

Skill 2 – Communicating for Results

There's a reason communication is the second essential *Skill*. Much of your success as a professional and a human being is determined by your ability to communicate well. Good communication, like any skill, can be learned, practiced, and perfected. It includes:

- How openly, candidly, and frequently you communicate

- How straightforward you are dealing with employees' performance

- How effectively you conduct team meetings

- How willing your employees are to bring up problems and issues

- How well you write

> Virtually every problem that would show up in your business can be traced back to communications; somebody didn't talk to somebody about something.
>
> *David Allen*

- How well you listen

- How effectively you scan the environment

- How well you present information to others

For more information about *Skill 2 – Communicating for Results*, turn to *Chapters 12-18*.

Skill 3 – **Building Successful Relationships**

According to executive coach Mary Jo Asmus, being a successful manager and leader is all about building successful, healthy relationships. To do this includes:

- Being supportive and helpful to employees

- Knowing how to effectively resolve conflict

- Being willing to confront tough issues

- Involving employees in setting their own goals

- Promoting teamwork

- Creating and sustaining an atmosphere of trust

> Alone we can so do little; together we can do so much.
>
> *Helen Keller*

For more information about *Skill 3 – Building Successful Relationships*, turn to *Chapters 19-21*.

Skill 4 – **Managing Others**

To succeed as a supervisor or manager, you must develop the ability to manage other people. After all, it's your team that needs to get the work done, and they won't be effective unless you manage their performance. This includes:

- Setting challenging objectives with and for your employees

- Being able to appropriately plan and coordinate the team's work

- Defining specific performance standards for each employee

- Meeting regularly with your employees to discuss their performance

- Helping your employees achieve high performance

- Discussing performance problems with employees and seeking their suggestions for improvement

- Using recognition and praise effectively to reward excellent performance

- Recognizing good performance more often than criticizing

- Being committed to developing your staff

For more information about *Skill 4 – Managing Others*, turn to *Chapters 22-25*.

Skill 5 –Managing Change

We live in a constantly changing world, and your ability to understand, implement, initiate, and manage change effectively is critical to your success as a manager. This includes:

- How well you understand and support change in your organization

- How willing you are to look for opportunities to improve your team's results

- How quickly and successfully you let people know when plans and goals change

- How you facilitate change within your group

- How easily you implement changes in direction, priorities, or projects

- How easily you accept imposed or mandated changes

- How willingly you seek out information about necessary changes

For more information about *Skill 5 – Managing Change*, turn to *Chapters 26-28*.

Skill 6 – **Solving Problems & Making Decisions**

An important part of being a supervisor or manager is being able to solve problems and make appropriate decisions about what you and your team need to do. This includes:

- Your willingness to make clear-cut decisions when needed

- Your willingness to involve employees and others in generating ideas, suggestions, and alternatives to complex problems

- Your willingness to consider new information, differing opinions, and viewpoints contrary to your own

- Your ability to solve problems and make decisions with incomplete information

- Your ability to understand the financial implications of your decisions

- Your ability to use critical thinking to weigh alternatives

- Your ability to provide guidance, support, and encouragement to others

A problem is a chance for you to do your best.

Duke Ellington

For more information about *Skill 6 – Solving Problems and Making Decisions,* turn to *Chapters 29-31.*

Skill 7 – **Leading & Empowering**

As your skills grow and you become successful at using the first six *Skills,* you'll develop the ability to empower and truly *lead* your team. Leading and empowering involve a series of high-level behaviors that include:

- Your ability to follow up on important issues and actions

- Your willingness to clarify individual responsibilities within the group

- Your willingness to be open and encourage people to express their feelings and viewpoints, including disagreements

- Your ability to deliberately and consciously empower individuals

- Your ability to keep a positive focus in front of the team

- Your willingness to help others overcome roadblocks and resistance to achieving goals

- Your commitment to individual and team development

The simplest definition of the word "Leadership" is, "the ability to produce change." We used to operate that way; now we operate this way.

Peter Senge

For more information about *Skill 7 – Leading and Empowering,* see *Chapters 32-34.*

Skill 8 – **Growing Yourself**

Success as a supervisor, manager, and leader today requires self-development. You must continually grow and refine your own skills and behaviors or you, your team, and potentially your entire organization will get left behind. This includes:

- Your ability to understand your own strengths, weaknesses, and opportunities for improvement

- Your willingness to ask for and use honest feedback from others

- Your willingness to create and effectively use a personal development action plan

- Your commitment to lifelong learning and personal growth

- Your persistence and willingness to try again and again until you achieve your goals

- Your resilience in the face of change and challenges

- Your willingness to actively encourage self-development in your employees and colleagues

> Leadership depends on influence rather than position, title, or power.
>
> *Robert Cooper*

For more information about *Skill 8 – Growing Yourself*, turn to *Chapters 35-36*.

You may have other ideas about skills and behaviors that help supervisors and managers succeed. As you'll see in the next chapter, too many times these and other useful skills seem to stay in the manager's toolbox. Why?

Chapter 3
Why Managers Fail

Two studies about management failure were conducted in the late 1990s by the Center for Creative Leadership and Manchester Partners. Both noted that approximately 40 percent of supervisors and managers fail *within the first 18 months* in their positions (defined as being fired, demoted, having their job reorganized, or otherwise having their responsibilities significantly changed). In addition, they noted that the vast majority of these new managers failed due to one or more of the following reasons:

- Not understanding their boss's expectations

- Being unwilling or unable to make tough decisions

- Taking too much time to learn the new job

- Failing to build partnerships & cooperative work relationships

- Lacking internal political savvy

- Maintaining an inappropriate work/personal life balance

The Big Six Reasons
Not Understanding Their Boss's Expectations

Expectations are always there. No matter who you are in the organization, you report to somebody else and that person is going to have expectations of you as a manager and supervisor. When those expectations are discussed out in the open and mutually understood, the odds of your success go up considerably. When those expectations are unstated or unclear, it's like stepping up to home plate with two strikes already against you.

Do *you* know what your boss expects from you? Have you discussed and mutually agreed to a shared vision of success for you and the organization? If you answered "no" to either of these

> The only industries that function well are the industries that take responsibility for training. The Japanese, you know, assume that when you first come to work you know absolutely nothing . . . . School isn't preparation for work and never was.
>
> *Peter Drucker*

questions, you have a great opportunity for improvement. First, make a list of what *you* think your boss's expectations are. Then schedule a time to sit down with them and have a discussion about expectations. And yes, this is a critical, top-priority item in your busy life; this may be the single most important meeting you'll have this year.

Being Unwilling or Unable to Make Tough Decisions

It's normal to make your first decisions carefully and thoughtfully. After all, being newly promoted or hired means upper management will keep a close eye on you for awhile. That's fine. And certainly your first or second personnel change will come under close scrutiny. The successful supervisor or manager makes personnel changes carefully, keeping at least their boss in the loop throughout the process.

It's not enough to be good if you have the ability to be better. It is not enough to be very good if you have the ability to be great.

Alberta C., Grade 8

In fact, most of the truly tough decisions you'll face are people-problem decisions. Certain issues can doom a new supervisor or manager to failure, such as being unwilling to confront poor performers positively and help them improve or move on, or ignoring interpersonal disagreements and conflicts. And while the toughest decisions are often people issues, they can also involve equipment, systems, or process problems; new product/service decisions; or other issues posing risk to your team or the organization.

Taking Too Much Time to Learn the New Job

This is the "not getting up to speed fast enough" problem. The days when managers were gradually brought along through a series of carefully planned steps are long gone. Our work force has become highly mobile as the old job-for-life concept has fallen away.

This means we must constantly take on new tasks and projects and operate outside of our comfort zone in an ever-evolving, dynamic, ambiguous environment. Rapid lifelong learning will always be necessary. You need to accept that you'll never feel you're really up to speed. So it's important for you to understand what your boss and others think that phrase means, and then give it your best shot.

Failing to Build Partnerships & Cooperative Work Relationships

Most successful organizations have effectively broken down the walls or silos that once existed among their internal units or teams. People move so frequently in larger organizations, and responsibilities change so quickly, that you can't be successful unless you build effective relationships. Your potential for success in higher levels of management depends on your ability to build partnerships and positive relationships with your boss, your employees, and your peers. In the end, being a successful manager and leader is all about relationships.

Lacking Internal Political Savvy

We may complain about it, but the reality is what we call "office politics" is often simply the relationships that help move an organization ahead. Having internal political savvy means understanding how decisions are made, who has real (positional) power, and who the informal leaders are in your organization. As a manager and leader it's essential that you build a solid internal network within the organization, and that you know how an agenda *you're* pushing will affect other parts of the organization.

> You have to accept whatever comes and the only important thing is that you meet it with the best you have to give.
>
> *Eleanor Roosevelt*

An important part of political savvy is the approach and tone you use. Constantly raising issues in an aggressive, complaining, tactless manner will be seen as being a P.I.A. (Pain In the Ass) by those above you in the organization. As one executive recently said, "If you are constantly in my face, run me down to others behind my back, and generally behave as a pain in my rear end, why would I want to promote you?"

Maintaining an Inappropriate Work/Personal Life Balance

Having balance in your life is generally viewed as desirable. It means taking time to build and nurture your family and other personal relationships as well as your professional network. It might mean volunteering in your community for a cause you believe in. And, yes, it means actually taking vacations. Balance means working hard but not becoming a workaholic. Research has shown that if your workweek regularly goes beyond 52-55 hours, your ability to be productive and make good decisions goes downhill quickly – something that no company wants. Routine 60-70 hour workweeks are a recipe for disaster.

There will be times when a long week (or even a few long weeks) might be necessary, but you can't effectively sustain that kind of schedule without paying a severe price personally. A failed marriage, missing your children's lives as they grow up, and generally not having a life other than work are the results of inappropriate balance. At the same time, if your boss can't count on you to be at work regularly because you're always gone with a family emergency or crisis, you'll be viewed as someone who isn't reliable. In the end it is, after all, a question of balance.

How to Succeed as a Supervisor/Manager

To avoid being one of the failed 40 percent of new managers, you need to learn how to think and act like a successful supervisor. To do this you need to keep several things in mind:

- Know yourself.
- Know your people.
- Know your organization.
- Gather support from those above you.
- Gather support from your direct reports.

Know Yourself

Have a realistic self-image. Know who you are – your strengths as well as your weaknesses. Know when you need to ask for help. Having a realistic understanding of yourself becomes much easier if you ask for and receive honest feedback from those around you – your boss, peers, and direct reports. There are well-designed 360° feedback instruments to help with this process, and the results will allow you to focus on your most promising areas for growth.

Know Your People

Get to know your employees and peers as individual human beings, rather than just slot-fillers. This will help you better manage your relationships at work. And when you focus on creating and improving relationships at work, you're more likely to see your personal relationships improve too.

> The two most important forms of intelligence are the ability to read other people and the ability to understand oneself.
>
> *Bruce Pandolfini*

Know Your Organization

Learn how your organization works, what it does, and how to get things done. Every organization has a culture, a way of operating that's part of the corporate DNA. Some are tightly structured, even quasi-military in their approach. Others are more laid back and loosely structured, with little attention paid to titles or hierarchy. Your understanding will grow over time, but within a few months of joining a new organization you should have the culture pretty well figured out.

Gather Support From Those Above You

Being successful in a front-line or mid-management role is much easier when you have the support of upper management. Having senior executives or leaders who clearly understand your role *as well as theirs* will give you the confidence to become a real leader, regardless of your position in the organizational pecking order.

Gather Support From Your Direct Reports

To lead, you need followers. Your employees will usually follow your lead *if* they believe you know what you're doing *and* you've built solid relationships with them. It's very simple. Without the support of your team, you won't be effective as a supervisor or manager. To improve your chances for success, make sure you provide your direct reports with:

- Clear authority and responsibility for their work assignments

- Clear priorities and prompt updates when priorities change

- A clear sense of the organization's mission, vision, values, goals, and expected results

- Accurate, adequate, and timely information, especially feedback about their performance

- Opportunities to learn, develop, grow, and contribute to the success of your unit and the entire organization

- A willingness to truly listen to their concerns, problems, and ideas

- A willingness to act fairly, consistently, and in their best interest, as well as the interests of the team and the organization

When your direct reports perceive you as a competent manager who has their best interests at heart, *and* they see you behave that way every day, your job will be much easier.

Now it's time to take a look at the expectations that define the job of a manager. On to *Chapter 4*.

Chapter 4
Great Expectations

Regardless of your role in your organization, there are certain attitudes and behaviors that are expected of you. These expectations typically come from five sources:

- The organization as a whole

- The employees who report to you or are on your team

- Your manager or the person you report to

- Your peers

- Yourself

How these expectations are expressed will, of course, vary depending on the setting. There may be certain expectations that are unique to your particular situation, but in this chapter we explore some of the most common ones.

Your Organization's Expectations

Big-picture expectations can be seen in the organization's goals and values, whatever they may be. When your personal values and the organization's goals and values are in sync, you're likely to feel that you've found a good fit. But when there's a mismatch, you may feel uneasy about your workplace and your role in it. Do your organization's values and goals match your own?

Listen with your full attention, Look for the good in others, Have a sense of humor, and Say thank you for a job well done.

Code of Conduct
J.M. Smucker & Co.

An organization's expectations might not be written down anywhere or posted on the company bulletin board or intranet. But those expectations are real and they will affect you and your work. Usually you can quickly figure them out by looking at the organization's goals and its corporate culture.

What are your organization's expectations of you as a manager? Here are a few examples that show up in just about any kind of organization:

- Have a clear understanding of its mission, vision, goals, and values and work to make them real.

- Select, develop, and retain highly motivated, well-trained employees.

- Use the authority of your position appropriately.

- Listen to and meet the needs of your customers or clients.

Take a minute and list the expectations your organization has for you. It will come in handy later.

Your Employees' Expectations

In addition to your organization's expectations, your employees also have certain expectations about how you should behave and how they should be treated. Here are a few examples:

- Provide clear information about what you (and the organization) expect them to do or accomplish.

- Listen to their ideas, concerns, problems, and proposed solutions.

- Treat them fairly.

- Recognize their accomplishments appropriately.

> Nobody cares how much you know until they know how much you care.
>
> *Theodore Roosevelt*

Team Expectations

Let's say you have solid individual performers reporting to you, but their success working together as a team isn't so great. This can occur with a group of individual contributors or professional specialists. They tend to be very competent in their own professional specialty, but not very knowledgeable about other areas. They might exaggerate their own importance or contribution and ignore or downplay the contributions of others. When this happens they'll expect you to meet two essential needs: (1) help each person get their own job done successfully, and (2) help the team members cooperate and work together successfully.

How would you describe the expectations of *your* employees? Don't supervise at the moment? No problem. Think about your teammates; what would they expect of you if you were their supervisor?

Your Manager's Expectations

In most situations you have another set of expectations to deal with: those of the person you report to, your manager. For the self-employed that could be a spouse or significant other. You might not report to them officially, but that relationship is clearly an important factor in your professional and personal success.

Of course, individual expectations will vary from one manager to another. Your boss's management style may be different from other managers in your organization. However, certain expectations are fairly common no matter what organization you work for, such as:

> If you pick the right people and give them the opportunity to spread their wings—and put compensation as a carrier behind it—you almost don't have to manage them.
>
> *Jack Welch*

- Solve daily problems on your own, using the resources available to you.

- Support your boss's ideas and decisions without being a "yes" person.

- Be a self-starter, trustworthy, honest, and reliable.

What would *your* manager put on their list of expectations for you?

Your Peers' Expectations

Unless you're the only manager in your organization, you're going to have relationships with peers – other managers at the same level or leaders of other functions. They'll have certain expectations of you and your team, such as:

- Pull your share of the load; make sure your team carries its workload with good results.

- Be supportive and cooperative in your dealings with them; have a positive, "can-do" focus.

- Hand off work products in a way that doesn't create problems downstream.

> Surround yourself with the best people you can find, delegate authority, and don't interfere as long as the policy you've decided upon is being carried out.
>
> *Ronald Reagan*

Think about how you expect your peers to act. You can be sure they have similar ideas about how they'd like you to do your job.

Your Own Expectations

Finally, you have certain expectations for yourself – personal standards of behavior, communication, and demeanor that govern how you operate as a person. Your expectations of yourself might include items like the following:

- Keep your manager in the loop about what is happening in your unit.

- Use the organization's resources wisely and efficiently.

- Maintain a healthy balance between work and home.

For a more complete look at expectations from all five of these sources, see the *Expectations Chart* on the following pages.

Here is the prime condition of success: Concentrate your energy, thought and capital exclusively upon the business in which you are engaged. Having begun on one line, resolve to fight it out on that line, to lead in it, adopt every improvement, have the best machinery, and know the most about it.

Andrew Carnegie

Expectations Chart

Organization	Employees	Manager
Take initiative to solve problems appropriate to your level in the organization	Manage under-performers so they either succeed or leave	Meet the expectations of the organization and your employees
Have a clear understanding of the mission, vision, goals, and values and work to make them real	Provide clear information about what you (and the organization) expect them to do or accomplish	Know your responsibilities and carry them out effectively without a lot of detailed instructions
Use the authority of your position appropriately	Listen to their ideas, concerns, problems, and proposed solutions	Be flexible in responding to shifts in priorities or direction
Select, develop, and retain highly motivated, well-trained employees	Provide recognition and appropriate rewards for good performance	Solve daily problems on your own, using the resources available to you
Evaluate employees' performance and provide them with meaningful feedback	Provide them with opportunities to grow and develop in their jobs and within the organization	Suggest improvements that will help the organization be more successful
Adhere to, support, administer, and enforce policies, procedures, and rules	Make sure they have the information, resources, and support they need to effectively do their jobs	Support their ideas and decisions without being a "yes" person
Be flexible and innovative; accept and introduce positive changes	Give performance feedback that is accurate, relevant, timely, and fair	As they arise, bring issues to their attention that need to be handled at their level
Provide solid leadership to employees	Use your authority appropriately, fairly, and with restraint	Carry out their instructions or directions promptly, successfully, and cheerfully
Keep on top of daily activities and operations	Treat them fairly	Keep them in the loop about what is happening in your unit
Set specific goals for yourself and your work group	Keep them informed about things that have a bearing on their work	Train, develop, and retain your staff so the work gets done effectively and efficiently
Be a self-starter, honest, trustworthy, and reliable	Be a self-starter, honest, trustworthy, and reliable	Be a self-starter, honest, trustworthy, and reliable

Expectations Chart

Peers	Yourself
Pull your share of the load; make sure your team carries its workload with good results	Meet the expectations of the organization, your manager, and your employees
Manage the performance of your individual team members effectively and take care of performance issues when they occur	Effectively use your personal and professional power for the good of your employees and the organization
Hand off work products in a way that doesn't create problems downstream	Understand your personal value system and operate within it daily
Solve daily problems on your own, using the resources available to you	Use the organization's resources wisely and efficiently
Be supportive and cooperative in your dealings with them; have a positive, "can-do" focus	Tell people what they need to know, not just what they want to hear
Share information that helps others get the job done successfully; don't use information as power	Maintain a healthy balance between work and home
Keep them informed about progress, issues, and ideas that help get the job done well	Operate effectively without the need for a lot of instructions from others
Train and develop your staff	Keep your manager in the loop about what is happening in your unit
Be an active member of the team; provide ideas, suggestions, and feedback	Be committed to your own and your employees' development and constant learning
Pitch in and help out whenever possible	Do your best and do the right thing, all the time
Be a self-starter, honest, trustworthy, and reliable	Be a self-starter, honest, trustworthy, and reliable

Common Ground

You've noticed by now that some expectations apply to all work relationships. The specific words you use might be slightly different, but there's some consistency – particularly when it comes to expectations about communication and your trustworthiness.

For instance, everyone – your boss as well as your employees – expects to be kept in the loop about issues and projects. You're expected to communicate openly and honestly about things that affect their ability to do their job. Depending on the situation and the relationship, your behavior will shape their confidence in you. How well you've met their expectations in the past will be a significant part of their confidence (or cynicism) regarding how well you'll meet their expectations in the future.

This might be a good place to ask yourself a couple of questions:

- If I could change one particular expectation in each group, what would that be?

- What can I do to help shift expectations to a more successful or positive level?

During the past 30 years we've seen many managers and leaders run into major problems due to unclear or conflicting expectations. The following case studies show some examples.

> Management is, above all, a practice where art, science, and craft meet.
>
> *Henry Mintzberg*

Case: Anita's Ethical Dilemma

Anita was a production manager in a large food distribution processing plant. One of the organization's major goals was to get its products processed, packed, and shipped with as little waste as possible. Senior management had decided that achieving this goal was important because every pound wasted on the processing lines meant lost revenue. While Anita understood that reducing waste was an important expectation, she also wanted to make sure the company's products were safe for consumers. Since spoilage is always an issue in the food processing industry, she knew that some amount of raw material would go bad before it could be handled and shipped.

Anita was personally committed to doing her very best to meet company expectations, but she also was committed to shipping healthy and safe products to her customers. When the company arbitrarily assigned Anita a production target that could only be met by shipping spoiled products, she was faced with a conflict: her personal commitment to take care of her customers by maintaining high quality versus the company's expectation that she would ship the maximum amount of products all the time, regardless of quality. Anita felt she was in a lose-lose situation: either (1) violate her personal values and resign herself to shipping spoiled products, or (2) look for a company with a different approach.

Lessons Learned

Anita experienced a clear conflict of expectations. Her expectation of herself centered on quality; the company's expectation centered on quantity. It looked like she'd have to either set aside her personal value system or look for another place to work. What would *you* do in this situation?

What people say, what people do, and what they say they do are entirely different things.

Margaret Mead

Case: Don's Derailment

Don was a manufacturing expert whose personal style of being "one of the guys" on the shop floor (including crude language and hard-drinking, back-slapping, dirty-joke-telling, in-your-face, confrontational communication) helped him turn around the operations of a large manufacturing company. An expert in lean manufacturing, he had been popular with the work force while obtaining excellent productivity from his employees.

Don moved from operations director to vice president and then to president over the course of two years. Then he began having problems with his board of directors. His demeanor hadn't changed from his "one of the guys" persona, and he failed to understand that the board expected him to become more diplomatic, more sophisticated, and more "presidential" in his demeanor, communications, and personal style. He aggressively argued with the board one too many times and was fired after barely six months in the corner office.

The board members didn't clarify their expectations prior to elevating Don to the presidency, and he didn't ask for clarification. Too bad. His considerable talents were lost to the company and Don was unemployed for more than a year before finding a plant manager position at a much smaller company.

Lessons Learned

As you move to progressively more responsible positions, your reporting relationships – and the expectations that go with them – are going to change. Don didn't take the time to step back, clarify expectations, and decide how his approach to others needed to shift. The board was unhappy when he didn't intuitively understand what they wanted. Do you think Don learned his lesson from what happened to him?

Case: Harry the Patriarch

During the past 25 years Harry had built a successful trucking business. The company had grown from four employees and three trucks to 150 employees and a fleet of more than 125 trucks. Harry was nearing 50 and wanted to slow down a bit. Most of his management team had been promoted from within, typically starting behind the wheel of a truck or in an entry-level office job.

As founder and CEO, Harry had been the focus of the business for all of those years: making the decisions, guiding and building the team, regularly driving trucks (just to remember where he came from), and otherwise acting as the center of the universe. He expected his long-time, dedicated employees to now make more decisions and take more initiative. Unfortunately, his "at the center of everything" approach for so many years meant his managers had little ability and willingness to step up to their new role; they hadn't been properly prepared. Harry had great difficulty letting go and was visibly impatient when his managers didn't immediately rise to the challenge. The management team expected Harry to stay around and be "daddy" for a lot longer so they wouldn't have to make tough decisions.

Lessons Learned

As an organization grows and expands, the role each person plays is likely to change too. Harry and the managers had mismatched expectations. Harry failed to understand that his expectations for sudden independent decision making were unrealistic given his history of having to be at the center of everything. The managers didn't understand why their usual expectations suddenly weren't being met. What would you have done in Harry's situation?

The bottom line of all this? Make sure you're clear about not only what you expect of yourself, but also the expectations of your organization, your employees, your boss, and your peers. It's a major factor in your professional success. Ignore expectations at your own peril!

Chapter 5
The First Step on the Ladder

Making the move into supervision and management can be an intimidating, scary experience. It represents a major change for you and for the people you're managing. So it may help if you understand how organizations fill front-line management positions.

Where do Supervisors Come From?

Most supervisory positions in organizations are filled from within the ranks of current employees, generally with those who have technical skills and a positive attitude. Internal promotions tend to be favored because:

- Employees already know how the organization functions.

- Employees often already know the people they will supervise. Even if they haven't worked together, their inside knowledge of the culture makes for an easier transition.

- Management knows a great deal about the work history and attitudes of the employees they're considering for promotion. All things being equal, an internal promotion is more likely to produce a smooth transition than an outside hire.

- Management knows that hiring from within motivates existing employees; they see opportunities for advancement.

> All our dreams can come true - if we have the courage to pursue them.
>
> *Walt Disney*

Supervisory positions also are filled by new college graduates with relevant majors (e.g., business, engineering, marketing) who have completed two-year and four-year programs in supervision and management. Most organizations place these newly minted graduates in an internal management development program. Often these programs are expanded versions of the general orientation or "on-boarding" process, helping the new hires to understand how the organization operates.

Selection Criteria

While specific selection criteria vary among organizations, there are certain common attributes most employers look for when hiring from within their ranks. They want employees with:

- A good work record and low absenteeism

- A positive, generally cheerful attitude

- A genuine interest in supervision (it's not for everyone!)

- Decent organizational skills

- The ability to get things done with limited direction

- Problem-solving skills

- A track record of reliability and follow-through

Organizations that are successful in helping new supervisors get started typically provide them with some initial training and development. In general, the more training new supervisors receive, the greater their chances for success.

In the middle of difficulty lies opportunity.

Albert Einstein

How Difficult is the Transition?

When middle managers move from one position to another, the transition is relatively straightforward because they're usually moving between similar positions. The technical requirements might be somewhat different, but the overall responsibilities are often the same. It's simply a matter of exercising similar skills and building new relationships at a higher level.

But some organizations have a practice of promoting in place. This can be a real challenge, particularly if you're now supervising the people who were previously your peers. When you move from being "one of the gang" to a supervisory role, you can expect to experience some (or maybe many) challenges. These could include:

- How quickly you adjust to what good performance meant for you as a team member and what it means now as a supervisor

- How quickly you understand and meet differences in expectations and perceptions (i.e., what others expect your new role, behaviors, attitudes, and output to be compared to those of your team members)

- How well team members understand your new role, and their willingness to accept and support your new duties

- How well you understand and adapt to the workload and pace associated with the responsibilities of your new job

- How well you understand and deal with the uncertainty, ambiguity, and need for multitasking associated with your new role

- How quickly you realize that your technical expertise and your success as an individual contributor no longer determine your success on the job

- How quickly you learn important administrative tasks that you aren't prepared for or experienced in

- How well you handle the wide variety of human resources, interpersonal communication, and people-focused issues that are part of your new job

> The only limit to our realization of tomorrow will be our doubts of today.
> *Franklin D. Roosevelt*

Now that you have a solid overview of what is involved in becoming a supervisor or manager, you may want to assess your current situation by using the *Management Skills Self-Assessment* tool in the *Appendix*. This will help you decide where you might want to focus your professional development efforts. After all, knowing where you are now is pretty important when you're trying to figure out how to get where you want to go!

Management Skills Self-Assessment

What is your *current* level of success in the *8 Essential Skills*?
Assess yourself using a 1 – 5 scale (5 highest)

Skill 1 - Managing Yourself

1. How you use time	
2. Your approach to accomplishing the goals and objectives of your unit and organization	
3. How you recognize and deal with the really important issues	
4. How open and approachable you are to your employees and others,	
5. Your willingness to keep up to date technically	
6. Your level of self-confidence and ego maturity	
7. Your willingness and ability to make decisions.	

Skill 2 – Communicating for Results

Skill 1
MANAGING YOURSELF

"One can never consent to creep when one feels an impulse to soar."

Helen Keller

Skill 1 – Managing Yourself

Most of us live in a fairly complex world. The term "multitasking," taken from the way modern computers handle a number of tasks simultaneously, reflects that reality. What we're really talking about is the pace and density of our personal and professional lives. The sheer volume of communication, information, commitments, projects, and tasks seems to grow all the time. And the further we progress in our careers and personal lives, the more complex the mix seems to become.

Part of this challenge is caused by how our work has changed. Years of mergers, acquisitions, economic disruptions, layoffs, budget shortfalls, outsourcing, and off-shoring, compounded by a major worldwide recession, have permanently changed the meaning of work.

Most of us have multiple jobs, or even multiple careers, during our working lives. Two-income households have become the norm. Most of us experience the "sandwich generation" squeeze at some point – juggling responsibilities for both aging parents and children. And as baby boomers reach their 50s and 60s, they're opting to work longer than their parents did – many from necessity and others by choice. This affects job and career opportunities for the following generations. Add broad economic and environmental changes, and it all can become overwhelming.

Your ability to be successful in your organizational role begins with how well you manage yourself in the midst of all this, and that's pretty much up to you. So understanding yourself is the first step if you want to become truly effective personally and professionally. Self-knowledge will help you capitalize on your strengths and become more aware of your blind spots and shortcomings. It will also help you understand other people better and value their individual differences. In the long run your ability to understand

There are three things extremely hard: steel, a diamond, and to know one's self.

Benjamin Franklin

To do good things in the world, first you must know who you are and what gives meaning in your life.

Paula P. Brownlee

and manage yourself effectively – *Skill 1* – will lead to your individual success as a supervisor and manager, but it will also contribute to your organization's success.

Keeping your head above water in these turbulent times requires some creative swimming. There's no one best way to improve your self-management skills. The key is to find a few ideas in these pages that appeal to you, try them out, keep the ones that work, and discard the rest. Then try out some more ideas.

All of us are in some sort of *transition* phase from what we did and who we were yesterday to what we will be doing next year or five years from now. The "who" we used to be is not the person we'll become. Some of you reading this book are in a major transition from a career that has disappeared, an occupation that has been outsourced, or a company that has closed. You might have been forced to retire early. Whatever the transition you're in, knowing yourself well is the most important part of effectively living your life in turbulent times.

Understanding Your Hardwiring

If you play it safe in life you've decided that you don't want to grow anymore.

Shirley Hufstedler

While each of us grow and develop throughout our lifetime, we have certain entrenched personal characteristics that form our unique individual personality. We refer to the combination of these characteristics as our individual "hardwiring." They tend to remain generally consistent over the years and are made up of four significant factors:

- Personality preferences

- Hemispheric dominance (right brain/left brain)

- Information processing preferences (visual, kinesthetic, auditory)

- Innate talents

Each of these four factors includes inborn traits. Together they make up your individuality, and understanding each of them is important to your ability to be successful as a manager *and* as a human being. Who you are as an individual is made up of nature as well as nurture – heredity and environment. It's the combination that makes you unique. We're going to briefly explore each of these four factors in the next three chapters.

A Note About Multitasking

Before we go any further, it's important to know that the term "multitasking" is really inaccurate. We don't actually do two things at exactly the same time. When we do what is called multitasking, we're really handling lots of different tasks and ideas, one at a time, extremely rapidly. (This is actually what a computer's CPU is doing, but at a speed that's unimaginable in human terms.)

Our brain is not physically wired for true multitasking; as far as we know it's physically impossible. So when you're paying attention to one thing while you're doing something else, you end up not doing either very well. We know that having a split focus like this causes problems (e.g., the increase in auto accidents caused by drivers texting or talking on their cell phones). In fact, recent research has shown that those who tend to multitask the most believe they're being very efficient. But they actually aren't accomplishing more. They're just more likely to have difficulty getting much of anything done effectively.

Chapter 6
Your Personality Preferences

Often people don't understand each other and things don't go the way you'd like with your team. This doesn't necessarily indicate deep-seated conflict or that you're a failure as a manager. It can simply be the result of normal differences in personality preferences.

Throughout this book you'll find references to personality preferences and the Myers-Briggs Type Indicator™ (MBTI). There are other tools for understanding human personality and behavior. However, our experience with several of these has shown the MBTI to be the most widely used, complete assessment. While it isn't the simplest approach to understanding human behavior, it seems to deliver the most consistent long-term results. A properly administered MBTI process with well-facilitated feedback can do wonders for almost any team of people by helping them understand normal personality preferences.

The MBTI was originally developed in the early 1940s, and it has been thoroughly researched and validated. It looks at eight personality preferences that all people use at different times. These eight preferences are organized into four groupings or dimensions. When a person completes the MBTI, the four dimensions they identify as most like them are combined into what is called a "type."

It's important to understand that the MBTI describes *preferences*, not skills or abilities. All preferences are equally important, and there are no "right" or "wrong" preferences or types.

While each person is clearly an individual, there are certain shared preferences and traits that will affect your success. How these show up in your behavior may vary depending on the situation you're in.

Distribution of MBTI Types

ISTJ 11.6%	ISFJ 13.8%	INFJ 1.5%	INTJ 2.1%
ISTP 5.4%	ISFP 8.8%	INFP 4.4%	INTP 3.3%
ESTP 4.3%	ESFP 8.5%	ENFP 8.1%	ENTP 3.2%
ESTJ 8.7%	ESFJ 12.3%	ENFJ 2.5%	ENTJ 1.8%

General U.S. Population
Percentage Distribution

After all, humans are complex individuals and their personality preferences are only one part of what makes them unique. Still, it's certainly worth exploring the role your personality preferences play in guiding your life.

The Dimensions of Personality

According to MBTI theory, the four general dimensions of human personality and behavior influence how we operate in all aspects of our lives, not just at work. They include:

- Extraversion & Introversion (E and I)
- Sensing & iNtuition (S and N)
- Thinking & Feeling (T and F)
- Judging & Perceiving (J and P)

Extraversion & Introversion

Our Source of Energy & Orientation

Extraverts (49% of U.S.). Extraverts (E's) get their energy from interacting with others. They prefer variety and action and can be impatient with long, slow jobs. They usually communicate well, like to have people around, and are good at greeting people. On the other hand, they often have difficulty listening and may interrupt others. Extraverts tend to:

- Prefer doing something rather than quietly thinking about it
- Enjoy jumping into things, sometimes without thinking
- Be naturally adept at meeting new people
- Prefer to communicate verbally
- Think things through by talking about a subject
- Have trouble listening actively
- Enjoy having other people around and find meetings useful

> Everything that irritates us about others can lead us to an understanding of ourselves.
>
> *Carl Jung*

> You've got to take the initiative and play your game . . . confidence makes the difference.
>
> *Chris Evert*

- Prefer discussion to thinking things through alone

- Operate from a "ready, fire, aim" approach

- Need to interact with others regularly during the workday

E's often exhibit what appears to be little or no connection between their brain and their mouth. For the Extravert, it is often a case of, "I have no idea what I'm going to say until I open my mouth and out it comes." As a result, their mouth tends to frequently run ahead of their brain.

The ideal weekend or vacation for an Extravert is usually filled with activities, often with a group of people. Partying, hanging out and talking, going on group excursions, or attending sporting or cultural events along with hundreds or thousands of others can be great fun for E's.

Half of the U.S. population is made up of Extraverts, while other cultures have a smaller proportion. For instance, in Japan E's represent only about 30 percent of the population.

Introverts (51% of U.S.). Introverts (I's) need to recharge their batteries alone after being around other people for extended periods. They're usually comfortable working alone, prefer a quiet workplace for concentration, and appreciate uninterrupted work on one subject. They're usually good listeners but may have some problems communicating with others.

> Stop talking about it and start doing it!
>
> *Julie Wainwright*

Introverts make up the other half of the U.S. population, although they are a clear majority in some other cultures. They're oriented toward, and get their energy from, their inner world of thoughts and ideas. They have a rich inner life and are actively thinking most of the time. Introverts tend to:

- Prefer to work quietly on their own, which helps them concentrate

- Prefer to communicate in writing rather than verbally

- Listen well, but have trouble communicating their thoughts quickly

- Find it tiring to interact extensively with others

- Need down time after work to recharge their batteries

- Constantly take in information, evaluate it, think about what it means, and use their brain for processing the world around them

- Think things through before acting, sometimes never reaching closure

The ideal weekend or vacation for an Introvert may consist of sleeping in, reading, or doing things with a small group of family members or close friends. Introverts use the term "friend" much more sparingly than Extraverts. For I's the term is reserved for a small group of individuals they have known quite well for a long time.

Recent research suggests that the brains of Extraverts and Introverts may be hardwired differently; that is, the way they process the same piece of information may follow different neural pathways. Marti Olsen Laney's excellent book, "The Introvert Advantage," discusses this idea.

To find qualified MBTI practitioners in your area, see *Other Recommended Readings and Resources* in the *Appendix* for the Association for Psychological Type International (APTi).

Sensing & iNtuition

How We Prefer to Gather Information

Sensors (73% of U.S.). Sensors (S's) are the consummate detail folks in any organization. They focus on gathering information that's concrete and "real" to them. S's are comfortable working with facts, numbers, data, and other specific information. They approach work as an orderly, step-by-step process, paying great attention to details. They usually dislike new problems unless there are standard ways to solve them. Sensors tend to:

- Prefer an established routine

- Work all the way through a project to reach a conclusion

- Have difficulty understanding or caring about theory or strategy

- Be bored by creative development and brainstorming processes

- Ask detailed questions and want detailed answers

- Prefer having a list of specific things that need to be done rather than a broad description of a future purpose or outcome

- Plan by developing an orderly, sequential, step-by-step approach to projects or assignments

> Small things done consistently in strategic places create major impact.
>
> *David Allen*

iNtuitives (27% of U.S.). iNtuitives (N's) tend to see the big picture first and often spot trends or see implications or patterns that Sensors don't see. They enjoy solving new problems and dislike doing the same thing over and over again. They may jump to conclusions, are impatient with routine details, and dislike taking time for precision. Knowing how a task or project fits into some broader purpose – the mission of the organization, the vision of the next five years – is of major importance. iNtuitives tend to:

- Dislike dealing with situations or problems in a routine way

- Prefer to create a new approach to an issue rather than use an established method

- Be comfortable starting almost anywhere in a project and skip steps to get the desired result

- Let details fall through the cracks and make factual errors

- Drag their feet and perceive a project as just more busywork unless they understand its overall purpose and value

- Put more emphasis on *why* something should be done rather than *how* it should be done

I'm long on ideas but short on time. I expect to live to be only about a hundred.

Thomas Edison

Thinking & Feeling

How We Prefer to Make Decisions

Thinkers (40% of U.S., 57% of Males). Thinkers (T's) make decisions based on logic and what they view as best for the organization and its bottom line. They prefer analysis, rationality, and putting things in logical order. They tend to focus more on people's errors and mistakes, are less likely to reward and praise good performance, and can appear to be hard-hearted or uncaring. Conflict and disagreement are often viewed as useful and constructive.

T's prefer a work environment where the focus is on getting things done, believing that people should leave their emotions and personal problems at home. Thinkers tend to:

- Be able to get along without interpersonal harmony, shrugging their shoulders and moving on when Feelers react emotionally

- Be concerned about treating people fairly and doing the right thing

- Relate well only to other Thinkers and think that Feelers are soft-hearted, overly emotional wimps

- Hurt people's feelings without realizing it and unwittingly damage work and personal relationships

Feelers (60% of U.S., 76% of Females). Feelers (F's) are quite aware of other people and their feelings, which helps them relate well to most people. They like to give and receive praise but tend to avoid conflict. They dislike telling people unpleasant things and often take conflict, disagreement, or criticism as a personal attack. However, their natural empathy and desire to please people means they provide recognition and praise easily and readily. Feelers tend to:

- Make decisions based on their value system, their relationship with the people involved, and their desire to do what is best for others

- Stretch the rules sometimes to please employees or maintain harmony

- Be seen by their employees as ideal supervisors, except when they fail to deal with a lazy or incompetent team member

- Carry grudges for a long time

- Believe that praise, recognition, and reinforcing the behavior desired is far more useful than pointing out real or imagined errors

- Postpone corrective or negative feedback for too long

> You don't get to choose how you're going to die. Or when. You can decide how you're going to live.
>
> *Joan Baez*

Judging & Perceiving

Our Lifestyle Orientation

Judgers (54% of U.S.). Judgers (J's) seem to operate most successfully when they can plan what they'll do and then work through that plan in an orderly way. They're driven to get things decided, and the quicker the better. Once closure has been reached about an issue they can be rather rigid, rejecting new information. ("We made that decision last week and we're going to implement it; don't try to change direction now.")

J's can be impatient with exploring alternatives before deciding on a direction, so they may neglect to try new approaches. They find Perceivers to be indecisive, disorganized, and somewhat messy. Judgers tend to:

- Continue to drive for a goal even when changing circumstances call for a shift in strategy

- Be impatient, wanting only the essential information required to get on with a task

- Find deadlines useful and will plan their work to meet them

- Be decisive; they usually can spot things that should or need to be done

- Be satisfied once they form a judgment about an idea, situation, or person

> Some people regard discipline as a chore. For me, it is a kind of order that sets me free to fly.
>
> *Julie Andrews*

Perceivers (46% of U.S.). For Perceivers (P's), life is a series of new opportunities. They often postpone decisions as long as possible (or even longer!), preferring to gather more information before deciding. They're usually good at adapting to changing situations and requirements. They may have difficulty making decisions, even routine ones like what to order for dinner in a restaurant. Their flexibility and openness makes P's good at handling emergencies and rapidly changing situations.

Perceivers find Judgers to be a bit anal, uptight, and overly organized. Perceivers tend to:

- Be willing to leave things undecided or unfinished

- Enjoy gathering new information on something already in progress

- Be spontaneous, preferring to handle issues and things as they occur rather than plan ahead

- Be frustrated by Judgers' impatient drive for closure and desire to have everything planned and organized

- Change their mind frequently, which can frustrate Judgers

Distribution of MBTI Types

ISTJ **11.6%**	**ISFJ** **13.8%**	**INFJ** **1.5%**	**INTJ** **2.1%**
ISTP **5.4%**	**ISFP** **8.8%**	**INFP** **4.4%**	**INTP** **3.3%**
ESTP **4.3%**	**ESFP** **8.5%**	**ENFP** **8.1%**	**ENTP** **3.2%**
ESTJ **8.7%**	**ESFJ** **12.3%**	**ENFJ** **2.5%**	**ENTJ** **1.8%**

General U.S. Population

Percentage Distribution

E 49.3%		T 40.2%
I 50.7%		F 59.8%
S 73.3%	SOURCE: (MBTI MANUAL, 1998)	J 54.1%
N 26.7%		P 45.9%

(See Appendix for U.S. Male and Female distribution tables.)

What This Means to You

Although your personality preferences are only one part of your individual hardwiring, they play an important part in how effective you are as a supervisor or manager. Your ability to get the job done – and your ultimate success – are directly influenced by how you take in and communicate information, how you make decisions, your approachability, your willingness to take on and complete tasks, and how all this is interpreted by the people around you.

Everyone is an individual, so your actual behavior may be different from someone with your same type preferences. Each of us uses both aspects of the four dimensions. Your particular type preference simply indicates your *preferred* way of dealing with the world. Even the most outgoing Extravert will behave in an Introverted fashion at least some of the time.

The key is to *know* what your personality preferences are and how they're expressed in your individual situation. That requires increasing your self-knowledge and becoming an informed observer of your own behavior.

Now it's time to learn more about the role your brain plays in your hardwiring. That's in *Chapter 7*.

If the success or failure of this planet and of human beings depended on how I am and what I do, how would I be and what would I do?

Buckminster Fuller

Chapter 7
Your Remarkable Brain

During the past 25 years we've have learned a lot about the human brain, how it operates, the role it plays in how we perceive the world, and how it helps to determine our behavior. But even with all of this scientific research, we're just beginning to understand this wonderful, complex organ.

The billions of neurons or nerve cells in your brain interact and interconnect in ways that create the capacity for incredible informational processing power. Thought develops from an incredibly complex web of electro-chemical signals – signals that move around the brain at warp speed along thousands of neuronal connections.

In this chapter we'll focus on three areas related to brain function:

- Your reticular system or filtering function

- Your interconnected (but separately functioning) right and left hemispheres

- Your information processing preferences

Understanding how your brain operates and the role it plays in managing yourself is an important step in becoming a successful manager. It isn't that your brain predetermines how you'll act in any given situation. But your brain has a lot to do with what seems "right" to you, what approaches seem to work well, and what kinds of information make the most sense to you. Understanding at least a little about how your brain functions will help you get a much better handle on the behavior that's driven by your own internal hardwiring.

The Reticular Formation

In your brain stem is an intricate network of nerves about the size of your little finger. This network is called the *reticular formation*. It receives and sends nerve impulses to and from all areas of your brain. It plays a critical role in keeping you awake, as well as several other automatic body functions.

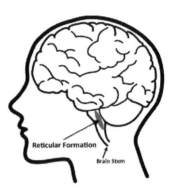

Reticular Formation

Brain Stem

The brain so needs pattern recognition it would prefer the familiar to the truth.

David Allen

The reticular formation monitors and filters information coming in through your senses. This portion of your brain has a great deal to do with what you pay attention to and what information gets through to your conscious mind. It helps keep you sane by filtering and limiting the overwhelming amount of sensory and other information you're exposed to every second.

This filtering function also has a powerful influence on how you translate your wishes into reality. Basically, the reticular formation helps you to create (and maintain) your paradigms – the beliefs and constructs you have about what is real. By filtering out information that doesn't match your paradigms, the reticular formation attempts to maintain the status quo. It excludes new information or input you don't want to pay attention to.

Of course, once you know how this process works, you can use it to your advantage by focusing on outcomes you *do* want and describing them as completely as possible. For example, setting goals is an important part of managing yourself. But merely setting a goal isn't enough. You need to *focus* your mind on that goal, particularly on the end result you want to achieve. What would it look like? What would be happening? What would you experience if you successfully met that goal?

When you focus on a desired outcome, your reticular formation essentially opens its filters. Information and experiences from the environment will start to show up in your consciousness. (The information is actually always out there and available, but your brain won't notice it until you need that information to achieve the outcome you want.) You'll start to think of actions you can take to move closer to your goal. And you'll tend to notice whether those actions are getting you there, which allows you to do course correction much earlier in the process.

Hemispheric Dominance

This bit of hardwiring has to do with how we learn and the role played by our dominant brain hemisphere. In general, the right hemisphere of your brain controls the left side of your body, and the left hemisphere of your brain controls your right side.

> It is the mind that makes the body.
>
> *Sojourner Truth*

In addition to thousands of other functions, each hemisphere has a distinct approach to accessing and processing information. You use both sides of your brain all the time. However, as an adult your neurological system tends to "listen" to one hemisphere more than the other, usually on about a 60/40 basis. The favored side is your dominant hemisphere. It's the one you rely on, particularly when you're under stress.

Hemispheric Dominance

Left Brain   Right Brain

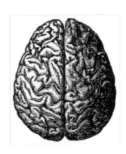

Left Hemisphere Dominance

If you're left-brain dominant, you tend to learn by focusing on facts and details and using language – often by reading, speaking, or listening. You understand a whole concept by understanding its component parts. Left-brained people tend to:

- Learn best via linear, factual, logic-oriented systems

- Learn best when information is presented in an organized manner

- Prefer objective (multiple choice/true-false) tests

- Be primarily interested in how things are done

If this sounds familiar, it's because Sensors are generally more likely to be left-brain dominant. Since Sensors are in the majority in many cultures, including the U.S., it's likely that most of the population is left-brain dominant.

Right Hemisphere Dominance

If you're right-brain dominant, learning is more of a visual process that focuses on patterns and the big picture. Your key to understanding a concept is to see the whole rather than the parts. Right-brained people tend to:

- Learn best when the information is accompanied by music, colors, visualization, and other creative endeavors

- Prefer information presented spatially or through models or diagrams

- Prefer subjective (essay) tests

- Be primarily interested in understanding why something needs to be done

- Be comfortable with intuitive decision making

Business organizations seem to be mostly left-brain entities; the prized behavior is logical, linear, data-detailed, and unemotional. Most managers seem to shut out the right-brain, imaginative, big-picture, holistic perspective. So if you're right-hemisphere dominant, you may feel out of sync with others. You might even discount your intuition about what feels like the best solution.

What This Means to You

Hemispheric dominance represents two different ways of thinking. One way is not better or worse than the other; they're just different. The important thing is to be aware that there are different ways of thinking and to know what your natural preference is.

If you want to increase your effectiveness, practice looking at situations from your non-dominant hemisphere. If you think you're left-brained, try making a small decision before all the data are in, based on your gut instinct for the situation. If you think you're right-brained, take a few minutes to look at the data. Practice reading the charts, not just the stories, in an annual report. Ultimately, your decisions will turn out to be more balanced and successful, and you'll be less likely to miss something important by relying too much on one hemisphere.

Information Processing Preferences

While you use all five senses to gather and process information coming in from the world, you use your three major senses – visual (sight), auditory (hearing), and kinesthetic (touch) – when learning and gathering new information. And you'll tend to use these three senses to significantly different degrees.

Early in your brain's development your nervous system developed a dominant pattern for processing information. One sense is the strongest (let's call it the "conscious" sense). One is a support function (the "subconscious" sense). And one is the weakest (the "unconscious" sense.) This pattern strongly influences how you learn and process information. While you use all three senses, you learn best when you utilize your dominant sense.

- *Auditory* learners prefer to hear material in order to learn it. Music and audiotapes are useful tools for them. They make up about 25-30 percent of the U. S. population.

- *Visual* learners prefer to see what they're learning, often using charts, diagrams, models, outlines, or films as tools. They make up about 65 percent of the U. S. population.

- *Kinesthetic* learners prefer to learn through experience and hands-on physical manipulation. They seem to learn best by doing. They make up about 5-10 percent of the U.S. population.

The various combinations of these dominant learning styles yield a total of six different patterns:

STRONGEST Conscious	SUPPORT Subconscious	WEAKEST Unconscious	PATTERN
Kinesthetic	Visual	Auditory	KVA
Kinesthetic	Auditory	Visual	KAV
Auditory	Kinesthetic	Visual	AKV
Auditory	Visual	Kinesthetic	AVK
Visual	Kinesthetic	Auditory	VKA
Visual	Auditory	Kinesthetic	VAK

Notice that in some cases two individuals with different patterns could end up communicating using their support (or subconscious) information processing preferences. For instance, someone who is primarily Kinesthetic and Visual (KVA) interacting with someone who is primarily Auditory and Visual (AVK) results in *neither* person using the sense that works best for them. This can make the communication process more challenging.

> In the *Appendix* you'll find a pair of simple, quick, self-assessment exercises created by Mary Blakely for her delightful book "Why Not You?". These assessments may help you better understand your own hemispheric and information processing preferences. While these assessments aren't extensive or scientifically validated, they can help you get a handle on your own hardwiring.

What This Means to You

When you're interacting with another person, especially in your role as a manager or supervisor, you need to be able to feel confident that the two of you are connecting accurately. Understanding your own information processing preferences and the preferences of your co-workers will help facilitate both learning and communication. For instance, if you're primarily Auditory and

Kinesthetic and I'm primarily Visual and Kinesthetic, you need to reinforce your verbal instructions with a hands-on demonstration or walk-through to make sure we agree about what needs to be accomplished.

Understanding how your internal hardwiring influences the way you look at the world, take in information, learn, and make decisions is a great beginning. The next chapter explores how you can become a more effective manager by identifying and nurturing your talents. While your innate talents are part of your hardwiring, it's only through learning and experience that you can turn them into strengths.

Chapter 8
Your Innate Talents

Each of us comes into the world with a set of innate gifts or talents. Research by the late Donald O. Clifton and others has shown that these talents can turn into personal strengths when combined with education, experience and/or practice. Clifton is often cited as the father of what has come to be called Strengths psychology. He believed that most of what we knew about psychology had come from the study of sick or abnormal people. He wanted to find out what could be learned from studying normal, well-adjusted, successful people.

> Too many people overvalue what they are not and undervalue what they are.
>
> *Malcolm Forbes*

Developing Your Strengths

Your strengths are the talents you've developed that allow you to produce consistent, near-perfect performance. You would happily do these things all the time because they feel natural to you. As for weaknesses – the things you don't do well – it's been shown that the most effective strategy is to manage *around* them and not spend a lot of time trying to overcome them.

We tend to assume that innate talents will grow and develop naturally – that they don't need much attention. There are exceptions to this belief in athletics and the arts, where we're much better at identifying and nurturing talent. For example, we don't say to athletes, "You're a natural at baseball but you make a poor football lineman; you should focus on bulking up and learning how to block better." Instead, we encourage them to practice, grow, and develop their talent. An example? Michael Jordan was one of the greatest basketball players in history, but his attempt to switch to baseball after his first retirement was unsuccessful.

> Argue for your limitations and, sure enough, they're yours.
>
> *Richard Bach*

How often have you heard (or maybe even said), "You can do anything if you want it badly enough." As a consultant, coach, and mentor, I've said that frequently over the years. You might have the idea that success is simply a matter of concentrated hard work. Education, practice, and hard work are needed to turn a talent into a reliable strength. But that same amount of effort won't lead to the same result if it's applied to an area where you lack talent.

Of course, there are weaknesses that need to be addressed in any professional development process. But it's critical to understand the relative importance of the skills required for various positions. Managers don't need to be equally good at everything in their job description to be very effective as managers.

Identifying Your Talents

Have you ever wondered what your own innate talents are? When I first ran across the Gallup organization's research findings about this topic, I wondered if there was an assessment tool available. It turned out that Clifton and his colleagues were working on that very task. This led to the publication of "Now, Discover Your Strengths" by Marcus Buckingham and Clifton. Known as the Clifton StrengthsFinder™, this easy online self-assessment is available in several versions through a one-time computer code contained in any of several books published by Gallup, Inc. After you complete the online assessment, you immediately receive a summary of the top five themes of talent that seem to be most accurate based on your responses.

For several years we have used the StrengthsFinder with hundreds of managers in a wide variety of organizations. Nearly everyone who has completed the self-assessment with a well-facilitated feedback session tells us that the results seem to be highly accurate. While this self-reporting has only what academics call "face validity" (i.e., participants agree that the results seem to measure what they're supposed to measure), most people find the assessment process accurate and useful.

I am careful not to confuse excellence with perfection. Excellence, I can reach for; perfection is God's business.

Michael J. Fox

What really matters is what you do with what you have.

Shirley Lord

But identifying your particular innate talents is only the beginning. After you've identified them, you need to answer several questions, such as:

- How do these talents show up in my professional and personal life?

- What experiences have I had that might help turn each talent into a strength?

- What skills do I use with my talents? Do I need any additional knowledge and/or practice for them to become strengths?

- How well do my talents match up with what I'm doing professionally?

> To feel valued, to know, even if only once in a while, that you can do a job well is an absolutely marvelous feeling.
>
> *Barbara Walters*

Your answers to these questions should provide you with clues about development or growth opportunities. At the same time, it makes sense to look at your teammates. What can you do to help them identify their particular talents and turn those into strengths?

What This Means to You

Your individual talents are part of the raw materials that make up the unique person that is *you*. Understanding what your talents are and determining how to turn them into strengths is where the rubber really hits the road. After all, a talent doesn't become a strength without education, experience, and practice.

Once you have a solid handle on your innate talents and understand how they affect your work, you'll be able to make better choices about where to focus your time and energy. Plus, knowing the talents and potential strengths of your teammates can give everyone's performance a significant boost. Think what it would be like if you and your teammates each fully used your talents, turning them into strengths every day!

Case: Martha & Her Talents

Martha was a middle manager in a manufacturing company. She had a talent for communication – for vividly passing on to others the company's and unit's vision and strategy. Like most managers at her level she also had budget responsibilities, for which she had little talent or interest.

Many companies would send Martha through a series of budget or financial training programs, trying to improve her skills. Over time she might become an average budget manager. Instead, Martha's company recognized her strengths. She went through a basic training program in the company's budget process and then delegated most of this responsibility to a trusted team member who understood the process and enjoyed working with financial data. This freed Martha to concentrate on doing what she liked and what she did best. She continues to work hard to improve her communication skills, keeps up to speed with industry developments, and is seen as a high-potential candidate for movement into corporate planning and executive management.

Lessons Learned

Thanks, in part, to her company's support, Martha was able to focus on one of her talents and turn it into a significant strength. By building on her talents and managing around her weakness in budgeting, she is in line for the executive suite and the company is growing a highly valuable employee.

An individual's self-concept is the core of his personality. It affects every aspect of human behavior: the ability to learn, the capacity to grow and change, the choice of friends, mates and careers. It is no exaggeration to say that a strong, positive self-image is the best possible preparation for success in life.

Dr. Joyce Brothers

Why Your Hardwiring Matters

As you've learned, the four components of individual hardwiring are:

- Personality preferences

- Hemispheric dominance

- Information processing preferences

- Innate talents

The potential combinations of these four components are almost limitless. Taken together with our upbringing and life experiences, they result in each of us becoming a unique human being.

Your ability to be successful as a manager and a fully functional person can be enhanced by increasing your knowledge about your own and others' hardwiring. Ultimately, why does this matter?

- The better you know yourself – warts and all – the better you'll be able to interact with other people.

- You'll be able to see yourself through more realistic eyes, which will increase your sensitivity to how you affect others.

- You'll naturally improve your communication skills.

- You'll be more likely to understand and value people whose hardwiring is different from your own.

- You'll be more comfortable seeking out differing viewpoints, which increases the level of trust within a group.

- Any fear in your relationships will be dramatically reduced or eliminated.

> The first trait that is common among those who are assured a place in history is that of being predisposed to continual self-improvement.
>
> *James Stockdale*

The end result is improved relationships with other people, greater involvement among your team members, and more open and honest communication – all hallmarks of a successful manager.

Chapter 9
A Cluttered Mind

Have you ever had the feeling that your brain is too full? It's a familiar feeling to most busy people. One of the major reasons is that most of us try to use our brain as a filing cabinet. Frankly, it wasn't designed for that purpose so it just doesn't work very well.

> It is more important to know where you're going than to get there fast.
>
> *Dale Carnegie*

What's on Your Mind?

All of us have lots of things on our mind . . . things we need and want to do . . . commitments we've made . . . things that bother us, worry us, bug us, and otherwise intrude on our ability to stay focused and productive. According to David Allen in his book "Getting Things Done," there are usually three reasons things are on your mind:

- The intended outcome you're seeking isn't clear.

- You haven't decided on the next physical action required to move things forward.

- Reminders about the outcome you seek and the next actions required aren't held in a system you trust.

The Intended Outcome Isn't Clear

This simply means you haven't determined what "done" or "success" looks like for a particular project or task. This happens when you don't allow yourself to imagine what will occur, what you'll be doing, and/or what will be different when you successfully accomplish the thing you have on your plate.

Let's say you think it would be a good idea to create a succession plan for your unit. However, all you have in mind is a vague notion that creating a succession plan would be a good idea. The problem is you haven't clarified what the end result will look like; your goal

> MBTI Theory:
> Extraverts (and especially Extraverted iNtuitives) are more likely to jump in and "just do it" with only a vague general idea of what is involved in a task or project.

isn't clear enough. What will be different *after* you've created the succession plan? Will your team function in a different way? Will you be doing different things than you're doing now?

You Haven't Decided on the Next Action

One of David Allen's key notions is the value of breaking down complex projects into a series of simple "next actions" that can be accomplished relatively quickly. How do you eat an elephant? One bite at a time!

If you're like most supervisors and managers, you can't set aside large blocks of time to work on big projects; the pace of your daily work is just too fast. Instead, you probably have only a few minutes between interruptions to work on moving a whole bunch of different projects forward. If you have just a few minutes before the next meeting, phone call, drop-in, crisis, or whatever, then you need to be clear about what the next physical action is on each of your current projects.

Reminders Aren't in a System

The person who says he is overworked is usually working the wrong way.

Unknown

The third leg of David Allen's approach requires that you find or create – and then consistently use – some sort of system, tool, or set of tools to keep track of all the outcomes (projects) and next actions (tasks) on your plate.

From personal experience I know David's take on this is right on target. You've probably experienced that jarring sensation that occurs when you realize you've forgotten to do something that turned out to be *really* important. This is your overtaxed, overwhelmed, mental self-management system saying, "Wake Up!" Your brain is trying to tell you that it was not designed as a filing cabinet or an onboard self-management toolkit. Your brain was made for thinking, planning, dreaming, imagining, and creating. Using it as a mental reminder system full of to-do lists is like using a super-computer just to play solitaire. Not a very appropriate use of that equipment.

The Power of Having a System

The idea of having a comprehensive overview of everything that's on your plate and on your mind is neither new nor radical. If you want to make sure those things that surface in your conscious mind have a good chance of becoming reality, write them down. This simple act is one of the most powerful self-management tools you'll ever use.

By the way, this approach holds true whether something surfaces from your subconscious or comes to mind through your senses (e.g., "Gee, that door trim needs painting"). Wherever it comes from, when you tell yourself you need to get something accomplished, even something simple, you have three options:

- *Option 1.* Do it right now, while you think of it.

- *Option 2.* Do it later, when you get the chance.

- *Option 3.* Do it never; forget about it.

If you select option 2, you have to trust your brain to remind you to do that thing, whatever it is. Or you have to immediately capture that thought in some fashion so you'll remember to do it later. The half-life for mental notes is measured in nanoseconds for most of us, so using some sort of tool to capture your thoughts just makes sense.

> Ideas can come from anywhere at any time. The problem with making mental notes is that the ink fades very rapidly.
>
> *Rolf Smith*

Creating some sort of system to track information, commitments, tasks, ideas, and other important material is generally attractive to about half of the population. The other half prefers to not plan or organize so much. If being organized appeals to you, or if you're feeling somewhat out of control in parts of your life, then creating a self-management system could help with your mind clutter.

The variety of personal organizational tools available today is staggering, and they range from silly to sophisticated. The tools you select will be determined by the way information, commitments, and projects arrive, move through, and leave your life. An important issue to consider when putting together a system is your comfort and involvement with electronic information. For some people a paper-based system works best. For others, computers and related technological support pieces drive the tool-selection process. Still others opt for a combination of paper and computer-based tools. There really is no single approach to self-management that works for everyone. You need to design and build your own system for managing everything on your plate.

Whatever you begin with, you'll find that your system naturally evolves over time. You never have to feel that you're stuck with something that no longer works. Paper-based systems can be as simple as a loose-leaf binder or notebook or as sophisticated as a top-of-the-line TimeDesign™ or Franklin-Covey™ binder system. You may find that electronic portability is a critical requirement for your life. Laptops, netbooks, tablets, PDAs, digital audio and video recorders, electronic notepads, sophisticated cell phones, and other assorted tools offer a lot of choices. If you like gadgets it's easy to get distracted by the array of new devices constantly coming to market. Still, it's possible to create a fairly seamless system without spending a lot of money or juggling multiple tools. There are lots of tools available out there. Start looking for one that fits where you think you are right now and then experiment.

Things turn out the best for the people who make the best of the way things turn out.

John Wooden

Recommended System Components

A good system to reduce mind clutter should contain at least the following items:

- *Daily/Weekly Plan.* A tool for daily appointments and reminders about tasks that require your attention on specific days.

- *List Section.* A way to track tasks and projects using various categories that fit the way you work.

- *Calendar Overview.* A way to look at future commitments and events for, say, each of the next three months, as well as an overview of the current year.

- *Projects Section.* A place to detail the steps necessary to meet each of your objectives, along with projected due dates.

- *Communications Section.* A section to record important conversations, recommendations, conclusions, and commitments made with important people you interact with regularly.

- *Contacts Directory.* A place to hold names, addresses, and other contact information about the people you know.

Clarifying the Truly Important

With all of the incoming information, assignments, tasks, and projects that show up every day, it's clear that getting *everything* accomplished is not realistic. Our lives are so full, complex, and ever-changing that at any given moment there will be a whole bunch of things you aren't getting done. So it's all a matter of the choices you make from among the wide variety of options available to you.

To do this effectively it makes sense to be clear about what is *truly important* to you, your relationships, and your organization. Having some sort of system to manage all your commitments, tasks, and projects frees your mind from having to track and remember all those details. In turn, this makes mind-space available to do what you really want to do and have some worry-free fun along the way.

So what is truly important in your world? The next chapter may help you figure that out.

It's a funny thing about life; if you refuse to accept anything but the best, you very often get it.

W. Somerset Maugham

Chapter 10
Choices, Choices, and More Choices

There's no doubt that you, like the rest of us, have *lots* to do. At the end of the day, week, or month you can look back and spot all sorts of things that you *should* have accomplished but didn't. So you've clearly made choices about what to do, what not to do, what to pay attention to, and what to ignore. You make hundreds of choices every day.

> I discovered I always have choices and sometimes it's only a choice of attitude.
>
> *Judith M. Knowlton*

Do you find that frustrating? Sure. But it doesn't have to be that way. You just need to understand how to choose what to do from all the alternatives you face. The choices you make must answer three basic questions:

- Who should address or resolve this issue?

- How important is this to me?

- What is the best use of my time, talent, and energy?

Span of Control, Sphere of Influence

You have various issues you can make decisions about, otherwise known as your "span of control." These are decisions you can make on your own, choosing what seems best to you. For example, if something is within your span of control, you may decide to keep your boss in the loop *after the fact*. You decide whether a given issue deserves the attention of someone at a higher level.

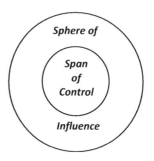

You also have issues, challenges, problems, and concerns that you have *some* influence over. This is your "sphere of influence." These issues are outside your span of control; your position and authority aren't enough to simply decide what to do. In this case you need the approval of someone else or the willingness of your boss to carry things forward. These issues tend to be things you care about and would like to have changed. So it pays to get good at raising issues, communicating critical information, and making recommendations so you can influence the person who actually *can* make the decision.

Learning to effectively use your *current* sphere of influence has a great deal to do with the *future* size of your span of control. Using and expanding your sphere of influence usually starts with your relationship with your own manager. You should quickly learn how they prefer to get your suggestions and ideas. Do they:

- Need a lot of data or just a general overview?

- Prefer to discuss your idea or issue, or see it in writing or via e-mail?

- Have a more receptive time of day?

- Need to perceive any new idea as their own?

> You can have anything you want, but you can't have everything you want.
>
> *Peter McWilliams*

This is all about your ability to *influence* the future direction of your team or unit. The goal is to provide your manager with the information needed so their decision will go the way you want it to. Obviously, you need to provide your boss with information that's truthful and complete. You don't want to leave out an essential piece of information that could prove to be a problem later. That would brand you as someone who doesn't think things through very well. Still, you can craft information and recommendations in such a way that they lead logically to the conclusion you prefer.

Often supervisors and managers are frustrated by an issue or problem outside their span of control. So they toss the issue to their boss without thinking about how they prefer to get input. When their boss rejects the idea or makes a decision they don't like, the frustration continues.

Case: Mary's Management Style

Mary was a department head in a large insurance company that had experienced steady growth during the past decade. She had promoted from within whenever possible, building a management team of seven loyal and hardworking managers.

Whenever one of the managers had a new idea or recommendation, Mary's initial response was almost always to say, "No." She believed that any idea could benefit from additional consideration, research, and thought. She wanted to make sure her managers did their homework so they really understood an issue before a decision was made. And she wanted to know they weren't just floating trial balloons. According to Mary, "If you don't bring up the issue or idea again, then you didn't think it was important enough to fight for it."

Lessons Learned

Once her management team realized this was Mary's preferred approach, they quickly figured out how to do the initial staff work needed to present her with fully developed proposals for changes and enhancements to the company's operation.

If you aren't getting the results you want from your approach, it's time to try a different approach. Ask yourself some basic questions, such as:

- What is the real problem or issue? How can I best describe it so my boss understands the essential facts?

- What specific outcome do I want? If this issue was in *my* span of control, what would I decide to do?

- Are there potential difficulties or problems associated with my approach? If so, what are they? What effect might they have on implementing my recommendation?

- What will be the benefits of following my recommendations?

- What will the payoff be to the organization and its customers?

- Who else supports my recommended approach?

Expanding both your span of control and your sphere of influence is a natural byproduct of life experiences. As you become more adept at managing yourself and the assignments, challenges, and opportunities that come your way, you "graduate" (David Allen's apt term) and take on new, higher-level challenges. Because of the confidence you develop in your own abilities, this growth process can continue as long as you're alive.

Using Time

Action is the foundational key to all success.

Pablo Picasso

Time is a resource, just like your staff, your budget, your equipment, your supplies, your skills, and your education. Like all resources it has limits. You and everyone else get exactly the same amount of this resource: 24 hours each day. In fact, time is the *only* resource that's available to everyone in exactly the same amount.

There is simply no way you can do *everything*. There are plenty of things that you need, want, and hope to do – all those things that pop into your head and into your in-basket. You may be able to do a great deal, but you have to let go of some things that you'd really like to do – or even some things that you think must be done. So, as we said before, it comes down to making choices. And sometimes they're tough.

Stephen Covey talks frequently about what he calls the four quadrants of what we do and where we focus our attention. I've always liked the way it so accurately describes most of what we do. His categories are:

- *Urgent & Important.* Crises, fires to put out, emergencies, surprises, and especially issues that hold the risk for major negative consequences.

- *Important but not Urgent.* Planning, strategizing, envisioning, re-creation (Covey's spelling), values clarification, proactive prevention. The big picture, "What do I want to accomplish" kind of activities that guide and shape our direction and results.

- *Urgent but not Important.* Interruptions, some meetings, some phone calls. Things that chew up time but contribute little to getting anything important accomplished.

- *Not Urgent & not Important.* Mindless activities that can be used to fill time when we are essentially brain-dead or exhausted. Going through junk mail, cleaning out desk drawers, or playing solitaire.

To be successful you need to spend most of your time in the "urgent and important" and "important but not urgent" quadrants.

When it comes to "not urgent and not important" – well, all of us occasionally need to chill out for a bit. Just be aware that spending more than a few minutes a day on these kinds of activities is a clue that you're not really invested in your work. Is it time for you to start thinking about what your next job looks like?

Covey also talks about what he calls the "tyranny of the urgent." This is the "urgent but not important" quadrant. It's a challenge to keep your focus on the truly important stuff while the stream of incoming demands on your time never ends. But your success depends on your ability to focus on the really important issues and not let urgent issues totally run your life.

> Time is precious. You can't get back the time you wasted yesterday.
>
> *Timothy Fong*

Whose Stuff is it?

Your sense of focus and accomplishment – and ultimately your ability to manage yourself – is reduced when you become overly involved in handling other people's priorities. Often this happens when others fail to plan, fail to keep their commitments, or let things slip through the cracks.

When it's your boss's priorities, you may have to adjust some of your own. When it's a peer or a teammate, you need to be supportive without letting their priorities pull you off-goal. Otherwise, you run the risk of underperforming in your own responsibilities. If the same few people constantly impinge on your priorities, it's time to have a conversation with them about expectations and roles – both yours and theirs.

Most managers say they want their employees to take initiative and be creative. But people will learn to delegate upward if their decisions are second-guessed. If you're truly interested in empowering your employees, your colleagues, and your growing children – and thus moving on to greater things yourself – you must be willing to trust their input and judgment. Of course, that doesn't mean you enable the aimlessly empowered; you don't hand off responsibility to someone without preparation. But once your employees have the information and resources to get the job done and know what results you expect, you should get out of the way and let them proceed. What a confidence builder that can be!

Part of making wise choices is the ability to manage your mental resources effectively. *Chapter 11* addresses the essential question: "Where is your focus?"

> It is necessary to try to pass one's self always; this occupation ought to last as long as life.
>
> *Queen Christina of Sweden*

Chapter 11
Managing Your Focus

"Am I doing the things that I *really* need to do? What about the things I *want* to do? Am I getting the kind of results I need?"

These are the kinds of questions most of us ask at some point. When you have a nagging feeling that the answer to one of these questions is "No," then you're probably struggling with your focus. It's pretty common to feel a bit overwhelmed under the barrage of requests, demands, and commitments coming your way. The difficulty comes when you feel overwhelmed more than just occasionally.

Focus – where you choose to put your attention and mental effort – is an issue on more than one level. There are the practical realities of your daily focus in your personal and professional roles. And then there are questions about your big-picture, long-range focus. For many of us the longer range tends to be neglected as our careers and lives take off and become more complex. Then, slowly but surely, we begin to feel overwhelmed every day.

Focus? So What?

As we discussed in *Chapter 10*, you *will not* be able to get everything done that you want to do. So you have to make choices. And to make good choices, you need to focus on what's important to you.

In *Chapter 7* you learned that the reticular formation in your brain helps determine what you focus on and pay attention to. When you clearly focus on a desired outcome, you acquire information, ideas, and approaches related to it. What you pay attention to creates ideas and thought patterns. Focus creates an "as if" reality both physiologically and psychologically; your mind experiences the desired outcome as if it were already happening. (For those who are

> The higher you lift your thoughts, the greater will be your achievements.
>
> *John E. Fetzer*

highly visual it can almost be like a video playing inside their brain.)

This isn't some kind of woo-woo theoretical stuff; what you focus on has very real, practical consequences. For example, research about goal setting has consistently shown one thing: people who set goals, write them down, and regularly review them are significantly more likely to say they're happy and successful than those who don't.

Instead of goals, let's think of this in terms of outcomes. Think about a specific outcome you'd like to achieve. What will be happening? What will people be doing? What will be different? The more clearly you can describe that outcome, using as much detail as possible, the more likely it is to actually occur. To some extent we do create our own reality through what we focus on.

> Failure to prepare is preparing to fail.
>
> *John Wooden*

Once again, an idea of David Allen's appeals to me. He views focus as a matter of *altitude*. If we think of things in terms of airspace, our daily tasks are the runway of life. Our current active projects – personal and professional – are like the 10,000-foot level of life. The 20,000-foot level consists of our major areas of responsibility right now, both personally and professionally. Looking out one or two years to the major goals we want to accomplish is the 30,000-foot level. Our vision of what the next three to five years will look like gives us the 40,000-foot perspective. And the really big questions – like "Why am I on the planet?" and "What is my mission in life?" – those are at the 50,000-foot level.

> I am only one, but still I am one. I cannot do everything, but still I can do something; and because I cannot do everything, I will not refuse to do something that I can do.
>
> *Helen Keller*

As a pilot I love this metaphor and it's easy to visualize. We all get better perspective from taking a look at the horizon at a higher elevation. Take at least a monthly look at the current month and the approaching two or three months. This will give you a good feel for the runway, 10,000-foot and 20,000-foot perspectives. A quarterly look at the 30,000-foot and 40,000-foot levels makes sense. An annual look at 50,000 feet, coupled with a 30,000-foot and 40,000-foot review, rounds out the year. A lot of people find that an annual review with a focus on what's next works well at the end of an old year or the beginning of a new one – whether it is a calendar or fiscal year.

Talking to Ourselves

We all talk to ourselves regularly. Every day, every hour, there's constant internal chatter going on inside your head. And for good or ill, you believe almost without question what you tell yourself. Often, without realizing it, you send messages to yourself about who you are, what you do, and how you do it. Do you have difficulty keeping commitments you make to yourself and others? Do you constantly criticize yourself? Do you tell yourself that you're a certain kind of person or that you're really not worth very much as a human being?

Shad Helmstetter has researched and written about this topic for many years. His work concentrates on better understanding how the human brain operates to provide us with information we use in our daily lives. He has shown that what we focus on with our internal self-talk profoundly affects the choices we make, what we believe, and the quality of life we have.

What Are You Focused On?

We've all had the experience. You focus on a new idea, project, need, or want and then information suddenly appears that helps you accomplish what you have in mind. As mentioned before, this is the reticular formation in your brain opening up to useful or supportive information.

There's an interesting flipside to focusing on desired outcomes. If you focus on what you *do not* want, the result is – yup – it will be more likely to show up in your life, even though you don't want it

No one can make you feel inferior without your consent.

Eleanor Roosevelt

to. This is the reality behind the saying, "Be careful what you ask for because you are likely to get it."

Much of what you've heard from other people has been negative in tone. This includes feedback from your parents and teachers when you were a child; the fault-finding, blame-fixing focus of many employers and managers at work; and even advertising messages telling you that you're less than you should/could be. This constant bombardment of negative messages and images can create a limiting, confining, constraining picture of who you are and what you can achieve. If you're like most people, you automatically see yourself in negative terms and your internal self-talk keeps reinforcing those beliefs. Over time that robs you of the confidence to change, to grow, and to see yourself as a winner . . . a proactive achiever . . . a person with unlimited possibilities for the future.

Using Affirmations

Do what you love
and the money will
follow.

Marsha Sinetar

So how do you change this? Helmstetter and others suggest the use of affirmations to help change self-programming. As Henry Ford said many years ago, "Whether you think you can or can't doesn't matter, 'cause you'll be right."

An affirmation is a positive statement about yourself that is at least 50 percent true. Through the consistent use of affirmations you can change the way you see yourself. Here are some basic rules of thumb for creating affirmations:

- Use the present tense. Create the affirmation as if the desired change has already taken place.

- Be precise. Carefully think through what you specifically want the end result to be.

- Use several affirmations around the same theme. This is particularly helpful when you're trying to change a habit.

- Make it simple. Use simple, easy-to-remember words and phrases.

Sample Affirmations

- I'm an excellent coach, teacher, and mentor, creating outstanding results that are widely recognized.
- Our clients place high value on our services and find working with us to be a great experience. We consistently exceed their expectations. We easily deliver more than anyone else ever could.
- I go to bed each night feeling grateful for my vibrant health and energy.
- I'm patient, open, and a good communicator. It's easy to support my family, my friends, and my colleagues.
- I'm grateful for my talents and gifts. I enjoy greater and greater success because I consistently act to achieve my goals.
- I have a complete overview of my direction, commitments, and priorities. I easily fulfill them every day.

Using affirmations that are personally meaningful and focused on what you want to become true in your life can, over time, replace negative, self-defeating habits and behaviors with positive, affirming, self-enhancing ones. Your self-talk can change.

What is Success?

Ultimately, all of the information in *Chapters 6-11* is about learning to manage yourself so you can be successful professionally and personally. But what does "success" mean? For some it's measured financially by salary, net worth, etc. For others it has to do with their job, position, or accomplishments. For still others it has to do with family, relationships, or a spiritual focus. Whatever success means to you, learning to effectively manage yourself will make a significant difference in achieving that success.

The secret of getting ahead is getting started.

Sally Berger

Although everyone is an individual, there seem to be four common attributes of successful people:

- Successful people know what they want and the results they want to achieve. They're clear about their goals and objectives and can describe what the desired outcome looks like.

- They take action. They get moving in the direction of their outcome or dream, and they do whatever they think the next step should be to achieve their outcome. They have a "What's the next action?" focus.

- They pay attention. They notice whether their actions are generating results that move them toward their desired outcome.

- They are flexible. They're willing to change course and try different things to reach their goal or desired outcome.

Successfully managing yourself is the first major *Skill* required to be an effective supervisor or manager. Without the ability to understand yourself and manage all of the incoming information, requests, assignments, wants, needs, and commitments you face, you simply won't be as successful as you could be.

Once you're seeing progress in your ability to manage yourself, the next step is to acquire *Skill 2 – Communicating for Results.*

Continuous improvement is better than delayed perfection.

Mark Twain

Skill 2

COMMUNICATING FOR RESULTS

"Be sincere; be brief; be seated."

Franklin D. Roosevelt

Skill 2 – Communicating for Results

Open and honest communication is at the heart of great work relationships. Your skill in using *all* methods of communication has a powerful influence on your own success and the success of your team and organization. In our work, when we examine why a manager's career has derailed we often find poor communication skills are a significant part of the problem.

Communication is the process by which information, ideas, and meaning are exchanged and understood by two or more people. In business the intent is to educate, inform, influence, or motivate.

As a manager you use verbal and written communication every day to influence another person's behavior or motivate them to accomplish something. You also use communication to achieve general organizational objectives, meet the mission, or implement some overall strategy. Regardless of your purpose, you want to create, transmit, and receive information as effectively as possible while building understanding and positive relationships.

> The quality of your communications is determined by the results you get.
>
> *Tony Robbins*

To communicate effectively you need to balance four major components:

- Verbal communication

- Nonverbal communication

- Written communication

- Listening

> Today, communication itself is the problem. We have become the world's first overcommunicated society. Each year we send more and receive less.
>
> *Al Ries*

The model on the next page shows an overview of these components and some examples of what goes into them.

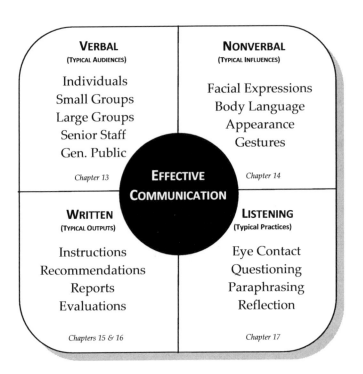

VERBAL
(TYPICAL AUDIENCES)

Individuals
Small Groups
Large Groups
Senior Staff
Gen. Public

Chapter 13

NONVERBAL
(TYPICAL INFLUENCES)

Facial Expressions
Body Language
Appearance
Gestures

Chapter 14

EFFECTIVE COMMUNICATION

WRITTEN
(TYPICAL OUTPUTS)

Instructions
Recommendations
Reports
Evaluations

Chapters 15 & 16

LISTENING
(Typical Practices)

Eye Contact
Questioning
Paraphrasing
Reflection

Chapter 17

Two monologues do
not make a dialogue.

Jeff Daly

Since communication is a *shared* process, it might fail when one of the parties has limited skills in one or more of these areas. How would you rate yourself today on each of these components?

For any organization, team, or group to be successful, people must understand each other, collaborate to define goals and tasks, and work together toward a common purpose. Interaction between people at work is essential to generate results. To accomplish this, face-to-face communication – either one-on-one or in group settings – is used frequently. Written memos are common, as are voicemail and e-mail messages, texting, and other electronic forms of communication.

Whatever the tools used, communication involves sending and receiving messages. The major goal of all interpersonal communication is to secure understanding, i.e., to create a solid match between the message sent and the message received. Why does this matter? Well, the better people who work together understand each other, the more efficient, effective, and creative they will be.

Visual Communication – Another Channel

There isn't room to explore the topic in this book, but in addition to listening, written, verbal, and nonverbal communication, we also communicate information and ideas through our visual sense. This includes graphics, signs, photos, billboards, videos, films, games, etc. During the past 20+ years we've become used to receiving a wide variety of messages visually. (Think YouTube, downloadable videos, TV commercials, flash-enhanced Web sites, and everything else that's emerging from Web 2.0 integrated communications). While often passive and one-way by its very nature, visual communication can be powerful. When done well it creates "sticky" impressions that stay with the viewer. For example, anyone who's old enough remembers the photo taken by AP photographer Nick Ut of a young Vietnamese girl running naked down a street after being severely burned by a South Vietnamese napalm attack. In the business world, think about the number of corporate logos that are instantly recognizable (e.g., Apple, AT&T) because of how they're used to communicate.

The art of communication is the language of leadership.

James Humes

Chapter 12
Communication 101

Seventy percent of the time we are awake we're engaged in some form of communication. According to a study by Air University (the Intellectual and Leadership Center of the U.S. Air Force), our communication time breaks down like this:

- 10 percent is spent writing.

- 15 percent is spent reading.

- 30 percent is spent talking.

- 45 percent is spent listening.

> The problem with communication . . . is the *illusion* that it has been accomplished.
>
> *George Bernard Shaw*

The Point of it All

When you communicate with others, you're usually trying to accomplish one or more of the following objectives:

- To be understood

- To understand others

- To gain acceptance or agreement

- To get something done

To Be Understood

You are trying to get something across so they understand what you mean. This "something" can be facts or your intentions, feelings, or frame of mind. Whatever method you use, you want others to understand you.

To Understand Others

You are trying to find out their point of view; you're seeking information to help you solve a problem or make a decision; or you're learning how they feel about a particular situation. This often takes the form of questioning, clarifying, listening, or probing for additional information.

To Gain Acceptance or Agreement

You are trying to get them to agree with you, give you a sympathetic hearing, or at least acknowledge that you have a point of view. This may include persuading them to change their attitude about something by showing it in a new light.

To Get Something Done

You are trying to move them toward action – to persuade them to do something because they understand what you want done, why they should do it, and perhaps something about how and when the task needs to be done.

Regardless of which objective(s) you're trying to meet, the more complex the task or project, the more important communication is. When you're responsible for a mission-critical project, you can't afford to get it right only 90 percent of the time and your organization can't either. Clear communication, usually using a variety of methods or channels, is absolutely essential for complex tasks.

Talking with someone (in person or on the phone) is suitable for conveying simple, nontechnical instructions. But when the process becomes more complex, you need something in written form. Using e-mailed instructions and information is a fast way to help support tasks and project work. But keep e-mails short and put the most critical information at the top; too often, information that's hidden below the bottom of the computer screen is ignored. (See *Chapter 16* for more ideas about e-mail and texting.)

Happiness is not a goal, it is a by-product.

Eleanor Roosevelt

Blessed is the man who, having nothing to say, abstains from giving us wordy evidence of the fact.

George Eliot

The Two-Way Street

When we think of communicating with someone, most of us (the Extraverts especially) think first of talking – the process of communicating verbally. According to research by Koneya and Barbour, the sum total of a one-on-one, face-to-face communication message is:

- Tone of voice   38%

- Body language and other nonverbals   55%

- Actual words   7%

You might consider the communication job finished when you've *sent* the message, i.e., when you've told your employee or teammate what you want done. But how do you know they heard you accurately?

When your nonverbal messages, your tone of voice, and your words are in sync, the chances increase that your face-to-face communication will succeed. But when your nonverbal messages and/or tone of voice aren't consistent with your words, communication is likely to derail. How many times have you said something, but the other person's facial expressions tell you the message wasn't received the way you anticipated?

It's important to remember that all communication is at least two-way. It's not just something that goes *from you to others*, but it's something that takes place *between you* and *others*. Unless you communicate with this in mind, you'll be as handicapped as if you worked wearing blinders and earplugs.

How important is communication to your success? Most managers spend about 80 percent of their workday on communication-related activities. The following graph is based on Henry Mintzberg's

Many attempts to communicate are nullified by saying too much.

Robert Greenleaf

The more elaborate our means of communication, the less we communicate.

Joseph Priestley

research from the 1970s, but the trend today isn't significantly different.

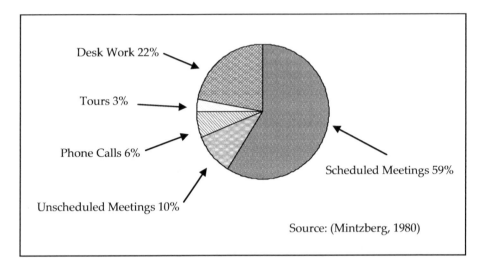

Source: (Mintzberg, 1980)

It's likely that at least some of the desk work shown in Mintzberg's findings is spent dealing with e-mail and texting. So the overall time the average manager or supervisor spends communicating may actually be higher than 80 percent. Our surveys show that most managers spend more than 90 percent of their day communicating in some fashion.

Are these findings substantially different from your workday? How much of the time do you spend communicating?

Why Communication Breaks Down

You cannot shake hands with a clenched fist.

Golda Meir

Why do people misunderstand each other? We've all experienced the look of confusion, the "40-yard stare," that people get on their face when they have no clue what we're trying to communicate. There are all kinds of reasons that communication breaks down. Some of them are:

- We don't ask the right questions of the right people.

- We don't actively listen to each other.

- We have significant personality differences or conflicting values.

- We believe the other person understood what was said, but don't check for comprehension.

- We tend to quickly evaluate and make judgments about what we hear or see.

- We are reluctant to ask questions when the other person is above us on the organizational ladder.

- We give too much information, too many details, too quickly.

- We give vague instructions or deliver them in a way that's hard to understand.

In addition, information can get lost or distorted in the sending and/or receiving. For example, noisy environments can make communication difficult or interrupt the interaction. But ultimately, misunderstanding occurs because we are individuals and our differences naturally create barriers to understanding each other.

The Anxiety of Interaction Overwhelm

Each of us interacts with other people and a lot of informational inputs every day. These inputs include:

- One-on-one meetings

- Staff/team/task force group meetings

- Casual/unscheduled/drop-in meetings and interruptions

- Phone calls/voice mail messages

- Electronic mail and text messages/document transfers

- Mail/memos/magazines and other "read and review" items

> One of the basic causes for all the trouble in the world today is that people talk too much and think too little. They act impulsively without thinking. I always try to think before I talk.
>
> *Margaret Chase Smith*

Several studies quoted in The Wall Street Journal indicate that the typical professional handles more than 170 interactions in an average workday. Is it any wonder that most managers and supervisors sometimes feel totally overwhelmed by their job? If you feel that way, you're not alone.

The bottom line is every one of your interactions involves some form of communication. So your competence with this key skill is critical to your success or failure as a manager. And that means that becoming adept at all aspects of *Skill 2* needs to be an important part of your professional development. The next several chapters will help you improve your communication skills.

The only tyrant I accept in this world is the still voice within.

Mohandas K. Gandhi

Chapter 13
Choices in Verbal Communication

Verbal communication is, in general, the process of expressing thoughts and feelings out loud. Since your thoughts and feelings are an internal process, you have to decide whether to express them aloud or not. (If you're a clear Extravert you might sometimes find yourself wishing you had chosen *not* to!)

Depending on your specific position and responsibilities, you may communicate verbally with a wide variety of different audiences (e.g., small groups, large groups, senior staff, and/or the general public). You will certainly devote much of your time to one-on-one communication. As a result, you'll need to pay attention to answering the following two questions:

- Who is the audience in this situation?

- What is the best way to communicate with them?

Verbal Communication Choices

As a supervisor or manager, you're a model for others, whether you want to be or not. As discussed in *Chapter 22 – Creating Outstanding Performance*, your attitudes, behaviors, and how you communicate will all be reflected in how your employees operate. This means you have to pay attention to what you say and what you *don't* say. Carefully consider how your thoughts are turned into spoken words. Once you've decided to speak your thoughts aloud, you have other choices to make, including:

- The specific words you use

- The sound of your voice

- The pace of your speech

> Wise men talk because they have something to say; fools, because they have to say something.
>
> *Plato*

- The volume of your voice

- The communication environment you choose

The Specific Words You Use

How can you best use language to express your thoughts? How you perceive the other people you're speaking with will certainly have an influence on the words you choose. You may use certain words or phrases with one person – like your boss – while using very different words with someone like your spouse.

The CPO Switches Gears

Some years ago I went through basic training at Great Lakes Naval Training Center outside of Chicago. One of the instructors was a grizzled Chief Petty Officer who used some very salty language in his lectures, including liberal use of the "f-bomb." As we neared the end of basic training this CPO was selected to deliver a talk to a group of family members about the training their sons, husbands, and fathers had received. The Chief knew that his salty language wouldn't go over too well with these civilians, so he slowed his pace, carefully thought about what he wanted to say, and got through the entire talk without a single cuss word. Of course, with his careful consideration of each word, he spoke in a very halting, choppy manner; I'm certain the assembled crowd thought he had some sort of speech impediment! But he understood that the words you choose do matter.

The Sound of Your Voice

People say conversation is a lost art; how often I have wished it were.

Edward R. Murrow

The sound or tone of your voice and how you use inflection or variation will also change depending on who you're talking with and the message you want to get across. By some estimates nearly 40 percent of our message is carried in how our voice sounds to the other person. For example diplomat and geopolitician Henry Kissinger and management philosopher Peter Drucker were both brilliant thinkers and had a huge influence on the world stage. But listening to them speak was often a challenge because they both had heavy accents and a monotone delivery style. Their ideas had extraordinary reach, but their lack of inflection made them hard to understand.

The Pace of Your Speech

There are often significant geographical differences in the pace or speed of delivery we use. In the U.S., those who grew up in the Northeast Corridor are often seen as speaking much more rapidly than, say, those who have lived their entire lives in the Deep South. People in their 60s and older often complain that young people talk too fast and speak as if they had a mouth full of marbles. Extraverts tend to speak more quickly (and use a *lot* more words) than Introverts; they often overwhelm others with the sheer number of words and a rapid-fire delivery. As you interact with different people, experiment with varying your pace. Find out what seems to be most effective in generating clear communication.

The Volume of Your Voice

Voice volume is an area where both sex and personality type influence communication. Most men have a built-in advantage over most women because their deeper-pitched voices tend to naturally sound louder and carry further. Also, Extraverts tend to deliver their torrent of words at a louder volume. Quieter Introverts (especially females) may have difficulty getting their message heard; fewer words spoken softly might not make it through the ambient noise level of the louder Extraverts. From personal experience I know that some Introverts simply give up trying to get their message across in the face of chattering Extraverts who tend to listen poorly.

The right to be heard does not automatically include the right to be taken seriously.

Hubert H. Humphrey

The Communication Environment You Choose

The environment you communicate in can have a major effect on the success you'll have getting your message across. Noisy environments – manufacturing plants, mechanical spaces, crowds, and poor acoustics – can cause parts of your message to be garbled or misunderstood. Relaying complex instructions verbally in a noisy workplace can be a crap shoot; the message sent and the message received may not be the same at all. Don't rely just on verbal communication in this situation.

> Communication is not only the essence of being human, but also a vital property of life.
>
> *John A. Piece*

Chapter 14
Nonverbals: The Silent Influencers

There are so many ways you can influence your communication through the nonverbal messages you send. As we mentioned before, nonverbal behavior makes up at least 55 percent of what you actually communicate in face-to-face encounters. Most of your nonverbal communication choices are made automatically, without conscious thought. In fact, unless you deliberately stop to think about it, you'll probably do what you've done in the past – an "automatic" nonverbal routine that feels right emotionally and physically.

Nonverbal Communication Is . . .

Nonverbal communication refers to the messages you send through your actions and behaviors rather than through the words you use. Nonverbal messages communicate your feelings and thoughts with far greater force than any words you say, no matter how carefully you choose your words.

Some examples of nonverbal communication include:

- Facial expressions

- Body movement & gestures

- Use of space, distance & territory

- Touching behaviors

- General appearance

- Physical appearance

> When I get ready to talk to people, I spend two thirds of the time thinking what they want to hear and one third thinking about what I want to say.
>
> *Abraham Lincoln*

Facial Expressions

This includes eye contact and eye movements as well as the rest of your face. The primary communicator of your emotions, your face can be difficult to control or manipulate. Sure, you can learn how to maintain a "poker face" when playing Texas Hold 'Em. But if you're like most people – particularly clear Extraverts – your emotions are playing out on your face all the time. Whether you're angry or happy with something another person has done or said, that feeling is going to be revealed, regardless of the words you say.

Body Movement & Gestures

This is sometimes referred to as "body language" and it can communicate a wide array of messages. For example, leaning forward and looking directly at the speaker conveys intense interest in what they're saying. Crossing your arms across the front of your body can communicate resistance, defensiveness, or lack of interest in what the other person is saying. Body movements and gestures have become a full-fledged field of study, and research has shown that what people do is strongly influenced by their culture and gender. Take a few seconds to consciously watch what others do with their bodies and gestures as they interact with you. You might see something interesting!

Use of Space, Distance & Territory

This includes the distance between people, your physical location, and the furnishings in the environment. Most of us like to have a certain amount of distance or "personal space" around us when we talk with someone. If another person gets too close (whatever distance that might be), we tend to be uncomfortable and may have difficulty focusing on the interaction. If you notice the person you're talking with taking a step backward, you might be invading their personal space. Don't follow them; just give them the space they want. Otherwise, you risk being perceived as trying to dominate, even if that's not your intention.

Offices say a lot nonverbally. For example, some managers seem to enjoy emphasizing their power by elevating their own chair or by

> The relationship is the communication bridge between people.
>
> *Alfred Kadushin*

using low side chairs to put visitors on a lower level. They think this makes them appear more powerful, even though most of us think it's silly. But it says something about the occupant's approach to communication. Remaining behind a desk (i.e., a barrier) conveys a more formal approach to interaction, while using a casual seating area away from the desk might indicate that discussion will be informal.

Touching Behaviors

Touch can communicate specific information about the relationship between people or how they regard each other. Feelers in particular seem to more readily touch other people as they interact. Holding a handshake while placing your other hand on the other person's arm is a technique that conveys connection and familiarity – something many elected officials seem to use while campaigning.

Both male and female managers have to be careful that their natural inclination to establish rapport and connection with others is not viewed as overly intimate or bordering on sexual harassment. After all, the appropriateness of touch is in the eyes of the person being touched, not the one initiating the touch. So learn to look for others' nonverbal reactions to how you use touch in your communication.

General Appearance

How you are dressed and groomed can symbolize to others your attitudes, values, station in life, identification with a particular group, cultural heritage, and other characteristics. We make value judgments about people who are neatly attired and wearing clothing appropriate to the situation. Dirty, sloppy, unkempt, or overly revealing clothes; extremely unusual hair styles; or dirty hands and fingernails say things about you as an individual. And whether you think it's fair or not, they also influence how seriously your message is taken by others. A neat appearance, with clothing and grooming appropriate to your situation and position, will tend

> I know that you believe you understand what you think I said, but I'm not sure you realize that what you heard is not what I meant.
>
> *Robert McCloskey*

to increase the weight of your message and make it more likely that your communication will be successful.

Physical Appearance

Your size, sex, skin color, and other obvious physical characteristics will affect how your communications are interpreted, especially during interactions early in a relationship. While it's true that your overall body type is based more on heredity than lifestyle, having your weight generally in proportion to your height will tend to make others feel more comfortable in your presence and pay more attention to the information you're trying to communicate. Tall people are generally perceived as being more powerful, although there are certainly plenty of examples of shorter people being highly successful.

As a supervisor or manager, you need to pay attention to your own nonverbal messages, making sure that your verbal and nonverbal communication match. At the same time, you need to be aware of what your colleagues, employees, and boss are saying with their own nonverbal messages.

Chapter 15
Writing: Communicating When You're Not There

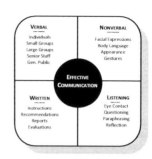

The amount of time you spend writing depends on your specific job responsibilities and the kind of organization you work in. Increasingly, the amount of work on computers required in most settings guarantees that at least some of your work is written. It's no longer unusual for supervisors and managers to spend several hours a day at the keyboard. And who predicted that computers would make the "paperless office" a reality?

"Improving my writing skills" shows up repeatedly in various professional development surveys as one of managers' top needs. But few organizations have internal business writing programs, and it's often assumed that when you become a manager you come equipped with reasonably good writing skills. In reality, a high percentage of supervisors and managers need help with their written communication. We can't teach you how to write well by reading this book. But this chapter gives you some tips and a quick overview of things to think about when you're writing.

Writing Realities

Depending on your previous experiences, writing can be scary, guilt-ridden, agonizing, a necessary evil, or – yes, it's possible – an interesting, fun challenge in communication. To start, let's look at a few realities about writing. They may not match things you learned in school or from your previous work experiences.

- Anyone can learn to write *clearly and simply*; that is what's at the heart of good writing.

- Good writing starts with a bit of thinking and planning – and then practice, practice, practice.

- Bulky writing — using large words and long sentences — isn't impressive and it doesn't make you sound smart.

> Verbosity leads to unclear, inarticulate things.
>
> *Dan Quayle*

It just makes things hard for your busy readers. Your goal is to be *clear and brief.*

- There are rules about grammar and sentence structure, but there's no *one* correct way to write.

- Many organizations have internal standards for written communication. If yours is one of those, take the time to learn and use them.

- Procrastination (i.e., putting off writing while you "think about it") doesn't help in the long run. Get started and put something on paper, even if it's just a general outline of what you want to say. Then go back, add more detail, review, and revise later.

- Boilerplate has its place (e.g., form letters), but it's usually better to start fresh each time. Previous writing won't save the day.

I love deadlines. I like the whooshing sound they make as they fly by.

Douglas Adams

Getting Started: The Basics

Every time you sit down to write, your real purpose is to communicate information in such a way that your readers say, "I get it!" You do this by making your writing simple, clear, and logical. "Great!" you say. "How do I do that?"

Grasp the subject, the words will follow.

Cato the Elder

Whether you're writing a set of instructions, a recommendation, a performance evaluation, or a major report, start with some basic planning by answering a few simple questions:

- Who is your audience – one person, a group? What do you know about them?

- What do they already know about your subject?

- What do you want to communicate? What information do you need to get across?

- What result do you want?

- What is the best way to reach them?

Your Readers

Like you, your readers are overwhelmed with the flow of information today. They have way too much to read in too little time in too many different formats (magazines, newspapers, e-mail, blogs, RSS feeds). Or their approach to handling incoming information isn't adequate to the task; and their personal system can't handle the overwhelming input. (Or both!)

How do you make sure *your* message gets their attention? By understanding how people decide what to read. Most people use four criteria:

- Is this something I'm interested in?

- Do I already know something about it?

- Is this important to me (for whatever reason)?

- Is this easy to read?

If your readers aren't interested, don't know much about the topic, believe it's unimportant, or find the writing hard to understand, your communication will be consigned to the heap of "someday, maybe" (if not the trash). You can't control your readers' interests, knowledge, or how important they think your topic is. *The only thing you can control is the quality and clarity of your writing*. If your message is too wordy or unfocused . . . if it doesn't speak to their self-interest or the interest of the organization . . . they simply won't read it.

The bottom line of all this? Before you start writing take a couple of minutes to think about your readers and what they already know

> To effectively communicate, we must realize that we are all different in the way we perceive the world and use this understanding as a guide to our communication with others.
>
> *Tony Robbins*

about your subject. What will stop them from immediately sending your writing to the electronic or physical wastebasket?

Your Purpose, Key Messages & Method

Purpose

Assuming your readers actually do read your document, what do you want them to *do*? What result do you want? Here are some of the many possibilities:

- You want them to learn something.

- You're trying to persuade them to do or believe something.

- You're delivering news – good or bad.

- You're asking/telling them to take some action.

You don't necessarily have to openly state your purpose. But whenever you write, you need to keep it in mind.

Key Messages

What, specifically, are you trying to get across? If you had only one minute during an elevator ride with your readers, what would be the most important points you'd need to make?

The hard part of this is being clear about what you want to say. You may find yourself quickly throwing a lot of words at your readers because you're not sure what you're trying to say. But that just makes things blurry and complex, increasing the chances your document will get pushed away unread. So before you start writing, take a minute to think about it. Sometimes, the easiest way to start is to make a bare-bones list of the key ideas you want to get across in your document.

Method

Also take a minute before you write to think about the best way to reach your readers. E-mails, memos, lists of instructions, detailed reports – you have a lot of choices, all of which have strengths and weaknesses. It pays to understand what format or approach will help your readers understand your writing under different circumstances.

Ending: Editing & Proofreading

After you've finished writing, it will save you all kinds of grief if you take a little extra time to double-check what you've created, even for a quick e-mail message. *Basic editing* is simply revising your document to make sure it says what you really want to say – and doing anything you can to help your readers understand what you're saying. *Proofreading* is the detailed work of looking for errors. The bottom line is NEVER send an important document without someone doing at least a quick edit/review and a thorough proofreading.

If you'd like to tackle this yourself, here are just a few of the things to look for:

- Is your content complete (i.e., did you forget anything)?

- Have you addressed all instructions, requirements, or requests?

- Is everything clear, consistent, and on topic?

- Can anything be trimmed, simplified, or eliminated?

- Does your document flow logically and make sense?

- Have you clearly stated any next actions and/or what you expect your readers to do with your message?

- Are there any typos or spelling mistakes (especially individuals' names!)?

> I have made this letter longer than usual, only because I have not had the time to make it shorter.
>
> *Blaise Pascal*

- Is the format consistent throughout the document?

- Is there any incorrect punctuation and capitalization?

- Are page numbers and other numerical sequences correct?

- Are there any math errors (subtraction, addition, etc.)

- Do you have any poorly aligned lists (especially important in financials, figures in tables, dates)?

Tips From the Pros

Here are five suggestions from a professional writer:

- Don't edit or revise while writing your first draft. Get your ideas down, then go back and revise.

- Proofread on hard copy, not your computer screen. (Paper activates a different part of your brain, and you'll see things on paper that you'll miss on the monitor.)

- For important documents, write your first draft and then sleep on it. You'll see things differently the next day.

- Put "time to write" cues into your work environment – anything that helps motivate or prepare you to write.

- Eliminate "I don't feel like it" from your vocabulary when it comes to writing. You're unlikely to ever feel like it. Just do it.

NOTE: If you're upset about something, go ahead and write about it, but then *do not* send it until you've set it aside for at least 24 hours. Since it's hard to get into trouble for something you *don't* say, waiting a day or two before hitting the "send" button on a flaming e-mail can prevent a career-limiting move.

Chapter 16
E-mail and Texting @ Work

WARNING!

Electronic messages are as private as the company bulletin board. If you'd be embarrassed to see your message posted on a bulletin board, don't put it out electronically.

E-mail, text messages, Facebook, Twitter, Skype™, blogs, RSS feeds (and other electronic tools that may have been invented within the last 24 hours) have permanently changed our communication patterns. But how do they apply to business and you as a manager or supervisor? In this chapter we look at the two tools you're likely to use most often: e-mail and text messaging.

When to Use E-mail

Although it's easy to use, e-mail isn't always the best way to communicate. Sometimes it pays to pick up the old pen and write a note by hand. So when should you use e-mail in business?

- You're in different time zones and/or contacting someone who's hard to reach by phone or in person.

- Your message is short and informal.

- You want to send the same message to several people within a short time.

- You're sending an advance notice, indicating you'll contact your recipients later with details.

- You're providing follow-up information after an initial contact.

> Electric communication will never be a substitute for the face of someone who with their soul encourages another person to be brave and true.
>
> *Charles Dickens*

E-mail Netiquette

A set of informal rules has developed over the years called the "netiquette" of e-mail in business. Most people receive between 25 and 50 messages a day (excluding spam), and some of us get as many as 200, 300, or even 500 each day. So it can be very helpful to your career if you know how to get your messages through the electronic pile.

Setting Up & Sending Messages

- Always fill in the subject line. Keep it punchy, short, and directly related to the topic(s) covered in the message.

- *Make sure* you've typed in the correct e-mail address. You may save yourself from severe embarrassment someday just by double-checking the recipient's address before you hit the "send" button!

- Send your message *only* to those who really need to read it (i.e., don't copy the whole office just because you already have them on a distribution list and you're in a hurry).

- Think three times before forwarding anything. Do you *really* need to forward this message? You don't want to become known as the person who forwards everything and whose messages are ignored by everyone.

- Limit your message to the equivalent of one screen page. If you need more room, put the rest in an attachment. Long, drawn-out e-mails with a task assignment or action step at the end usually don't work.

- Don't get exotic visually. Use a common typeface that will display well on everyone's computer (e.g., Times New Roman).

Writing a Message

- Be professional. All the rules of good writing apply to e-mail. Be as careful with your grammar, punctuation, paragraph formation, and spelling as you would in a printed memo on company letterhead.

- Put a friendly opening and the person's name on the first line.

- Don't use ALL CAPS. They're hard to read and using them is considered the equivalent of shouting at someone in cyberspace.

- There are hundreds of emoticons and abbreviations used as shorthand in cyberspace (e.g., BTW means "by the way" and IMHO means "in my humble opinion"). Don't use them in your corporate e-mail unless you're absolutely certain all of your recipients will understand them. Even then, use them sparingly; they can detract from your message.

- Request a specific action or response within a set time frame. If no response or action is needed write a sentence like, "No action needed."

- Include your name, company, telephone number, and e-mail address at the end. E-mail software lets you create signature files so your contact information will be generated automatically with every outgoing message.

- When replying to a message, refer to the contents of the sender's original message. They need to know what you're responding to.

- When responding to a current message, it's best not to throw in a new topic. Important comments, ideas, and actions get lost that way. Start a new message instead so you can clearly trace the new thread.

- Close with a friendly sentence or a "thank you."

> Words are, of course, the most powerful drug used by mankind.
>
> *Rudyard Kipling*

Finally . . .

Do your part to keep your network manager happy. Don't use e-mail to just say "Hi." Clean out your "Inbox" and "Sent" folders regularly. If you need to keep multiple versions of a file, archive offline everything except the most recent version.

When to Use Text Messages

Text messaging and other short messaging systems have developed their own vocabulary and spelling rules. They don't apply in any other business format.

Like e-mail, text messaging isn't always the best way to communicate. It's an immediate, very casual form of communication that works best for short bursts. So when should you use a text message in business?

- Your message is very short and informal.

- You need to communicate a small amount of information, *and* it must go out immediately, *and* you don't have other communications options available.

- You're sure that the person you need to communicate with has access to text messaging *and* is familiar with its use.

Text Message Etiquette

Like e-mail, text messaging has its own etiquette or rules of polite usage, such as:

- Composing, sending, and responding to text messages while you're in a meeting is just plain rude. Yes, a lot of people do this during meetings instead of participating in the discussion, but resist the temptation to join in. Set a good example for your team. Turn off your phone or PDA, pay attention, and participate.

> Good communication is as stimulating as black coffee, and just as hard to sleep after.
>
> *Anne Morrow Lindbergh*

- Text messaging is informal – very informal – so it isn't suitable for anything other than very short, informal communication.

- Simple and straightforward are important in any communication, but especially in text messaging. The medium has enough limitations, so using sarcasm or irony is asking for misunderstanding. Simple, clear words and sentences work best.

I'm convinced that the increased use of text messaging and thumb keyboards on smartphones has contributed to the poor sentence construction and horrid grammar we regularly see in e-mails and other writing. Take just a bit of care in how your message looks when using text messaging. It will make a big difference in how you're viewed by others. Simple things like beginning each sentence with a capital letter, using a bit of punctuation to more clearly convey your message, and not using truncated words (e.g., "you're right" instead of "u r rt") will help your readers and get your message across clearly.

Chapter 17
The Active Art of Listening

"We have two ears and one mouth so that we can listen twice as much as we speak."

This ancient proverb is often attributed to the Greek philosopher, Epictetus. While this statement may ring true, the simple fact is most of us *don't* listen very well. We may receive training in writing, speech, public presentations, and even nonverbal communication, but we seldom get training in improving our listening skills. Even though we instinctively understand that listening is an important part of effective communication, we tend to take it for granted.

Hearing is an *innate* skill, while listening is an *acquired* skill. By some estimates, we retain only about 10 to 20 percent of the information we hear. If you only "get" a small percentage of what you hear, you better hope what you retain is the really important stuff!

The problem is that we're usually merely *hearing* rather than truly *listening*. Much of the time we're simply passively taking in the information we hear instead of actively listening. Active listening means your brain is fully engaged. You're making a conscious effort to understand not only the words being said but also the *meaning* of the total message being sent.

All of us have had conversations with people who are clearly not listening actively. They don't respond in any way . . . they're distracted by someone else or their cell phone . . . you wonder whether anything you're saying is actually getting through. Well, it isn't. Communication is failing.

You never saw a fish on the wall with its mouth shut.

Sally Berger

To listen well is as powerful a means of communication and influence as to talk well.

John Marshall

Paying Attention

The first step in truly listening is simply *paying attention*. There's no way you can listen actively unless you're engaged in the communication. That means both your ears and your brain are attending to what the other person is saying. In other words, you're "present" in the sense that you're open to receiving their message and you're listening to what they're saying. Your brain's reticular filter has been opened, which allows you to focus on the incoming message and (hopefully) submerge or ignore any distractions from the environment.

Silence is the
ultimate weapon of
power.

Charles de Gaulle

Handling Distractions

Several years ago I was meeting with a key partner in a seminar room prior to the start of a public presentation. One of my staff members was in the room, laying out materials for the upcoming presentation. My focus on the discussion with the partner kept drifting because the staff member's actions didn't match the expectation I had for how he was to set out the materials.

Wisely, my colleague said, "Excuse me Paul, but you seem a bit distracted. Is there something you need to take care of before we continue?" I was relieved at her observation. I readily agreed with her assessment and proceeded to have a brief conversation with the staff person to make sure he and I were on the same page. Then I returned to my colleague and was able to fully focus on that conversation. My ability to pay attention was strong at first but decreased markedly as I observed my staff member's behavior. After I handled that I was able to pay attention again.

Understanding

Paying attention is only the first step in the listening process. Being open to receiving the other person's message is one thing, but *understanding* that message is something else altogether. Our ability to truly understand incoming communication is affected by many things, such as:

- Language barriers (accents, dialects, colloquialisms, etc.)

- Environmental issues (noise, movement, weather, etc.)

- Previous interactions with the other person (positive/negative)

- Positional differences (job, expertise, specialization, etc.)

- Our mindset (distractions, emotions, non-work issues, etc.)

- Our individual hardwiring and health (personality preferences, upbringing, hearing loss, etc.)

Individual differences of all kinds may limit our ability to truly understand the other person's message, regardless of how well we attend to and hear it. For instance, when you say, "I'll call you at 2 p.m.," my perception is 2 p.m., give or take no more than five minutes. But you may actually mean, "Maybe around 2 p.m. or perhaps later if I get tied up with something." At the end of this communication we don't know it, but we have very different notions of when that phone call will occur. There's been hearing, listening, and even some communication, but understanding has failed.

> Seek first to understand, *then* to be understood.
>
> *Stephen Covey*

> When people talk, listen completely. Most people never listen.
>
> *Ernest Hemingway*

Good Listening Practices

Here are some of the practices commonly associated with good and poor listeners. As you review this table you may come up with additional examples from your own experiences.

Good Listeners Tend to ...	Poor Listeners Tend to ...
Make and sustain eye contact	Have limited or no eye contact
Show nonverbal interest	Keep on working while the other person is speaking
Ask questions to clarify	Be nonresponsive, ask no questions, provide no feedback
Repeat or paraphrase	Interrupt or cut the other person off
Pay attention to the other person's body language	React emotionally or dismissively, ignore the other person's body language
Defer judgment	Jump to conclusions

Improving Your Listening Skills

Most people seem to think they are good listeners, even though they may only be hearing what another is saying. Becoming a good listener involves a set of behaviors and skills that must be developed and practiced. Becoming an active listener means not only paying attention to the other person, but also making a conscious effort to process and understand what is being said. So how can you improve your ability to listen effectively? Here are some key ideas:

- Paraphrase
- Question
- Reflect
- Reinforce
- Be patient

Paraphrase

Rewording what the other person is saying and feeding it back to them demonstrates that you've understood what they're saying. In addition, if you actually *didn't* understand them, they can try another approach to more fully explain what they meant. This helps ensure that both of you are on the same page as the communication goes along.

Question

Asking open-ended questions can help both you and the other person think more about the particular issue or situation you're discussing. Again, this helps clarify and refine your communication. It also shows that you *are* paying attention and are interested in what they have to say. This increases the chances that the outcome of the communication will be positive.

Reflect

When a person says something that expresses a *feeling* about an event or situation, you can reflect that feeling or emotion back to them to show you understand what they're saying. For instance, they might say something like, "I'm fed up with Joe's laziness! I've had enough!" You might respond by saying, "It sounds like you're pretty frustrated." In this case you're not repeating or paraphrasing what they *said*, but are reflecting back to them what you heard them say they *feel*. Reflecting helps to demonstrate that you're truly listening and understand their feelings. It also gives the other person a chance to amplify, clarify, or refine their message – which improves the quality of communication.

Reinforce

Letting others know that you *are* indeed listening helps reinforce your own efforts. Nodding your head from time to time or a simple "uh huh" reinforces the idea that you're listening and will help you focus. When combined with looking directly at the other person, the

It seemed rather incongruous that in a society of supersophisticated communication, we often suffer from a shortage of listeners.

Erma Bombeck

message you're sending says, "I'm paying attention." Although direct eye contact is useful in most situations in many cultures, it isn't used universally. So be aware of when it is appropriate to use this kind of eye contact.

Be Patient

Especially for Extraverts, it pays to curb the innate tendency to interrupt. Let the other person finish. In your desire to get your own point across you may inadvertently step on the end of people's sentences, and that *really ticks people off.* Part of good listening is being aware of the subtle cues from others. Just because someone pauses briefly doesn't mean they're finished speaking. (This is especially true of Introverts, who need to time to think before they speak.)

I have never been hurt by what I have not said.

Calvin Coolidge

Listening is not a passive process. You must be *actively* involved and engaged in the communication. You must be prepared, which means having done your homework (if that's needed) so you're up to speed on the topic. It also means asking questions to clarify and ensure you actually understand the message. And it means refraining from distracting activities such as taking phone calls, hunting for your pen, reading e-mail or text messages, or tracking off on some unrelated train of thought. Open your ears and your brain, and pay attention. It *will* improve your communication!

Chapter 18
Not *Another* Meeting

In nearly every organization we've worked with during the past 25 years, we've heard many complaints about ineffective meetings. The sum total of wasted minutes, hours, and days devoted to useless, ineffective, confusing, or downright mind-numbingly boring meetings, conferences, off-sites, and training programs is incredible. But with a bit of care, planning, and thinking, you can make *your* meetings truly useful and highly effective for you and your team. What does it take?

Usually, ineffective meetings are the result of poor planning and no process for conducting the meeting. Without some general planning and guidelines, meetings can easily fail to accomplish much of anything – other than to waste everyone's time.

Some companies have written rules about how meetings are managed. The following list from the Kellogg Company is as good a suggested set of ground rules as I've seen:

- Say what you need to say IN the meeting.

- Take responsibility to surface issues and offer solutions.

- Surface and resolve conflicts.

- Listen, respond, build on others' ideas.

- Take risks and support others as they do.

Extraverts seem to find meetings useful, while Introverts think they're primarily a place where Extraverts go to talk to each other. Scheduling, agenda-setting, and meeting facilitation tasks all seem to appeal to Extraverts and Judgers – those outgoing, organized planners who value action and closure on issues. In most organizations they're in the majority in upper management, so the company culture will tend to reflect their preference for meetings.

> You can't sit in a boring meeting, in a boring conference room and expect to generate much beyond boring ideas.
>
> *Andy Stefanovich*

A regular staff meeting is *not* the place to talk about poor performance. That conversation needs to take place one-on-one. It's also not the place to pound your fist and yell at people. That will only lead them to shut down, possibly permanently.

Why Have a Meeting?

There are five basic reasons to have a meeting. The first four were suggested by Andy Grove, cofounder of Intel, while the fifth was suggested by David Allen. The first two are leader focused and the last three are more team focused:

- Give information.

- Receive information.

- Develop options.

- Make decisions.

- Maintain contact.

Give Information

Interdependency
requires lavish
communication.

Max DePree

The main purpose is to transmit information to the group so they know what's going on. This includes new product announcements, future plans, or updates about the performance of the team or organization (e.g., shareholder meetings). The goal is to make sure the information provided is clear and understood by the participants. This type of meeting is often more formal than other types, and it may require some additional planning if you want to involve the audience as more than passive listeners.

Receive Information

The main purpose is to gather updates on a series of projects or tasks, brief other staff on a recommended approach to an issue, or gather input about pending items. The goal is usually to gather as much information as possible, even if the results are nowhere near consensus. You'll typically want to capture the information on a flipchart, white board, and/or computer, and then feed back the results to the participants.

Develop Options

Brainstorming, mind-mapping, and problem-solving meetings can be used to develop alternatives before making a decision. Having people use their imagination and creativity, and gathering ideas from multiple perspectives, are typical goals for this type of meeting. Because opinions are likely to vary considerably, you may want to use an outside facilitator – someone from outside the team or unit who can keep things on track and prevent different points of view from turning into pitched battles.

Make Decisions

This type of meeting involves discussing the pros and cons of one or more alternatives, with a focus on deciding what to do next. Planning who will participate is important since you want the right people to be present. That means: (1) having those with the power to make decisions in the room, (2) making sure they have the information needed to make a good decision, and (3) managing or facilitating the discussion to keep the meeting on goal and on track. Since disagreements are typically over which alternative is finally chosen, it's a good place to practice your conflict resolution skills. (See *Skill 6 – Solving Problems and Making Decisions* for additional information.)

Maintain Contact

Sometimes it's important to get the team together to keep everybody focused on goals and objectives, or just to maintain or improve the work relationships within the team.

By the way, having multiple purposes for holding a meeting is fine, as long as everyone is aware of the purpose(s) at the start. Once

> If I am to speak ten minutes, I need a week for preparation; if fifteen minutes, three days; if half an hour, two days; if an hour, I am ready now.
>
> *Woodrow Wilson*

you're clear about the *purpose* you can move on to creating a successful meeting.

Meeting Basics

Assuming you want to have an effective meeting, a bit of planning ahead is a good idea. To do this, ask yourself some basic questions, such as:

- Is this meeting with a group or an individual?

- What results do I want from this meeting?

- What is the best venue for this meeting?

- Does this meeting need to be formal, informal, or unscheduled (i.e., "I'll catch Bill when I see him")?

- How much advance notice to participants would be useful?

- Do we need an agenda for the meeting? If so, who will prepare it and when should it be distributed?

- Would it be helpful if the participants did something prior to the meeting (e.g., review a project file, read a report or supporting information, or develop a recommendation)?

Meeting Guidelines

Here are five basics for running an effective meeting:

- Start on time.

- End on time.

- Assign roles.

- Define the next action.

- Identify who, when & how.

Start on Time

When you have a 9:00 meeting and people are still straggling in at 9:15, you don't really have a 9:00 meeting. You have a 9:15 meeting and everyone knows it. Start by announcing that from today on, all meetings will start on time and there will be no time devoted to bringing late arrivals up to speed. Then when the appointed time arrives, start the meeting. People will quickly learn that they need to be on time.

End on Time

When your meeting is scheduled for 9:00–10:00, you need to make sure you end by 10:00. People often are scheduled back-to-back with meetings, and if you don't end on time they'll be late to their next meeting. I've seen this situation cascade through a whole organization because the boss kept talking past the scheduled end time, which caused all subsequent meetings to be behind schedule. By the end of the day everyone was running late and was cranky from constantly playing catch-up all day.

Assign Roles

Depending on the kind of meeting you're holding, you might want to assign certain roles to be filled by participants, such as:

- *Facilitator*. This person helps make sure the meeting stays on track and keeps the group moving through the agenda. Their role is to deflect things that are off-subject and keep the group focused.

- *Recorder*. This person tracks the discussion, and especially any task assignments that emerge, so people understand afterward what has been decided. The recorder basically tracks action items as the meeting progresses.

- *Clarifier*. This person's role is to sum up the end results of discussion on a particular agenda item and make sure

It takes less time to do a thing right than to explain why you did it wrong.

Henry Wadsworth Longfellow

everyone is clear about what the outcomes are. The clarifier paraphrases the conclusions and checks for understanding and agreement.

NOTE: All three of these roles can be handled by the same person or they can be spread among the participants.

Define the Next Action

David Allen's classic question – what is the next action? – will help keep the group focused on the results expected from the meeting. Often there will be multiple action items that flow from a multi-topic meeting. Make sure everyone is clear about what is supposed to happen next.

Identify Who, When & How

Not only is it important to capture the expected next action steps, but you also need to be sure everyone is clear about *who* is going to perform each action step, *when* those steps should occur, and *how* the tasks will be done (if that's relevant to the project). Will there be any follow-up communication from the people doing the tasks? Or will there be an update provided at another meeting the next day, next week, etc.?

Learning how to plan and conduct effective meetings is an essential skill if you expect to be successful as a manager. The larger the organization and the higher you go in your career, the more likely you'll spend a considerable amount of time in meetings. If you do it well, you'll gather more appreciation from others than you can imagine!

Self-expression must pass into communication for its fulfillment.

Pearl Buck

Skill 3

BUILDING SUCCESSFUL
RELATIONSHIPS

"Establishing good working relationships can help us
secure the cooperation of the people we need to
accomplish our tasks. If we delay building good
relationships until we really need them, it will be
too late."

Lois Frankel

Skill 3 – Building Successful Relationships

Your ultimate success as a manager and leader will depend on two abilities: (1) how effectively you get things done or accomplish tasks, and (2) how well you forge and sustain positive relationships. True leadership means focusing on *both* tasks *and* relationships. No matter how driven, focused, and hardworking you are, you won't be effective unless you can develop solid, healthy relationships.

These days, your ability to build successful relationships with your employees, peers, boss, and customers is a key skill – one that will help move you and your unit ahead or hold you back. It takes hard work and constant effort to create and maintain those relationships. When your work relationships are solid, you'll be able to effectively lead your team to get the job done. But when your relationships are poor, you won't get the results you and your organization need. You'll have a team that isn't actively engaged in doing a good job. Your people will be unhappy, unproductive, and may well "vote with their feet" by leaving. Research clearly shows that employees don't leave *jobs*, they leave *managers*.

> The best index to a person's character is how he treats people who can't do him any good, and how he treats people who can't fight back.
>
> *Abigail Van Buren*

Being smart and having great technical skills is a start, but it isn't enough. By some estimates as much as 90 percent of professional success flows from your ability to develop positive, healthy relationships with those around you. Getting good at *Skill 3* can give your career a major boost; the lack of it can derail you.

When work relationships are healthy, a lot of good things happen for the team and the organization. More work gets done, and the general look and feel of the workplace is more positive and upbeat. Quality tends to be higher, fewer mistakes are made, and the endless CYA that goes on in so many places is simply unnecessary.

Unfortunately, some organizations are filled with decidedly unhealthy work relationships. I once heard a newly-promoted CEO say to a group of front-line supervisors, "Over the years we have developed a negatively-focused, blame-fixing, punishment-oriented culture and if we don't change it we are doomed to failure." Since the CEO had spent his entire career in that organization, he was speaking from experience. He recognized that fear and negativity were driving away good people and leading employees to focus on staying out of trouble rather than their jobs. What a recipe for mediocre performance, lots of CYA, and high turnover.

If you truly want to be successful, you'll focus part of your attention on having a healthy relationship with your own manager. Managing upward – building a healthy relationship with the next level up in the organization – is just as important as your relationships with your team and your peers. In *Chapter 4* we talked about the *expectations* that those around you have for how you do your job. Now, as you work to improve your abilities in *Skill 3*, you'll need to analyze how well you're meeting the expectations of your manager. If you and your boss are clear about these expectations and their relative importance in your position, your relationship is more likely to be healthy. When you and your boss aren't on the same page, you have a great opportunity to improve a key relationship in your work life.

Front-line supervisors and mid-level managers are the most important factor in setting an organization's tone and building a successful work group or team. This means that you, more than anyone else, are responsible for creating a positive, productive, and successful work environment. Do it well and you and your organization benefit. Do it poorly and everyone pays the price. As my colleague and coach Mary Jo Asmus says, "It's all about the relationships." In this section you'll learn how to nurture and develop those key relationships.

Life is relationships; the rest is just details.

Gary Smalley

Chapter 19
Healthy Relationships

When work relationships are healthy, you and your organization will see five clear benefits:

- Productivity increases.

- People feel better.

- Communication improves.

- People are more engaged in their work.

- People are more committed to the organization.

Five Benefits of Healthy Relationships

Productivity Increases

When your relationships aren't solid, your employees won't give their jobs their full attention and focus. In fact, they might be actively disengaged from their jobs, looking for ways to mess with you. There's a bottom line to good relationships; they improve productivity. Employees will spend less time watching their back and more time and energy doing their job. They may actually *want* to do a good job for the team and for you as their leader.

People Feel Better

When your relationships are strong your employees will feel better about themselves, about you as their manager, and about the whole organization. They're more likely to have positive self-esteem and believe that you're working in their best interests. But when your relationships are poor, your employees will believe that most management decisions (not just yours) are designed to be malicious. They'll have more of an "us vs. them" mindset – with you as one of "them." They may feel like they're helpless cogs in a wheel rather

> Help those around you all you can. Every bit of help you give others will come back to you tenfold.
>
> *E. B. Gallaher*

than contributing team members working together for everyone's benefit.

Communication Improves

When your relationships are solid, employees will tend to raise issues and concerns in a positive manner; they won't whine or gripe very much. They'll tend to trust that management actually cares about what they think. But when your employees don't trust you, they'll usually stop communicating with you. When this happens, problems go unresolved, goldbricking increases, and they'll look for ways to get out of doing work. This really counts when hard times hit. In organizations with healthy relationships, employees *know* that senior management will minimize the disruption and pain of layoffs as much as possible and keep them informed about what is happening.

People are More Engaged

Power in organizations is the capacity generated by relationships.

Margaret Wheatley

Solid, positive relationships tend to promote individual job satisfaction. Employees will take pride in doing a great job, will be committed to achieving the organization's goals (and their own performance goals), and will offer positive feedback and encouragement to each other. Next time you watch a well-coached football team notice what happens after a missed field goal. Instead of berating the place kicker for the missed attempt, the coaches and players will recognize the mistake with "Nice try . . . you'll get it next time . . ." The result is the place kicker will try even harder the next time he's on the field. And you'll see him on the sidelines practicing for that next attempt. When work relationships are healthy and supportive, your employees will show pride in a job well done and will treat errors and mistakes as learning experiences.

People are More Committed

In the long run, healthy relationships help employees understand and focus on the organization's mission, values, and goals. When people feel safe and supported in their work relationships, they tend to be better at seeing the big picture – not just focused on surviving in their job. And when this happens, they can't help but be more committed to achieving results. In this kind of work environment, when difficult times show up (and they always do, sooner or later), your employees will be less likely to jump ship. They'll be more likely to ask, "How can I help us get through these challenges?" They'll volunteer to work extra, help trim expenses, and help each other and the organization weather the tough times.

Components of Healthy Relationships

Components of Healthy Relationships

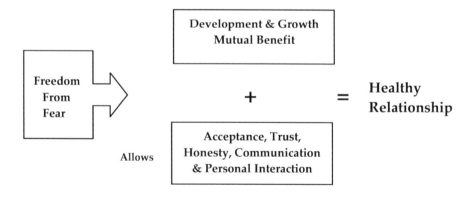

Creating and sustaining healthy relationships is easier once you understand what they look like. Here are some of the basic components of healthy relationships:

- Freedom from fear

- Acceptance

- Trust

- Honesty

- Communication

- Personal interaction

- Development & growth

- Mutual benefit

Freedom From Fear

Time and again people refuse to invest in improving work relationships because of *fear*. If another person intimidates or threatens you . . . if your boss demeans you when you make mistakes or blames you for their own errors . . . you'll naturally operate from a *fear-full* position. This happens when your past interactions with another person have been painful or generated negative results. Freedom from fear is the *bedrock foundation* of a healthy relationship. When fear permeates a relationship, it's impossible for that relationship to be healthy and positive. Without fear, a relationship has the potential to become healthy and mutually supportive. Then the other components required for a healthy relationship *might* develop.

Acceptance

In a healthy relationship you'll tend to be less judgmental about the thoughts and ideas of others. You'll also be more patient and less likely to jump to conclusions. When a relationship is healthy, disagreements aren't a big issue. The two of you simply see the situation from different perspectives, and each of you understands that. Applying Stephen Covey's notion, "Seek first to understand, then to be understood," will bring about an automatic increase in acceptance. When you disagree but honestly try to understand the other person's point of view, you have a chance to build the mutual trust that's needed for the relationship to be truly healthy.

Often times it happens that we live our lives in chains and we never even know we have the key.

The Eagles
"Already Gone"

Trust

Once others know you as a human being – a person with a family, hobbies, and interests outside of work – they *may* begin to trust you. But building a work relationship that includes mutual trust takes time. If you want to be trusted by your employees and colleagues, your behavior must inspire that trust. For instance, as a manager and leader you'll be told things that are confidential. How you treat this information will affect the level of trust in that relationship. Respecting confidences builds trust; breaking them damages trust and could be a career-derailing move.

Honesty

When one (or worse yet, both) of the parties in a relationship is dishonest, you have a win-lose or lose-lose situation. Wherever there's dishonesty, the relationship is based on fear. If you lie to your employees, you can count on the outcome – that lie is going to be discovered at some point. And when that occurs, they'll become disillusioned, fearful, resentful, and withdraw from meaningful interaction. This is a classic example of what Stephen Covey calls *a massive withdrawal from the emotional bank account.* A single lie can damage (or even destroy) your relationship with your entire team.

Communication

Max DePree, the visionary former CEO of the office furniture manufacturer Herman Miller, encourages us to "communicate lavishly." As we noted in *Skill 2*, improving your ability to communicate with others pays huge dividends in great work relationships. Successful communication means keeping your people in the loop about what's happening, making sure they have the information they need to successfully do their jobs, and helping them understand how their efforts fit into the greater purpose of the organization. Often managers use information as a club: "This is on a need-to-know basis, and *you* don't need to know!" Manipulative and dishonest communication like this creates an environment where your employees will mistrust your motives, everything you say, and everything you do. On the other hand, open and honest communication promotes even more successful communication.

Personal Interaction

Any review of current trends in technology shows the same thing: technology can reduce the amount of face-to-face interaction with others. It may be quicker and more convenient to communicate via e-mail and voice mail, but that doesn't necessarily help to maintain or improve relationships. Healthy work relationships require regular personal interaction, especially when they're important to your own and your team's success. In recent years we've seen a marked increase in the number of remote workers – those who work on a contractual basis and/or out of a home office, travel extensively, or seldom interact in person with their manager and co-workers. Creating opportunities for everyone involved in a project to get together as a group helps provide the cement required to get everyone working together. The more personal interaction you have with your teammates, the more likely you'll be to lead a true *team*, regardless of the employment status of each team member.

Development & Growth

Over time a healthy relationship can become something more than just two people who happen to work together fairly effectively. It can grow into a relationship that provides opportunities for learning and development. When you interact regularly with team members, you get to know each person as an individual. You'll find yourself seeking opportunities to help them grow and develop. You'll better understand their individual talents and strengths, and you'll be more likely to assign tasks and form project teams that take advantage of those strengths. And, as the manager or team leader, you'll find yourself looking for ways to help each person add to the value they bring to the team and the organization. When this happens, your team members will help each other grow and

> Be who you are and say what you feel, because those who mind don't matter, and those who matter don't mind.
>
> *Dr. Seuss*

> I believe that we are solely responsible for our choices, and we have to accept the consequences of every deed, word, and thought throughout our lifetime.
>
> *Elisabeth Kubler-Ross*

develop. When work relationships are healthy, the feeling of "We're all in this together" increases and the group becomes a real team, focused on working toward a shared goal.

Mutual Benefit

Finally, in a healthy relationship both parties gain benefit as they work toward the goals of the team and the organization. Each person has something to teach the other; the sum total of the relationship produces results that are greater than just two people getting along well. Each party is attuned to the other's strengths and weaknesses, providing support and guidance as needed. In military terms this would be a version of "I have your back" or "I'm your wingman." When both parties clearly value and benefit from the relationship, the results can be remarkable!

> Treasure your relationships, not your possessions.
>
> *Anthony D'Angelo*

Behaviors That Build Healthy Relationships

Successful and healthy work relationships are built as people interact. They're a function of the personal characteristics you each bring to the party and how you behave as you work together. Some behaviors that help build healthy relationships include:

- Show empathy & sensitivity to others.

- Seek feedback.

- Deal with & resolve conflict.

- Identify & accept the other person's frame of reference.

Show Empathy & Sensitivity to Others

Healthy work relationships are more likely to occur when each person is sensitive to others and displays empathy and caring. This means caring about them as individuals and understanding that they won't be in top form every day. Everyone has personal issues and problems to deal with at times, and it's unrealistic to expect people to check their personal life at the door.

Seek Feedback

All aspects of communication are important to building successful relationships. But none is more overlooked than the willingness to seek feedback from other people. You may want to try a simple, yet powerful, exercise. On a sheet of paper write the following requests:

- List three things you wish I would do more of.

- List three things you wish I would do less of.

- List one thing I do that drives you crazy.

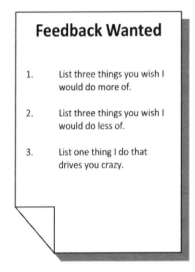

Feedback Wanted

1. List three things you wish I would do more of.

2. List three things you wish I would do less of.

3. List one thing I do that drives you crazy.

Then run off enough copies of the form to give to each of your employees. Ask them to complete the assignment. Then have one person collect the responses, transcribe them (to maintain anonymity), and give you the transcribed list. You'll be amazed at the consistency of the responses you receive. And the simple act of asking others for feedback will do wonders to build healthier work relationships – as long as you don't ignore the results of this exercise, of course!

> When you ask others for feedback they'll expect you to actually do something with it. If you don't want to change, don't ask for feedback!

Deal With & Resolve Conflict

Disagreements and conflicts occur naturally. People have opinions (often strongly held) about what's important, what issues need attention, and how the team should deal with those issues. These differences are shaped by previous experiences and when those viewpoints clash, conflict happens. You *can* learn how to successfully resolve conflicts. One of the most important skills is the willingness to consider the viewpoints of others. When combined with a solid understanding of how to resolve disagreements, you can have productive discussions that ultimately lead to agreement.

> When angry, count ten before you speak; if very angry, one hundred.
>
> *Thomas Jefferson*

Identify & Accept the Other Person's Frame of Reference

Sometimes you simply don't see the world in quite the same way as someone else. And you may both be right, depending on your individual experiences. In other words, there's no one right way to view a situation or challenge. When I can understand where you're coming from, we may discover we're not so far apart after all. So make the effort to understand someone's frame of reference in a given situation; you might be able to meet each other halfway. And if that isn't possible, it's fine to just agree to disagree.

As a general rule the better two people understand each other, the easier it is for them to work together, resolve conflicts, reach reasonable agreements, and cooperate for mutual success. This means their work relationship is more likely to be satisfying. In essence, we end up singing in harmony from the same piece of music as we interact. This includes how you interact with your boss – which is what *Chapter 20* is about.

> The hardest challenge is to be yourself in a world where everyone is trying to make you be somebody else.
>
> *e. e. cummings*

Chapter 20
Managing Your Boss

The relationship with your own manager – your boss – is one of the most important work relationships you have. The quality of that relationship has a lot to do with how much you enjoy your work each day. When you and your boss are generally on the same page, have good rapport, and communicate reasonably well, you're much more likely to enjoy your job. On the other hand, if your relationship with your boss is strained, you don't have good communication, and your ideas about how to get things done are substantially different, your daily interactions can quickly become a grind.

If you really want something you can figure out how to make it happen.

Cher

How's your relationship with your boss? Is it all it could be? Or could it stand some improvement? If it could be better, *you* will be the one who has to work on changing the relationship. Your boss is unlikely to invest much time and energy to improve the relationship unless you make the first move.

Expectations: You and Your Boss

What kinds of expectations do you think your boss has of you? What are the things you generally do to keep your boss in the loop? As we noted in *Chapter 4*, some of the expectations a manager might have of you as their direct report include:

- Meet the expectations of the organization and your employees.

- Know your responsibilities and carry them out effectively without a lot of detailed instructions.

- Be flexible in responding to shifts in priorities or direction.

- Solve daily problems on your own, using the resources available to you.

- Suggest improvements that will help the organization be more successful.

- Support their ideas and decisions without being a "yes" person.

- Bring issues to their attention, as they arise, that need to be handled at their level.

- Carry out their instructions or directions promptly, successfully, and cheerfully.

- Keep them in the loop about what is happening in your unit.

- Train, develop, and retain your staff so the work gets done effectively and efficiently.

- Be a self-starter, trustworthy, honest, and reliable.

What other expectations do you think your manager has? If you aren't sure, maybe it's time to *ask* them. After all, if you aren't clear about what is expected, it's going to be difficult to improve the relationship with your manager.

A wish changes nothing. A decision changes everything.
Unknown

We live in a world that's dynamic, fluid, and fast-paced. Priorities change and external events present new challenges. Try sitting down with your boss. Say to them, "Here are the things I'm currently working on. Here's my perspective on what you expect of me in my current role. I just want to make sure we're on the same page about priorities and whether you think I'm focusing on the right things."

Help your boss manage you. Think about how the relationship with your manager might change if you asked, "How can I help *you* manage *me* more successfully? What kinds of information would help you get your job done the best way possible? What can I do to help make your job easier?"

This approach (or something similar to it) will initially catch your boss a bit off guard; most managers never get that kind of request from an employee. But you're likely to get some valuable information from that conversation. If nothing else, it shows your boss that you take your job seriously and want to do your best.

At the same time you may want to get clear about your own expectations of your boss. What do you expect them to do as your manager? What kind of information do you expect to receive? How often do you expect to get together to review your progress? How much latitude do you expect in how you get your job done? These are all legitimate issues for you to consider.

Is the relationship with your boss positive and solid enough that you can have an open discussion about expectations? If not, then consider how unmet expectations might be influencing your job satisfaction. If your boss seems to be incapable of meeting your expectations (even if they're unspoken), then you have a choice to make. Can the relationship be improved to the point where you could have a productive discussion about expectations? Or do you need to look for a different person as your manager? Either way, this is reality check time. After all, one person's jerk boss may be someone else's perfect boss.

A leader is someone who has more faith in us than we have in ourselves.

Margaret Wheatley

The Issue of Relative Importance

Every aspect of your job is not equally important. Some of the roles you play, the projects you work on, and the teams you're a member of are more important than others.

When we conduct 360° assessments for managers, we have them rank order various components of leadership and management on their importance to their job. We also suggest that they ask their boss to do the same thing for that manager's job. When the rank order lists are fairly similar, the manager being assessed is usually perceived as having a good handle on their priorities. When the rank order is quite different, it creates a great opportunity for a productive discussion between the manager and their boss.

For more information about 360° assessment tools, visit our Web site at www.MidwGroup.com.

> What you need are people who know how to take groups that have different agendas and goals but have to work together and find that area of mutuality.
>
> *J. Lipman-Blumen*

Chapter 21
Creating a Great Work Environment

Most people would like to work in an organization that's really great – a place where they can make a meaningful contribution to an important cause, are treated with respect and fairness, and are compensated appropriately. Since we're all individuals, the definition of a great work environment varies. But no organization is likely to be viewed as a great place to work unless certain fundamental components are in place. So how do you help create that great place to work?

Organizational Culture & Management Style

As a supervisor or manager, you're responsible for getting results – the results your boss and the organization need from your unit or team. Organizational cultures differ. Some are quasi-military and hierarchical in their approach, like police and fire departments. Some are team-oriented, open, fluid, and free-wheeling, like start-up software development companies. And there's everything in between.

In some organizations you may be a "desk jockey" – pushing paper, answering the phone, going to meetings, running the numbers, and otherwise having little direct personal contact with your employees. In other organizations you might be heavily involved with your staff and communicate with them daily. Your level of involvement will have a distinct effect on the results they'll produce for you and the organization. Most front-line supervisors work *with* their team, sleeves rolled up, right in there pitching. But as your career develops and you take on more responsibility, you may have less personal interaction with your employees.

Being concerned about your employees is simply part of being a good manager. Being willing to become involved when they ask for

> If you show that you truly pay attention to ideas - even the small, seemingly insignificant ones - then you'll create an environment in which people feel comfortable generating and offering them.
>
> *Rolf Smith*

help (or stepping up when you think they need help but they're not asking) demonstrates a higher level of concern. This requires a different view of your role as a manager. It means seeing each of your employees in a holistic sense – as a whole person. And it means understanding that your employees are much more than just a resource to be used up.

In far too many cases senior management claims, "Our people are our most important resource," and then acts in ways to prove that statement is just more baloney. When tough times come, and they always do, look to see what senior management *does* rather than what they *say*. Do they cut their own pay and eliminate their own bonuses first? Or do they start by cutting staff? How this is handled is a reflection of the organization's culture and whether it truly is a great place to work.

> We are what we repeatedly do. Excellence, then, is not an act, but a habit.
>
> *Aristotle*

Pay Attention to What They DO!

When the economy tanked in 2008, the Big Three American auto companies announced massive layoffs and plant closings. Then the company executives flew to Washington, D.C., on their corporate jets to ask for a handout from the American taxpayers. Yes, these were the same guys who had led their companies so well that they had eliminated several hundred thousand jobs. They couldn't have done anything more to damage their relationships with employees, vendors, customers, and the general public if they had tried.

When an organization has to eliminate positions, watch how it's done. Is it done with caring and empathy for the lives that are being affected? Are transition assistance, severance pay, and bridging medical insurance provided? Or are the employees suddenly told they are being laid off – just before they're coldly escorted by security to remove their personal effects and then shown the door? What do you suppose the laid-off employees will have to say about their former workplace? A great place to work? Not likely.

Be a Model

When you manage people, your attitudes and behaviors serve as the model for your employees' attitudes and behaviors. Whatever *you* do, they will do. If you project the attitude that you care about doing a great job – if you work hard to create a cooperative work environment – so will your employees. But if your attitude and behaviors project "I don't care" about your employees' well-being, they're more likely to worry and be uneasy. They'll perceive that you don't really care about them. Telling your staff, "Do as I say, not as I do" is foolish. They'll do as you do regardless of what you say. If they perceive you as distant and uncaring, don't expect them to be cooperative, open, and friendly.

Be an Advocate

When you become an advocate for your people in making the work environment as good as possible, then you're really doing your job as a supervisor. From a hazardous upturned corner on a rug . . . to hazardous chemicals in the plant . . . to being aware of whose behaviors have undergone a change . . . to support for at-home issues . . . this is where the rubber meets the road in creating a great work environment. Advocacy means you're *proactive* and take responsibility for addressing issues when they arise.

> Just go out there and do what you've got to do.
> *Martina Navratilova*

Somebody Else's Job?

When it comes to creating a great work environment, there's no such thing as "not my job" for a supervisor or manager. Certainly, upper management needs to be committed to creating a great work environment. But it's at the supervisory and mid-manager levels that real problems get handled. Supervisors will see and sense things that higher level managers won't pay attention to or even notice.

Workplace Safety

Employees cannot and will not give 100 percent if they're worried (even subconsciously) about safety. This means both physical and psychological safety. When their concern is about physical safety, it may be related to the risk of injury caused by machinery, physical facilities, hazardous materials, or even assault by co-workers or others. Psychological concerns often relate to fear – the fear of being disciplined or fired . . . of verbal or physical abuse . . . of illness brought on by overwork or stress . . . or any of a number of other workplace issues.

Physical Safety is Job A1

In the days of wooden sailing ships safety awareness took the form of an old saying, "One hand for the ship, one hand for you." That focus on safety was necessary because the work environment was dangerous and qualified seamen were hard to find. Physical safety awareness, and practicing skills and behaviors that keep you and others safe, is of primary importance to anyone who works in any field. While the risk of injury is obviously higher for a police officer, a steeplejack, or a commercial fisherman in the Bering Sea, there are less obvious risks for other occupations that are just as real.

The bottom line is actually pretty simple: failure to keep workplace safety first and foremost can result in injury or death. High awareness of physical safety helps to create a better work environment. When employees believe that physical risks have been minimized as much as possible and risk awareness is high, they'll turn more of their focus toward getting their job done.

Psychological Safety is Job A2

Psychological safety varies as much as physical safety from one organization to another. The number of interpersonal conflicts and disagreements *and how they are handled* has a big influence on psychological safety. Conflict and disagreements are going to

> Because how we spend our days is, of course, how we spend our lives.
>
> *Annie Dillard*

happen as a normal part of human interaction. How effectively and positively conflict is handled, and the management style the organization uses, both have a direct bearing on psychological safety.

Your success at helping employees feel psychologically safe is determined, in part, by how they perceive *your* behavior. If, for instance, you tolerate sexual harassment, racial or ethnic jokes, or other unethical (or illegal) practices, how psychologically safe do you think the workplace will be? So doing the right thing and walking your talk just makes good sense.

Improving Relationships – Tips & Suggestions

If you'd like to improve your work relationships, waiting for others to change their behaviors, perceptions, and viewpoints isn't going to get the job done. If you want a relationship to change, *the change must begin with you*. This isn't just a "touchy-feely" notion – it's cold, hard reality. When was the last time your boss, a co-worker, or an employee had a spontaneous major change in the way they dealt with you all on their own?

So, if it's up to you, how can you create change in a relationship? Here are 11 tips and suggestions that might be helpful:

Luck, Watson, is a curious thing. I have found that it comes most often to those who are prepared to receive it.

Sherlock Holmes

- Take it easy!
- Be clear about goals & expectations.
- Encourage learning in a "fear-free" environment.
- Practice your listening skills.
- Listen to alternatives.
- Criticize performance, not people.
- Be flexible.

- Ask for input & give frequent feedback.
- Practice servant leadership.
- Build the team.
- Be a career coach.

Take it Easy!

If you make a major change in your behavior, demeanor, or outlook all at once, almost no one will take you seriously. Instead, take gradual steps, try out new approaches, and use them daily until they become part of who you are and how you operate. People need to practice a new behavior daily for at least three weeks before it becomes a new habit. You can't effectively change overnight; neither can your boss, peers, or employees. So be patient.

Be Clear About Goals & Expectations

People perform more effectively when they're clear about what's expected of them. Make sure the goals and objectives you set are clear, mutually agreed to, and regularly communicated using a variety of methods. Remember, different people get the message in different ways. Strong relationships are built when people know you're trying to reach out to them in a way *they* understand.

Encourage Learning in a "Fear-Free" Environment

Even if you're on the right track, you'll get run over if you just sit there.

Will Rogers

For an organization to grow everyone must be able to learn new skills and behaviors and adapt to ever-changing circumstances. All of us make mistakes and get it less than perfectly right when we're learning something new. So create a learning environment where employees feel free to try out new things without fear of ridicule or criticism. This will speed up the learning process and make it easier to take on new challenges in the future. Expect your employees to succeed, to overcome obstacles, and to learn new skills without being punished, and you'll be amazed at the positive relationships you'll build.

Practice Your Listening Skills

Make sure everyone has the chance to voice their opinion. Avoid the tendency to dominate meeting/discussion time. Some people take longer to express their thoughts. If you're an Extravert, make a contract with yourself to give the Introverts time for reflection before pressing for a decision. If you're an Introvert make a contract with yourself to allow Extraverts their thinking-out-loud time. Take time to really listen to the work problems faced by your team. Ask questions; don't try to solve all the problems yourself. Team members can often figure out what needs to be done. They just need you to listen and give them encouragement.

Listen to Alternatives

Part of good listening is being open to alternatives. It's easy to unintentionally dismiss new options or ways of doing things and miss out on a really great idea. If you're a hard-driving, highly decisive supervisor who has a tendency to push others toward closure, try setting aside enough time during planning to allow all options to be heard and considered. This is particularly important during brainstorming or creative development, when you might feel that you want to shut off generating alternatives and just pick something – anything – to get closure and begin implementation.

Criticize Performance, Not People

Some supervisors seem to take delight in letting their employees know when they've made a mistake. This criticism is often personal, focusing on the person rather than their behavior. The only thing worse than attacking employees personally for an error is to do it in front of their co-workers. If you do that, it leads to a truly massive withdrawal from your emotional bank account with the other person. At the other extreme, managers who prefer to avoid conflict need to realize that the world won't come to an end if they take an unpopular stand. Growth and positive change often result from

> Great works are performed not by strength but by perseverance.
>
> *Samuel Johnson*

healthy disagreement. And employees don't respect managers who fail to confront performance and behavior issues.

Be Flexible

Circumstances, information, and priorities change all the time. So you need to develop techniques that will help you effectively manage that change. For example, when changes are necessary, involve your employees in planning for them. Enlist their help in making the implementation as smooth as possible. Explain the reasons behind any changes that are made. Your team needs to understand the rationale for the change and the possible downside or losses as well as the expected benefits.

Ask for Input & Give Frequent Feedback

Ask your team members what you can do to help them perform more effectively. Agree to at least one action for each person, and then do it. This can provide a tremendous boost to your credibility; it shows that you really do care and that you're committed to improving your work relationships. Ask your employees to list the major barriers that keep them from performing more effectively on the job. Then work in a positive, sincere fashion to remove or minimize those barriers. Finally, provide frequent feedback about how each employee is doing compared to the goals, objectives, standards, and expectations for their position. Employees are more highly motivated when they know how they're doing; lack of feedback breeds doubt and uncertainty.

Practice Servant Leadership

If you view your role as one of service to others, you'll be much more successful as a supervisor and have stronger relationships. See your job as helping your employees to get their jobs done more effectively, removing barriers to their success, encouraging them through expressions of confidence in their abilities, and providing regular coaching advice.

One of the things I learned the hard way was that it doesn't pay to get discouraged. Keeping busy and making optimism a way of life can restore your faith in yourself.

Lucille Ball

It is one of the most beautiful compensations of this life that no man can sincerely try to help another without helping himself.

Ralph Waldo Emerson

Build the Team

Try to establish a group identity in your unit. Establish group goals and group rewards whenever possible. While you should avoid an "us vs. them" mindset, find opportunities for the unit to see itself as a team. Use staff meetings to improve teamwork. Provide a chance for all team members to express their opinions or offer constructive comments about the work of the group. Reward people for cooperating with their colleagues inside and outside the department. When someone in another unit helps someone in your unit, make sure that person's supervisor knows about it.

Be a Career Coach

Meet with your employees individually to discuss their career goals and identify the skills they need. Then work with your human resources department and other resources to help your people move toward their goals.

It's Up to You!

If you really want to change your work relationships, it's up to you to take the first step. In fact, you may have to take the first six steps! It will be worth the time and effort because it's so much easier to effectively manage your team when your work relationships are healthy and solid. For some practical ideas about how to do this, turn to the next section: *Skill 4 – Managing Others.*

Skill 4

MANAGING OTHERS

"First comes thought, then organization of that thought into ideas and plans; then transformation of those plans into reality. The beginning, as you will observe, is in your imagination."

Napoleon Hill

Skill 4 - Managing Others

Managers *must* focus on achieving the results needed by their organization and the people it serves. Meeting the expectations of your organization and delivering consistent, solid results becomes possible when you acquire the fourth *Essential Skill – Managing Others.*

Learning to manage others is at the heart of becoming a successful supervisor and, frankly, it has very little to do with filling out an annual performance appraisal form. Effective management is the cumulative result of your daily interactions with those you supervise. And that is where *real* leadership in management is demonstrated every day. Ultimately, you aren't going to be able to lead your team effectively unless you're adept at managing the performance of the people you supervise.

To manage others successfully, you need to:

- Create an environment where others are able to perform well.

- Understand what sustained, solid performance means in your organization.

- Realize how your expectations and attitudes affect others' performance, and then behave accordingly.

- Provide effective feedback to team members, some of whom may not be performing well.

- Use a variety of techniques to help employees improve their performance

Unless you supervise only one other individual, you'll probably use a variety of approaches to managing. As Hersey, Blanchard, and Johnson first suggested years ago in their book "Management of Organizational Behavior," different people are at different points at

> Focus on a few key objectives . . . . I only have three things to do. I have to choose the right people, allocate the right number of dollars, and transmit ideas from one division to another with the speed of light. So I'm really in the business of being the gatekeeper and the transmitter of ideas.
>
> *Jack Welch*

> Never tell people how to do things. Tell them what to do and they will surprise you with their ingenuity.
>
> *George S. Patton*

different times. Their Situational Leadership™ model suggests that you'll be more successful if you determine where each of your employees is right now and then proceed to manage them where they are – rather than where you would *like* them to be. (See *Skill 7 – Leading and Empowering* for a more extensive discussion of this and other approaches to leadership.) Whatever your approach to managing your team, a large part of your success will be driven by your ability to get your people to perform well.

> You can't motivate a group of people or a Team. You have to motivate people individually, and that motivation has to be in an environment in which that person has a goal - something they want to accomplish in their lives.
>
> *Lou Holtz*

The Successful Performance Model

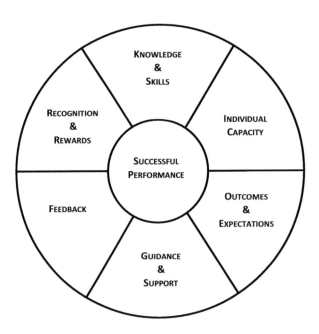

What does it take for people to perform successfully? Consistently successful performance is driven by a combination of six factors, as shown in the model above. *Chapter 23* explains the Successful Performance Model. But before we explore it in detail, let's take a look at two issues that can have a major effect on how well your employees perform: (1) the climate you and your team operate in, and (2) the lesson of the self-fulfilling prophecy.

Chapter 22
Creating Outstanding Performance

In addition to creating a great work environment, you need to create an atmosphere where your employees can deliver consistently great performance. This will be influenced by your daily interactions with your team. The attitude, commitment, and results of your people are hugely influenced by *yours*. You're an example to those you supervise, whether you think so or not. You may be a great example or a poor one, but you can't escape being an example. So if your team members aren't producing the results you need and you want things to be different, look in the mirror first.

Creating a climate so your team can perform well and produce great results is the sum total of a lot of daily activities. It goes far beyond just doing good performance reviews. If you're going to improve the performance of your unit, you need to make sure that your people *are able to* perform well. Then your behavior and communication with them will increase the chances that they'll perform at their very best.

Creating that high-performance climate isn't easy. If it were, everyone would do it all the time. But the good news is if you're truly committed to improving your own and your employees' performance, *you will be able to do it!*

If you're like every other supervisor, you have an imperfect team. You'll probably have some very good performers and some who are not so good. After all, you're working with human beings and each person has strengths and weaknesses. To create an environment where success is expected and delivered, you must be able to lead a team that functions well together regardless of who its members are. Usually, you inherit a team when you become a supervisor or move into middle management. Unless you were promoted in place and now supervise your former peers, you may not be able to

> Good people are in short supply. No matter who you are or where you work, you need to pay more attention to employee motivation and human relations.
>
> *Esther Dyson*

remove players and recruit new ones. You have the talent you have, and it's up to you to make the most of it.

Let's assume that your human resource folks didn't go out and recruit some dummies just to make you work harder. With very few exceptions, each of the people on your team met at least the minimum requirements to work in your organization. So you have to ask yourself, do any of these jobs require somebody who's a genius? If so, you're in trouble because geniuses are hard (and expensive) to find.

> You don't manage people; you manage things. You *lead* people.
>
> *Admiral Grace Hooper*

Instead, you have some raw material to work with. Some of your people may have extensive experience . . . some may be relatively new to the organization or their role . . . some may have wanted your job too and now harbor resentment . . . some may see you as "book smart and common sense dumb" . . . and some may just be waiting for the right supervisor to come along so they can blossom into star performers. So whatever your situation, you've got who you've got.

You can create this success even if your organizational climate isn't perfect or all that progressive. The reality is that *you* can play an important role in changing the climate of your entire organization. Don't believe it? Just try out some of the ideas presented in the next few chapters. They'll help you learn how to become a supervisor of champions!

Organizational Setting & Management Style

Much of what is done in an organization is framed by its culture and by the attitudes of its management and leadership. When leaders or managers at any level have identified an organizational weakness (especially one related to establishing a positive climate for good performance), they should set a course to correct it.

For example, if your organization sends the message that employees are children who must be *controlled* by management, they will eventually act like children. They might become more passive, abandon initiative, and wait for your instructions before doing anything. They might become less cooperative, less collaborative, and less creative in looking for ways to improve work processes or performance. And small frustrations might blossom into major conflicts or disagreements.

On the other hand, if your organization sends the message that employees are adults who need some *coaching and support* – and that management is prepared to provide that – they will act like adults. And that can only enhance performance.

What we're talking about is creating an environment where employees are expected to make a commitment . . . behave appropriately . . . perform well . . . be successful . . . treat their colleagues and others with dignity and respect . . . and focus on doing the best possible job in the best possible way. All of the time.

In his book "The Human Side of Enterprise," Douglas McGregor referred to two different ways of managing as Theory X and Theory Y. In his view Theory X was a more authoritarian style, based on the notion that "Management must counteract an inherent human tendency to avoid work." This management style was the dominant approach in most organizations during the middle third of the 20th century. It's still used by many managers in all kinds of organizations.

Theory Y is a more participative management style. It presumes that people are essentially self-directed, self-controlled, and will work cooperatively to achieve the organization's goals once they're committed to those goals. Under Theory Y your main responsibility as a manager is to enhance and support that commitment.

> In looking for people to hire, you look for three qualities: integrity, intelligence, and energy. If they don't have the first, the other two will kill you.
>
> *Warren Buffet*

If a team doesn't perform well Theory X lets management off the hook because, after all, people are generally lazy and don't want to work hard. Theory Y puts more of the responsibility for poor team performance on the manager; you haven't met your peoples' needs for information, self-respect, and/or achievement.

Most managers realize that success is not a matter of simply using one approach versus another. But you can be certain that your attitude – and the organization's attitude – toward employees has a huge effect on how involved, engaged, committed, and productive they're going to be every day. In the end, the climate you create is up to you.

> The only disability is a bad attitude.
>
> *Scott Hamilton*

The Self-Fulfilling Prophecy

Most of us know the basic story of Professor Henry Higgins and Eliza Doolittle in the play "My Fair Lady." The play and two movies have illustrated how expectations can become reality – what has come to be called the Pygmalion effect. (Named after George Bernard Shaw's play "Pygmalion," in which a professor makes a successful bet that he can teach a poor British flower girl to speak and act like an upper-class lady.) Rooted in fiction, the relevance of the self-fulfilling prophecy has been proven repeatedly in real life.

What is the Self-Fulfilling Prophecy?

> Whether you think you can or can't doesn't matter, 'cause you'll be right.
>
> *Henry Ford*

Here's what happens. *An expectation that is not necessarily true becomes true when people act on that expectation.* Our expectations, either positive or negative, influence the actual outcome. That's the self-fulfilling prophecy. What we expect or predict will occur happens because of our own behavior.

For instance, the Great Depression of the 1930s saw bank runs. Solvent, healthy banks were forced to close because people acted on the fear that they needed to get their money out before the bank collapsed. Their negative expectations created the very reality they feared. More recently the economic collapse of 2008 – the Great Recession – occurred in part because so many people panicked. The tightening of credit due to foreclosures in sub-prime mortgages, combined with falling real estate market values, helped speed a freefall in stock prices. The results were far worse than they needed to be given underlying values, but once again expectations created reality.

Similarly, our personal and professional expectations about other people might eventually lead them to behave in ways that tend to reinforce or confirm those expectations. The model below illustrates how the self-fulfilling prophecy becomes reality.

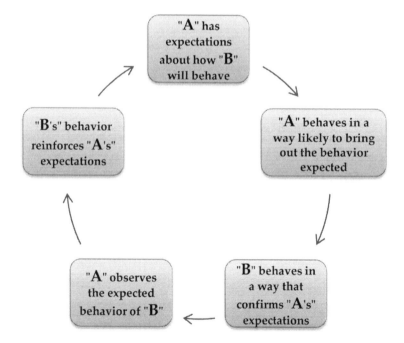

Hundreds of experiments conducted in the last 40 years have proven the reality of the self-fulfilling prophecy. Students who are expected to succeed do better than those viewed as average or "slow." Employees who are identified as having high potential will perform better than those viewed as being average performers.

> In matters of style, swim with the current; in matters of principle, stand like a rock.
>
> *Thomas Jefferson*

Where Expectations Begin

Where do these self-fulfilling expectations come from? We all have them, even though they don't seem to make sense. Why would you expect one person to be successful and another to fail? Why do you expect some people to accomplish less than others? As we saw in *Chapter 4*, the nature of supervisors' and managers' work is filled with expectations.

Understanding how your expectations are formed is a first step in using them to your benefit. If you're like most people the challenge is this: are you allowing your past history, prejudices, or preconceptions to negatively affect how another person behaves? Answering this question requires some introspection, the ability to step back a bit, gain some perspective, and take a relatively unbiased objective look at your own attitudes and beliefs.

What's important to remember is that *the behavior you expect is the behavior you'll get*. If you want to change someone's behavior give them some attention when they do it right. After all, you're the one in charge of *your* expectations about another person's behavior.

What a testing of
character adversity is.

Harry Emerson Fosdick

Chapter 23
Improving Individual Performance

Most managers agree that most people (themselves included) show up at the beginning of a workday *wanting* to do a good job. And most agree that their people are bright enough, talented enough, and have the resources to do a good job.

How about you? Does everyone on your team perform well? Are you getting the results you need from everyone? Is your boss pleased with your team's performance? Are your peers satisfied with your group's output?

If your team isn't as successful as you'd like, or if you answered "No" to any of these questions, the cause is most likely somewhere in the system they're working in. Or it's at least partially in your attitude and approach to your team. Deep down, are you more of a Theory X manager? Have you and/or the organization's culture effectively robbed your employees of their desire to take initiative and be responsible for achieving success?

As we mentioned in *Chapter 22*, supervisors and managers need to create a work environment that will help people achieve individual and team success. When individuals perform well in their jobs, they support the success of the organization's mission, vision, values, and strategy. In fact, the only way an organization can be successful in the long run is to have high-performing people at all levels.

The Six Keys to Successful Performance

Experienced managers know that all employees are not created equal. Individuals have their own strengths and weaknesses and their own quirks, qualities, and issues. So how do you improve the chances that your team members will regularly turn in knock-your-socks-off performance? Here is a fairly simple process.

> We call it the "Rule of Crappy People." Bad managers hire very, very bad employees, because they're threatened by anybody who is anywhere near as good as they are.
>
> *Marc Andreessen*

> Without discipline, there is no life at all.
>
> *Katherine Hepburn*

- Determine knowledge & skills needed.

- Determine individual capacities.

- Set outcomes & expectations.

- Provide guidance & support.

- Provide feedback.

- Provide recognition & rewards.

It's important to understand that this process is *not* a linear, sequential set of separate activities. The key to success is to make sure you've covered all of the issues shown in the model. Ultimately, how you approach this is going to be determined by your past history with each employee, the complexity of the task, and other factors.

Determine Knowledge & Skills Needed

Start with the basics. Does each of your team members have the knowledge necessary to perform their assigned tasks? Do they have the skills required for good performance? Have they been well trained, or do they have sufficient experience with similar tasks? Do they understand why the desired end result is important?

When faced with a new and unfamiliar task, most people will look at it through the lens of their previous experience. That's fine *if* the new task is a lot like something they've done before. However, a new assignment might require one or more of your employees to learn some specialized information or a new skill. As the manager it's your responsibility to make sure they have the knowledge and skills necessary to perform successfully.

Determine Individual Capacities

While there are few jobs that require membership in MENSA, you need to match specific assignments to the employees' individual abilities. Do each of your employees have the mental capacity to perform well (i.e., are they bright enough to do their job)? Do they have the physical and emotional abilities needed to perform well? Does their current workload allow them to take on a new assignment?

Sometimes team members can't perform well due to outside issues or problems – difficulties at home or health problems, for example. Or the task or project at hand might require special skills that are outside their current capabilities. Or their current workload might be so heavy that adding a new assignment is setting them up for failure. In any of these situations you'll want to explore alternatives. Are there tasks that can be postponed, delegated, simplified, or otherwise adjusted? What will generate success for your employees, you, and the organization?

Set Outcomes & Expectations

This is the first step in the performance appraisal process. Do your employees understand and agree with what needs to be done? Have they had an opportunity to ask relevant questions to clarify the goals? Do you have clear standards or benchmarks for evaluating their work? Do your employees believe the standards and intended results are realistic?

Whether you're talking about a short-term project or a long-term strategic initiative, you need to set appropriate expectations with the people who will do the work. To do this, of course, you need to be clear about *your own* expectations for the task. And it makes sense for this expectation-setting process to be a discussion, not a monologue. The bottom line for all this is simple. If your employees don't know what the expectations are for their jobs, how can they deliver the kind of results the organization is seeking?

> If you treat an individual as he is, he will remain as he is. But if you treat him as if he were what he ought to be and could be, he will become what he ought to be and could be.
>
> *Goethe*

Provide Guidance & Support

Once you believe that outcomes and expectations are clear, the path to good performance begins to appear. Are the necessary resources available to complete the task? Does the proposed approach make sense to you and your employees? Take time to reconfirm that everyone is on the same page; ask your employees to describe to you *in their own words* what they believe the outcomes, expectations, and goals are that you've all agreed to.

> Life is a test; it is only a test. If it had been real, more instructions would have been provided.
>
> *Jack Canfield*

Next, ask your employees for their initial ideas about appropriate next step(s). This will give them an opportunity to clarify, question, discuss, explore, and think out loud about the project or task. Have them identify what they would like to have you do to support their efforts. (Remember that Introverts may need to think about it on their own and then come back for that discussion; just make sure it happens.)

If the task is complex, get the main facts and points down on paper. The key is to provide *guidance* along with advice and suggestions. Don't provide a step-by-step checklist of instructions unless that's the only way to get the job done or it's legally mandated. And if you think your team might face some resistance or obstacles, be sure to alert them to that fact.

Provide Feedback

The amount and quality of feedback you give to employees is critical to their ability to perform successfully. Do your employees routinely receive information about their performance? Can they count on you to give them feedback without them having to ask for it? Is the feedback specific and timely enough so they can easily connect what you say with their performance? Is it accurate based upon actual results?

When projects begin to go off track you may not notice it right away unless you're keeping a close eye on your employees' progress. While you don't want to become a micromanager and constantly look over their shoulders, a bit of well-crafted feedback and check-in can keep things from going seriously off course. Look for opportunities to support and assist employees by giving them information and guidance that will help them to succeed. For ideas and suggestions about high-quality feedback, see *Chapter 25*.

Provide Recognition & Rewards

Recognition and rewards, even small ones, help motivate marginal employees and can "re-recruit" good ones. Do your employees *believe* that their performance is appreciated, recognized, and rewarded in ways other than their paycheck? Do they consider the organization's rewards for good performance to be meaningful? Are recognition and/or rewards given in a timely manner relative to their performance?

Most people don't need constant recognition to perform well. Often a simple, "Thank you for your good work on this project; we appreciate it!" can go a long way toward ensuring more good work from your team members. But if there's no difference between the recognition and/or rewards given to great and barely adequate performers, there's little incentive for excellent workers to continue their high performance. Don't make the mistake of thinking that rewards have to be monetary. Sometimes a small token like a new book, a gift card to a favorite store, or even a nice lunch at a good restaurant can make a huge difference to those good performers.

Aligning Capacities & Expectations

As you're doing all this you need to perform a "sanity check" before deciding who should take on new tasks and projects. Do the people you have in mind have the personal capacity to perform the task – i.e., the mental, emotional, and technical capacity to get the job done? How should you adjust their current workloads to make sure they have the time they'll need?

It does no good to keep adding to your star performers' workloads because they're so good. If you don't balance things correctly they won't be stars for long; they'll just burn out and leave. (Really great performers are hard to come by and highly valued; they usually don't have much difficulty finding another job.) On high-performing teams it's common for employees to shift and trade off responsibilities to take advantage of each person's strengths.

God does not ask your ability or your inability. He asks only your availability.

Mary Kay Ash

To sum up, when expectations and performance/quality standards are clear and tasks are matched to team members' capabilities, people can perform well. When they receive specific, timely, positively focused feedback about how they're performing, they become more motivated and tend to perform more successfully. When accountabilities match expectations . . . feedback is frequent and positive . . . appropriate rewards are given . . . and you're seen as someone who's interested in helping your employees succeed . . . the people on your team can and will perform better. It all comes together.

So what kind of expectations do *you* have for your individual employees? Could you make a list of those expectations that apply (or *should* apply) to everyone? How about expectations that are specific to certain positions or units? You may want to take a few minutes to make a preliminary list. (See *Chapter 4* for some examples.)

Chapter 24
Managing Your Team's Performance

A good manager knows when to lead, when to be a good team member, and when to follow. No matter how awesome and outstanding you are as a manager, there are times when someone else is better equipped to run the show. Most of the time though, your team needs you to lead.

When Things Go Right

Have you ever worked as part of a team that regularly performed well? What was that like? Regardless of the setting, I'll bet the following things occurred:

- Everyone knew their own role on the team.

- Everyone pulled together, communicating, collaborating, and cooperating effectively.

- Results produced by the team met or exceeded expectations – yours', your managers', your customers', and your organizations'.

- Team members voluntarily stepped up to assist their teammates when needed.

- New team members were welcomed, oriented, and successfully integrated into the team.

Some of us will do our jobs well and some will not, but we will all be judged by only one thing - the result.

Vince Lombardi

When things go right your team's output is consistently high quality, other units inside the organization can count on your team to carry the ball successfully, and your customers know they can count on you, even when errors occur. The challenge, of course, is that all teams have at least some difficulty consistently performing at a high level. Why? Because things have a tendency to go wrong.

The time is always right to do what is right.

Martin Luther King, Jr.

When Things Go Wrong

When performance problems occur many supervisors chose one of several actions:

- Ignore

- Coach & counsel

- Retrain

- Threaten

Ignore. The first thing that managers do is to simply ignore the problem, hoping it will go away or spontaneously correct itself. But when was the last time you saw a poor performer improve without help? Right. I've never seen it either.

When a person isn't performing up to standards or expectations you *have* to intervene. Failing to address performance shortcomings isn't an option. If you don't address them, there will be no improvement and they may get worse. The rest of the team knows who isn't pulling their weight, and they're probably getting impatient waiting for *you* to do something about it.

When employees underperform, a leader tells them so.

Jack Welch

Coach & Counsel. Another favorite approach is to coach and counsel poor employees in an attempt to improve their motivation or change their behavior. You might assume something is wrong with these employees without really knowing *why* they aren't performing well.

So much of what we call management consists in making it difficult for people to work.

Peter Drucker

In this case, you've jumped to the conclusion that there must be some flaw in the employees when their results don't match your expectations. But if you dig a little deeper you might discover that the information or instructions given to the employees were flawed, incomplete, or confusing. So coaching and counseling at this point seems premature.

Retrain. Another approach is to give employees more training in the procedure they're doing incorrectly. A bit of refresher training is useful for most of us, but you can't assume that retraining is the answer. If it turns out the procedure itself is flawed, retraining will simply reinforce the flawed behavior.

Threaten. If none of these tactics work, you might feel you have to resort to threatening them with negative consequences unless they "get their act together" and start performing (behaving) differently. This is like saying to your crying child, "If you don't stop crying I'll give you something to really cry about!" It's not a very effective strategy with either 7-year–olds or employees.

Here's the bottom line. You still haven't answered the basic question at the root of nearly all performance problems: if these team members are bright enough to do the job and they aren't performing as we expect, then *why* aren't they performing successfully?

In all of these approaches the focus is on the *employee* as the root of the performance problem. Each approach assumes that fixing them will solve the problem. In other words, whatever the performance problem, the cause is always the people. But automatically focusing on employees as the root cause of performance problems ignores the fact that they're simply *one part of the system* that affects performance.

Creating Positive Performance Expectations

How do you make sure your focus is on helping people perform well, rather than finding out who screwed up and how to punish them? To a great extent it's about expectations. If you expect people to perform poorly, your self-fulfilling prophecy is very likely to produce the kind of results you *don't* want from your team.

Life does not have to be perfect to be wonderful.

Annette Funicello

You can use the following items as a checklist to see if your performance expectations are truly useful. Well-developed, clear expectations generally have the following characteristics:

- They focus on specific results.

- They are realistic & attainable.

- They relate to what is truly important about the job.

- They contribute directly to achieving job, team & organizational goals.

- They are in writing, particularly for important initiatives or projects.

- They are measurable.

Focus on Results

If you chase two rabbits, both will escape.

Unknown

Your expectations for your team should be focused on specific results to be achieved rather than just vague, big-picture objectives. The overall objective is important (especially for iNtuitives), but you need to pay attention to the specific outcomes that define success for an assignment. Since about 70 percent of your work force is likely to be people who prefer detailed information (Sensors), you'll want to flesh out your instructions a bit more than you might think is needed.

In some cases the particular task or project might be rather ill-defined, especially if it's a problem to be resolved. In those situations there may not be a lot of details until the issue is in process, so you'll find that frequent updates and course corrections are helpful.

Are Realistic & Attainable

Expectations must be realistic and attainable, but they should require that employees stretch somewhat to be successful. Employees who have grown in their abilities should be ready for more challenging assignments or higher standards of performance. Most of what people do is routine so raising the bar a bit gives employees something to shoot for and helps to stir any sleeping competitive juices. This turns the project or task into another opportunity for them to learn and succeed.

While setting the bar higher usually helps employees, setting it too high can be demoralizing as they struggle to meet unrealistic expectations. The reverse is also true. Setting the bar too low may lead them to perceive the task as unimportant and not worth doing well. Like many things in life, it's a balancing act for you as the manager.

Relate to What's Important

Your expectations should be prioritized and/or weighted to reflect the importance of various tasks compared to other responsibilities and assignments. Not everything you do is of equal weight or importance, and the same is true of your employees' jobs. Make sure you and they are on the same page about the kinds of tasks and projects that are most important. It will make your job and their lives much better.

Contribute to Goals

Your expectations need to align with the goals of your team, your unit, and your organization. Show employees how projects and tasks relate to the overall goals of your team or business unit; this will help them understand the context of their daily activities. When they understand how their work relates to a clearly articulated mission and vision, they'll begin to see how what they do affects the entire organization. Employees who understand their part in the success of an enterprise tend to be more engaged in their work.

Live in such a way that you would not be ashamed to sell your parrot to the town gossip.

Will Rogers

Are in Writing

While not all expectations need to be in writing, those that are should be clearly worded and easy to understand. Both you and your employees must be confident you're on the same page. Vague expectations delivered verbally are almost guaranteed to generate unanticipated (and unwanted) results. A project with any degree of complexity should include at least a written outline of the project, the desired outcome, and the guiding expectations. Often an exchange of e-mails or memos is enough to informally but clearly lay out the parameters of the project and get it underway.

Are Measurable

Fortune favors the prepared mind.

Louis Pasteur

Expectations are clearer when they're measurable. Then both you and your employees can easily see and agree on the end results – how much, by when, etc. You can't measure everything, and everything that's easy to measure may not be important. However, if there's a way to quantify the desired change or outcome, that can offer a tangible target and a way to evaluate results.

The focus of doing all this is to make sure that you and your employees are in agreement about what needs to be done, what the results need to look like, and what the project timeframe should be.

It's All About the Team

The secret of managing is to keep the guys who hate you away from the guys who are undecided.

Casey Stengel

Unless you're completely self-employed and have nobody working with you, you're part of a team. Two people can be a team, just as 20 or 200 can be a team. When your job is to manage and lead the team, you have to be clear about the objectives to be met and your expectations about how that will happen. Since everyone on the team doesn't take in and process information the same way, you'll need to communicate the important information in several different ways. The next case shows what can happen when you don't.

Case: Bill & the Company Goals

Bill was CEO of a 1,400-employee manufacturing company making precision components for the aircraft industry. His vice presidents seemed to be unclear about the overall goals and strategy of the company as the industry and marketplace were going through some rapid changes. When this confusion was first mentioned to Bill, he got visibly agitated and said, "I don't get it. I told them the goals six months ago!" When he was asked if the goals were in writing, his response was, "No! If you write that stuff down your competition can find it out."

There wasn't much danger of the competition finding out because Bill's own vice presidents didn't even know! As a result no one else under them did either. The company continued to falter as employees tried to meet goals no one understood.

Lessons Learned

A verbal list of goals spoken in one meeting more than six months earlier wasn't sufficient in this case. If Bill really wanted his vice presidents to "get it," he should have provided the goals in writing, reviewed them with the team, and then discussed with each vice president how their particular area was going to accomplish those goals.

You can probably think of other expectations in your own organization's culture that influence your team's performance. Just remember that the individual manager at the unit level has more to do with the commitment, engagement, and ultimate performance of the unit than any other factor. If you're in that position, that means you!

Chapter 25
Feedback and Evaluation

Providing ongoing performance feedback to your team will help improve its success. But this is seldom done well. Most managers are much more likely to let their employees know what's going wrong than what's going right. While most organizations have some sort of periodic written performance appraisal process, that's mostly a paperwork exercise for legal purposes. Filling out some forms has little to do with sustaining or improving performance.

It's probably obvious, but if you aren't well informed about how your employees are doing and the results they're getting, you can't expect to be an effective manager. So visibility and data are good places to begin.

> He who knows best knows how little he knows.
>
> *Thomas Jefferson*

Any performance expectations you develop should include measurable targets. Interim measurement points will help, providing clues along the way so you know how a project is coming. Routine benchmarks can easily be reviewed using common statistical tools (e.g., Microsoft SharePoint) to display important data. Commonly called "dashboards," visual presentations of status and data can be extremely helpful in monitoring performance on a variety of people, projects, and activities.

Evaluating Performance

Okay, so you and your employees are clear about what needs to be done and by whom, the standards for success have been agreed to, and you have all the resources you need. Everything should be moving smoothly toward getting the job done, right?

Not really. Life happens and the performance you expect doesn't always end up being the performance you get. When you're juggling so many projects and have so many balls in the air, it may take you awhile to notice that the results you anticipated aren't quite there. When that happens, it's time to make some corrections.

Ability is of little value without dependability.
Unknown

Formal Reviews

Most organizations have some sort of process in place to evaluate performance. If the formal process is well designed . . . if supervisors and managers are well trained in how to use that process . . . and if they *actually use* the process properly . . . these systems can be a positive force for improvement. That's quite a few "ifs," but some organizations have gotten pretty good at their formal process.

If you don't want to get tackled, don't carry the ball.
Ann McKay Thompson

Typically, performance appraisal systems call for at least an annual evaluation in writing, with a required one-on-one discussion. This annual review is "for the record" and it ends up in the employee's personnel file. The annual appraisal supplies input for decisions about promotions, pay raises, succession planning, training programs, and other administrative and legal processes. However, once a year doesn't tend to generate the best outcomes. The best approach seems to combine quarterly semi-formal discussions with a more in-depth annual process.

Informal Reviews

Most really good supervisors and managers have performance-focused conversations with their people more frequently – perhaps weekly or monthly. "How are we doing on this project against our targets? What can I do to help you stay on track and achieve the expected results? Any problems or roadblocks you could use some help with? I'm confident you'll be successful. I'm here to help." Frequent interactions with questions and comments like these help keep employees focused, on task, positive, and moving forward. In these conversations you need to concentrate on expectations and results, offer assistance, and express your confidence in them.

Performance feedback can be informal, but it needs to be based on documented results and your own observations of each person's work. That means you have to be there, seeing what's going on at least some of the time. And you need to keep up with any metrics, statistics, or other measurables generated by each of your team members. You should sit down regularly and go over progress to date with each employee. This lets you compare their individual progress with stated expectations, objectives, goals, and standards.

Providing Effective Feedback

Both the contents of performance feedback and how it is given make a difference in how well employees understand and accept it. This is true whether the feedback is given to reinforce successful performance or improve substandard performance. How do you give effective feedback?

- Focus on behaviors, not the person.

- Focus on observations, what you see going on.

- Focus on descriptions, not judgments.

- Focus on specifics, not generalities.

Focus on Behaviors

Good feedback focuses on behaviors rather than the person. Refer to what the employees *do*, rather than describing who you think they *are* as people. You aren't dissatisfied with *them;* you're dissatisfied with the *results* you're getting. When you focus on behaviors, people are less likely to feel like they're being attacked.

Focus on Observations

Good feedback focuses on observations, on what you directly observe about the work process or an employee's behaviors. You can't rely solely on what others tell you about a team member's performance, although that information can help you decide what performance problems might need attention. Depending on the situation, you may want to discuss how an employee's behavior affects you or others. Sometimes people are simply unaware of how their behavior affects others. And sometimes they just need a bit of guidance about how to do or say things to improve their outcomes.

Focus on Descriptions

Good feedback focuses on descriptions rather than judgments. When we *describe*, we report what has occurred. When we pass *judgment*, we evaluate what has happened as being right or wrong, good or bad. This is a good time to seek first to understand, then to be understood. Review the expectations. ("Here is what we said we were trying to accomplish.") Then describe the results *as you see them.* ("Help me understand where we are from your perspective and how we're doing against the expectations.") Many times, employees know precisely where they're succeeding and falling short. Asking for their perspective usually gets the results you're seeking: they reconnect with the expectations, they see what isn't working, and they suggest steps to get the project back on track. Of course, sometimes your perspective might be different from an individual employee's. But this approach gives you a chance to help your employees perform their own course corrections.

A good plan today is better than a perfect plan tomorrow.

George S. Patton

Focus on Specifics

Good feedback focuses on behavior related to a *specific* situation, rather than commenting on *general* behavior. "You're doing a heck of a job" is nice but too general. This kind of feedback is less effective because it doesn't give people the specifics that help them understand what—and why—they should attempt to change. Since Sensors usually do better with details and specifics anyway, you'll want to practice observing and communicating about specific behaviors and situations. From personal experience I can tell you that this can be a challenge for iNtuitives. It takes practice and persistence to get good at it if this isn't your natural approach. But it's worth the effort since nearly everyone prefers to get practical, specific feedback about what is working well and what could stand improvement.

A final observation. In analyzing 360° feedback results from thousands of managers and leaders, I've noticed that employees almost always give *lower* scores about the amount and quality of feedback they receive from their managers than the scores managers give themselves. Most managers simply don't offer anywhere near the amount of feedback their employees would like – and they don't know that until it's pointed out to them. Whatever amount *you* are currently providing, set yourself a goal to double it within the next three months. Your employees (and your boss) will thank you for it, and your life will be easier.

Keeping Your Balance

Effective feedback is balanced. It contains comments about superior and acceptable performance as well as what needs improvement. Some managers like to use what's called the "sandwich" method of feedback: a positive observation, followed by a corrective observation, followed by another positive observation. My own experience shows that sometimes the "meat" in that sandwich

You can have a great day or a lousy day; it's totally up to you.

Ed Foreman

doesn't register on the employee's radar screen as clearly as the positive comments.

Other managers try to operate on a one-to-one or even four-to-one ratio of positive to corrective feedback. I agree that it's a good idea to have some sort of overall balance when comparing positive to corrective feedback. I also agree that having more positive than corrective feedback is a great idea. However, it *doesn't* make sense to *delay* corrective feedback until you have a positive observation for balance. It makes more sense to provide feedback *as soon as possible.* The more directly feedback is linked to a specific behavior in real time, the more likely the feedback will stick with the employee.

The Three "C's"

When you're preparing for a periodic review of your employees' performance, use the following categories to help organize your thoughts and the review process.

Continue

What activities or behaviors do you want them to continue doing? What parts of their jobs or areas of responsibility are they doing well? Compare expectations to results to reveal which areas are being covered adequately. (Positive reinforcement and acknowledging their results will help keep them moving in the right direction.)

Change

Which activities or behaviors do you want them to handle differently? Which areas deserve more attention or a different approach? What results have not been meeting expectations? Do you have a good idea of what you want to have them change? Ask them what ideas they have for changes or course adjustments.

Create

Are there any assignments, changes in duties, or projects you want your various employees to take on? Are there ways you can help them capitalize on their talents or strengths? If you'd like to see them stretch a bit, ask them what they would like to take on. Identify and highlight two or three areas where you or other team members need some help; suggest they give you some ideas in one or more of those areas.

Performance Improvement Plans

Creating a performance improvement Action Plan is not reserved for employees with major performance problems. Having employees who take on performance improvement as their own responsibility helps to create a great organization. In larger organizations this process may be fairly formal. But smaller organizations have enjoyed excellent success and growth by making performance improvement a daily part of the way they do business.

For example, at Gazelle Sports – a three-store, community focused sporting goods company based in Kalamazoo, Mich. – everyone is involved in performance improvement. Since they opened their first store 25 years ago, the owners have provided every employee, full- and part-time, with the opportunity to grow, develop, stretch, and take on new assignments. This simple yet constant search for how to do their work, serve their customers, serve their communities, and serve their employees better has led to long-term sustainability and success.

The most effective type of Action Plan for performance improvement is one that:

- Relates to specific performance problems or areas needing improvement.

> I've failed over and over and over again in my life. And that is why I succeed.
>
> *Michael Jordan*

- Contains realistic steps that can occur within an appropriate timeframe.

- Reflects an accurate understanding of key performance expectations, responsibilities, or standards.

- Describes specific steps or actions that can be monitored and measured, including checkpoints for progress reviews.

There's no one best format for a performance improvement plan. But the process generally works better if each employee takes the lead in defining the corrective actions they plan to take, then runs the plan by you for input and approval. You may need to provide some direction or guidance, but you should avoid imposing your preferred plan on your employees. Employee commitment and self-confidence are usually higher for self-developed plans than those imposed from above. If an Action Plan starts out as "your plan" to "fix" an employee's performance, it's unlikely to ever become "their plan" or to be successful.

Some Final Tips & Suggestions

Being clear about expectations, creating an environment where people can perform well, and providing good feedback all contribute to good performance, successful outcomes, and fewer errors or false starts. Still, you'll find yourself occasionally needing to have a performance discussion to help an employee improve. And some people will get upset or defensive when they receive corrective feedback, even when that feedback is well delivered. Here are some additional tips and suggestions for giving feedback.

Catch someone doing something right.

Kenneth Blanchard & Spencer Johnson

- Performance feedback should be given face-to-face, in a private conversation.

- Do your homework. If you plan to talk about a performance problem, be sure you have evidence to back up your perceptions.

- The purpose of corrective feedback is to help employees improve their performance. There's no need to apologize for giving them feedback about areas or issues that need improvement; you're providing feedback to help them be more successful.

- Don't discuss the performance or behavior of other employees. If they bring up the behavior of others as justification for their results, don't get dragged into that discussion. Immediately bring the conversation back to the performance of the employee you're talking with.

- In discussing changes in performance, make sure you focus on the job itself – the results they're getting and how they're behaving on the job.

- Keep accurate records (in whatever format is comfortable for you or required by your organization), but limit what you write to the following types of information:

  - Job performance and results, compared to expectations

  - Performance-related observations about behavior

  - What the two of you discussed as ways to improve performance

  - What you told the employee would happen as the "next step"

- Actively seek opportunities to observe the employee's performance, and get feedback from other key people who regularly observe the employee at work.

- Have a performance-focused discussion with each employee at least quarterly. It doesn't need to be formal, with written forms, but it should be based on your observations and notes you've made along the way. This offers a chance for you to do some coaching, encouragement, and corrective suggestions. It also provides an opportunity to make adjustments in expectations and results as business conditions change.

- If an employee's performance is seriously sub-standard, you might need to discuss the most likely outcomes if their behavior or results don't change.

- Have employees evaluate their own performance using the expectations and accountabilities you established together. Most competent performers are tougher on themselves than others might be, and you may discover that your ratings of their performance are higher than their own.

> Our deeds determine us, as much as we determine our deeds.
>
> *George Eliot*

Managing other people – *Skill 4* – is a critical role in any organization of any size. The primary responsibility of any managerial position is to work with and guide the work of others. However, if you expect to successfully manage others, you also need to master the next essential skill, *Skill 5 – Managing Change.*

Skill 5

MANAGING CHANGE

"How wonderful it is that nobody need wait a single moment before starting to improve the world."

Anne Frank

Skill 5 - Managing Change

Every time I lead a workshop, seminar, or course segment that deals with change I ask the participants, "How many of you see today's world as changing much more rapidly than 10 years ago?" Regardless of age, position, education, or regional differences, their response is always nearly 100 percent "Yes."

Almost everyone agrees that the pace, degree, and effects of change are increasing, and many of us don't like it. Whether change seems to be accelerating in your own life or not, you live and work in an environment where change is pretty much a constant. In fact, change may be the *only* constant in daily life. You can definitely count on things being different in the future.

> Change is the norm. . . . unless an organization sees that its task is to lead change, that organization will not survive.
>
> *Peter Drucker*

As recently as the 1980s, if you worked for most large organizations you could pretty much count on being employed for a long time – perhaps until you retired. With decent performance you could expect your career to evolve over time with that same organization. Today, of course, the picture is much different. The unwritten contract between employers and employees – exchanging job security for loyalty to the company – has become irrelevant.

Change is Tough

Change doesn't happen easily and painlessly. The status quo is strongly attractive to individuals. Think back to the various changes you've personally attempted over the years: the New Years' resolutions to get organized, the exercise programs, the diets, the desire to get out of an awful job (or get away from that jerk of a boss). The simple reality is that most of us have a lot more "starts" than "finishes" when it comes to changing our habits and our circumstances.

The same thing is true for organizations. How many major change initiatives has your workplace undertaken in the past decade? And how many of those fizzled out or were put on the back burner to be replaced by some other "flavor of the month"? Most of the major quality improvement efforts undertaken by U.S. organizations fail shortly after they begin. More than half of all major change initiatives also fail over the long haul. Why? Why do we have such a difficult time building and sustaining positive change as individuals and in our organizations? It may be because we don't understand the true nature of change.

Chapter 26
The Dynamics of Change

Change isn't easy, primarily because of the power of the status quo. As human beings, we're hard-wired to think and act based on how we view the world around us. We look for information, interpret events, see opportunities, and make choices based on our *mental model* or perception of reality. Information that doesn't fit into this model is often ignored, discounted, or viewed as threatening or just plain wrong – and that's if we're willing to recognize that it exists. When we don't understand our own mental model and aren't aware of how it influences us, we often view change negatively. We're stuck like glue to our mental model and are often unaware that we're stuck.

> There is no sin punished more implacably by nature than the sin of resistance to change.
> *Anne Morrow Lindbergh*

The Stickiness of Mental Models

Your mental model can prevent you from recognizing that your present way of operating isn't producing the results you want. You might redouble your efforts along the same path without understanding that the path has changed. Or you may fail to recognize that the goal you're working toward is no longer appropriate. You may not even see that the world has changed; or you may see the changes but resist doing anything about them.

For example, Al Gore and others were roundly dismissed and derided for sounding the alarm about global warming until the video "An Inconvenient Truth" brought the issue to the attention of a wider audience. Setting aside arguments about the accuracy of its content, the point is our collective mental model simply couldn't accept the notion it proposed – that we need concerted action to reduce the use of fossil fuels.

> Life is change. Growth is optional. Choose wisely.
> *Karen Kaiser Clark*

Your mental model can also prevent you from finding a process or developing strategies that will produce and reinforce new behaviors. You may be so invested in your current perceptions and behavior patterns that you're unable to see that you *can* change. If you believe the changing world around you is threatening and hostile, you may see yourself as the victim of change rather than the agent of change in your own life. And even if you believe you can change, you might not see *how* to change. When this happens, it's easy to abandon efforts to change at the first hurdle or roadblock.

Organizations also have mental models. Businesses, government, and nonprofits are operating in a rapidly changing, fluid environment, so they need to be flexible, adaptive, and forward-focused. But resistance to change in organizations can be even more powerful than what you face as an individual.

> Conformity is the jailer of freedom and the enemy of growth.
>
> *John F. Kennedy*

Perhaps no better example of excessively rigid corporate mental models exists than the Big Three U.S. auto manufacturers. Their resistance to improving vehicle quality in the 1980s created huge opportunities for Japanese and German automakers. The Big Three's mental models consistently led them to resist calls for higher fuel economy and alternative fuel vehicles even as petroleum prices skyrocketed.

The EV1 Story

From 1996 to 1999 General Motors Corporation produced a remarkable vehicle called the EV1. It was designed in response to a ruling by the California Air Resources Board (CARB) that a percentage of all vehicles sold in the state must be zero-emission vehicles. When GM unveiled its original Impact concept car in 1990, Chairman Roger Smith touted it as the wave of the future and gave the go-ahead to design an all-electric car for mass production. This led the CARB to mandate that two percent of all vehicles sold in California would have to be emission-free beginning in 1998, five percent by 2001, and 10 percent by 2003 — generating a ready-made market for the first company that created the right car.

By 1996 GM had developed the EV1 production sport coupe. It began leasing (not selling) EV1s through Saturn dealers in Los Angeles, Phoenix, and Tucson. A year later Sacramento and San Francisco were added.

When the first 50 test vehicles were loaned to consumers for a week or two, the demand for test drives was overwhelming. In Los Angeles GM expected about 80 volunteers; they shut down the phone lines after 10,000 calls. A proposed test in New York City generated 14,000 calls before the lines were turned off. The test cars got favorable reviews from consumer and auto magazines. A modified Impact set a land speed record for electric vehicles at 183 mph. The car was clearly a winner and consumer demand continued to grow.

The second-generation EV1 debuted in 1999 to rave reviews and enthusiasm among the environmentally aware. By this time, though, GM was led by a different set of executives. Their long-term plans did not include the EV1. The vehicle had always been considered something of a poor stepchild to the rest of GM, where corporate policy had been to fight and delay the CARB mandate as much as possible. Eventually GM and other manufacturers persuaded a federal judge that part of the CARB mandate was unconstitutional, so the CARB postponed the implementation of its ruling.

When the EV1 production line shut down in 1999, there were 1,100 lessees who immediately became concerned about what would happen at the end of their leases. In 2003 CEO Rick Wagoner officially cancelled the EV1 program, saying the company could not sell enough of them to make a profit. The CARB mandate was eventually scrapped. In late 2003 GM began reclaiming the cars. They were gradually withdrawn and stored, to eventually be shredded or crushed.

Update: The EV1 became the subject of the 2006 documentary, "Who Killed the Electric Car?" In 2008 former GM Chairman Wagoner cited the cancellation of the EV1 and lack of support for hybrids as his worst decision. GM declared bankruptcy in 2009, emerging as a much smaller company with fewer car lines and far behind the competition in developing fuel-efficient vehicles.

Even when organizations try to change, many of those attempts are unsuccessful. Back in 1993, the international consulting firm Watson-Wyatt reported on a study of more than 500 companies that had extensively restructured their operations. This research showed that the most frequent barriers to successful organizational change were (1) employee resistance to the change initiative, and/or (2) a dysfunctional organizational culture.

For example, think about the high number of unsuccessful mergers and acquisitions (M&As) during the past 20 years. Too many times the M&A is made for entirely the wrong reasons: executive egos run amuck . . . a desire to cash out . . . senior management's failure to turn around a struggling company . . . the examples are endless.

So why do so many M&As fail so miserably?

- The initiative's leaders don't understand the nature of change.

- The organizations have very different cultures, which rarely makes for a successful corporate marriage.

- The people in the organizations are stuck and aren't ready for change, or they're burned out from too much change.

Stages of the Change Process

So how can individuals and organizations *ever* change? What makes them willing to break their mental models? Years of real-life (rather than purely academic) research seems to have cracked the code on understanding change. The generally accepted model for behavioral change shows a predictable process that includes:

- Precontemplation of change

- Contemplation of change

- Preparation for change

- Action

- Maintenance & consolidation

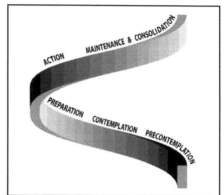

Precontemplation of Change

This stage is firmly focused on the status quo. As an individual or an organization, we have no real intention to do things differently. In fact, in this stage we often deny that any change is needed. When a situation requiring change comes up we feel pressured, we avoid talking about it, and we might feel helpless to see any solution to the problem. An individual in this phase might ignore increasing weight or other health warning signs until some precipitating event (e.g., heart attack, having to buy a larger wardrobe) causes them to shift to the next phase.

The most difficult thing is the decision to act. The rest is merely tenacity. You can do anything you decide to do. You can act to change and control your life; and the procedure, the process, is its own reward.

Amelia Earhart

Contemplation of Change

In this stage we understand that some sort of problem exists. We may even acknowledge that changes are needed. While we haven't decided specifically what we'll do or what the new approach needs to be, we're beginning to look at potential solutions or alternative approaches. In this phase we may start moving toward taking some action. Or we might decide to abort the change process and return to the status quo.

Preparation for Change

By this point in the change process we've examined various alternatives and are developing plans to take some sort of action fairly soon, most likely within the next 30 days. We're fine-tuning our plans – perhaps seeking new information or making final adjustments before actually starting the new behavior. To enhance our chances of success, we may learn more about how the change process works, preparing ourselves for the next phase.

Action

In this phase we're actively implementing the change in our behavior, habits, or approach. Active change takes time, energy, and effort to be successful. Not all aspects of the plan will be equally effective, so we may need some form of course correction and adjustment as we move forward. Depending on the nature of the change, this phase can take days, weeks, or even months. When changing a personal habit or behavior, we usually need to do the new behavior every day for three or four weeks before it starts to become the norm. For a large organization, this active change phase may last *months* before becoming part of accepted practice.

Maintenance & Consolidation

Once the new approach or behavior has been implemented the process is *not* over. The change may seem to be fully installed, but the challenge at this point is to sustain the new behavior or approach long enough to really make it permanent. When the change is major or complex it's easy to lapse into our former behavior – especially when we're under pressure. This natural tendency needs to be overcome for the new way of doing things to actually become "the way we do things around here."

We frequently see organizational change programs die a premature death because senior managers get impatient with how long it's taking. Since those who are leading the change have been discussing and debating the situation for some time, they're further into this five-step process. They may already be fully on board (i.e., ready for action) before the rest of the organization even knows about the change (i.e., at precontemplation of change). Unless upper management understands and acts on this dynamic, there will be frustration all around.

You're a human being, so you've had personal and professional changes that haven't lasted or have gone off track along the way. Even when you're highly motivated to make a change, attempting to bypass a step in the process usually sabotages your change initiative and causes it to derail or just stop.

So how can you help create successful change in your team and organization? Turn to the next chapter for some answers.

> In the battle that goes on for life
> I ask for a field that is fair
> A chance that is equal with all in strife
> The courage to do and dare.
> If I should win let it be by the code
> My faith and my honor held high.
> If I should lose, let me stand by the road
> And cheer as the winner goes by.
>
> *Knute Rockne*

Chapter 27
Creating Successful Change

What would constitute a major change right now for you or your organization? Of all the things going on in your personal and professional life, what would you like to be significantly different? I'm sure you can think of more than one.

In the mid 1990s a number of U.S. aerospace companies were getting up to 70 percent of their sales from military contracts. They had helped to equip a military expansion, largely as a deterrent to the USSR. With the collapse of that threat, military contracts were scaled back and a lot of that business disappeared during the next several years. Converting military product lines to civilian markets was a major change for those companies. Some successfully made the transition. Others failed and were absorbed or went out of business.

> Both tears and sweat are salty, but they render a different result. Tears will get you sympathy, sweat will get you change.
>
> *Jesse Jackson*

What Drives Change?

For major change to occur, two important ingredients must be present: pain and remedy.

Pain

In this context pain means a critical mass of information/input that justifies breaking with the status quo. In other words, information begins to accumulate that suggests your current behavior or approach is not producing the results you seek. Before anything can change, you need to have enough of this information – the current situation must be painful enough – that you'll consider doing something different. You don't know exactly what you'll do differently at this point; you just know that the current reality is getting increasingly uncomfortable.

> There is no birth of consciousness without pain.
>
> *Carl Jung*

There came a time when the risk to remain tight in the bud was more painful than the risk it took to blossom.

Anais Nin

Remedy

This means desirable, viable actions you can take to solve a problem or take advantage of an opportunity. Once you're uncomfortable enough with the current situation, you can start looking for potential new ways to behave. This is the point when organizations examine alternative strategies, look more closely at the competition, and research best practices to see what possible changes might be useful.

Case: A Bad Decision at Daimler-Benz

When the management board at Daimler-Benz finally figured out that Jurgen Schrempp's strategy in acquiring Chrysler was a financial and brand-focus mistake, they cast about for appropriate remedies. They finally selected two: (1) force Schrempp into an early retirement, then elevate the popular Dieter Zetsche into the top spot, and (2) support Zetsche's strategy of selling off 80 percent of the money-losing Chrysler division to private equity firm Cerberus. This change wasn't as risky as it sounds. Since Zetsche had run Chrysler just prior to ascending to the top spot, he knew whether selling Chrysler was a good idea or not. Smart thinking, as it has turned out. Schrempp had been the architect of several acquisitions that ended up costing Daimler-Benz billions of Deutsche Marks, including Mitsubishi Motors and Fokker Aircraft.

Lessons Learned

It seems that even highly successful global corporations can resist change much longer than is healthy. In this case, Daimler-Benz eventually found the pain of multi-billion Mark losses sufficient to seek a remedy that included the replacement of Schrempp with Zetsche.

Although you probably aren't dealing with changes that are as complex and volatile as Daimler-Benz's in your daily work, you still might want to keep the following in mind:

- Without sufficient pain, the status quo remains attractive enough to prevent change from occurring. An interest in change may flicker briefly across your mind, but you're unlikely to do anything to change your present state. If you aren't sufficiently uncomfortable, maintaining the status quo will be more attractive than the perceived value of change.

- If the pain of the present situation is enough for you to seriously contemplate change, the remedy must be more desirable than the difficulty of undergoing that change. You must believe that, in the end, you'll reduce your pain enough to have made the work of change worthwhile.

> If we keep on doing what we've always done, we'll keep on getting what we always got.
>
> *Barbara Lyons*

When the pain of the present is greater than uncertainty about the future, *and* when a viable new behavior or opportunity is attractive enough, then change can occur. Until both of these conditions are met it simply won't happen.

Natural Reactions to Change

There are at least seven natural reactions that humans have when faced with change. The important word here is "natural." Most people don't relish change and eagerly go for it as part of how they naturally react to events. We have to work at change to get comfortable with it. These reactions include:

> One of the best ways to properly evaluate and adapt to the many environmental stresses of life is to simply view them as normal.
>
> *Dennis Waitley*

- Fight or flight

- Seeking control

- Target fixation

- Denial & rejection

- Fear/avoidance of ambiguity

- Malicious compliance

- Passivity & helplessness

Change can be likened to an unplanned journey into uncharted waters in a leaky boat with a mutinous crew.

Michael Fullan

Fight or Flight

This is our first instinctive reaction to any new or uncomfortable situation. Our natural tendency is to react with aggression or defensiveness or to run away. Fight or flight is hardwired into our bodies, and it's as old as the human race. These were often the only options for Cave Man. We either run from the predator/change (and hope we're faster), or we stand and fight the predator/change (and hope we win). The third option is being eaten by the predator or overwhelmed by the change. The point is even when change is not life-threatening, we react biologically as though it were.

Seeking Control

This often hides under the guise of needing more information, attempting to get our arms around the situation, and/or pushing away the change by seeking to manage what's going on. We often see this in organizations that create committees to address challenges. Unfortunately, too often committees get bogged down in over-analyzing and delaying decisions. This attempt to slow down and control the change may not be intentional, it may not even be conscious, but it's often there.

Target Fixation

This reaction surfaces when we're heavily invested in achieving a certain goal or objective *and* rapidly changing circumstances require a refocusing or shift in the target. The term target fixation grows out of combat training – i.e., when soldiers are so focused on hitting a certain target that they ignore a new, more dangerous enemy who has outflanked them.

Denial & Rejection

This ranges from denying that a problem even exists to coming up with lots of reasons why all possible solutions will not work. Operating from a negative, fault-finding focus, this reaction grows out of fear and represents a head-in-the-sand perspective. This reaction often appears when we're faced with an emerging problem or trend and we don't like where things are heading.

Fear/Avoidance of Ambiguity

Fear of the unknown is a normal, hardwired human reaction. But an overwhelming desire to avoid ambiguous situations and change is often marked by seeking order, facts, and details or by creating extensive contingency plans. We cannot plan for every eventuality and we cannot foresee the future with great accuracy. We can, however, deal with most situations that are likely to occur – as long as we realize we'll never have all the information we'd like to have.

Malicious Compliance

This reaction is insidious because it exists in silence. The thought processes go something like: "I think this is a dumb idea/solution/approach. Nobody asked me what I thought. (Of course I didn't offer my opinion, but they don't care anyway.) I'm not going to support this decision. I'll just do the minimum necessary and only when I absolutely have to." This subtle kind of resistance to change is often at the root of change initiatives that start with big hoopla only to gradually wither and die.

Passivity & Helplessness

This reaction often takes the form of "victimhood." It can sometimes be seen in a long face, whining, complaining about others, or just silent hopelessness. In organizations that are going through layoffs or downsizing you can see numerous examples – people walking the halls and staring off into space as they sit in their cubes,

> All adventures, especially into new territory, are scary.
>
> *Sally Ride*

They say that time
changes things, but
you actually have to
change them
yourself.

Andy Warhol

wondering if they'll be next. The amount and quality of the work that does get done deteriorates.

The Comfort Zone

Since we tend to equate change with pain and we want to avoid pain, we usually stick with what we've done before. It's comfortable and it's gotten us to where we are today. But, as the saying goes, "If you always do what you've always done, you'll always get what you always got." If you want to change something, you have to do something other than what you've been doing.

Your home has a thermostat that controls its heating and cooling system. In addition to degree markings the thermostat may have an area (usually around 65-75 degrees) called the Comfort Zone. (This was more common in the days before digital readouts). When the temperature is in the comfort zone, most people feel comfortable and the HVAC system is sitting idle. When the temperature is either above or below this range, the system will turn on to bring the temperature back into the comfort zone. Once the comfort zone is reached, the system goes back to idle.

Each of us also has a personal comfort zone. It's the comfortable feeling you get when things are going along pretty well. You're not too challenged. There's just enough new stuff going on to keep from getting bored, but not so much that you feel threatened. Everyone has a different comfort zone "setting," and the boundaries of your comfort zone may determine how easily you adapt to change.

Case: Jack, Jill & the Comfort Zone

Jack, the client services manager in a large nonprofit agency, had a fairly wide comfort zone. He was an easy-going fellow, comfortable with uncertainty, change, and ambiguity. He had a philosophy of taking life as it comes, and was generally able to deal well with events as they happened. Jack had grown up in a free-wheeling household where the rules consisted of general guidelines and deviations from the norm were handled in a fear-free, learning-oriented manner.

Jill, the financial manager in the same agency, had a much narrower comfort zone. She liked to have things very well defined, planned, scheduled, and ordered. Unexpected events, even fairly minor ones, caused her a lot of stress. Jill had spent most of her career at the agency doing work with a lot of very clear, precise rules and regulations. She had grown up in a strict family where deviation from her parents' rules and standards brought instant criticism or punishment.

Lessons Learned

The same amount of ambiguity and change that fell within Jack's comfort zone drove Jill up the wall. They were both ideally suited for their respective jobs. But the executive director knew that Jill was much more likely to perceive change as a threat than Jack, so she made sure that Jill was one of the first to know when any change was on the horizon.

Adjusting your Comfort Zone

How wide is your individual comfort zone? If daily events and changes that seem to be "no sweat" for most people make you anxious, your comfort zone may not be broad enough. Even if you're generally pretty comfortable with most situations, there are likely to be certain areas of your personal and professional life that cause you stress or discomfort. Remember, all of us operate from within our mental model, and changing circumstances are bound to bump against our way of viewing the world at some point. That's when we discover the size of our comfort zone.

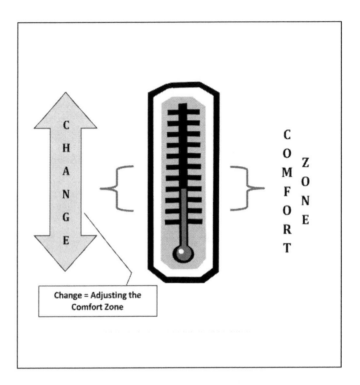

So how do you go about adjusting your comfort zone if you'd like it to be wider? David Allen tells us that the boundaries of our comfort zone are really all about *standards* – patterns of behavior and limits that define how we think and act. If you want to change your comfort zone, you need to change your standards.

Nearly 30 years ago, when I first took his personal productivity workshop, I recall David talked about our individual comfort zone and how it relates to the amount of cash we need to have in our bank account. For instance, if our standard (i.e., our mental model) about money says we need to have a minimum of $1,000 in our checking account, we're likely to get very creative about saving and curtail spending when we find our account balance is only $600. We also have a standard about the maximum or top of our comfort

There's only one corner of the universe you can be certain of improving, and that's your own self.

Aldous Huxley

zone. When we find our bank balance is above our top standard (say \$4,000 when we think \$2,500 is more than enough), we'll also get very creative about spending ourselves back down into our comfort zone.

So . . . want to have more money? Change your standard. Decide and commit to the notion that the minimum standard you'll accept in your checking account is \$2,000 and your new top standard is \$5,000. Over time, you'll find ways to make that happen and your comfort zone will have changed. In other words, if you want to change anything in your comfort zone (including something as fuzzy as how much fun you have in your life), change your standards. Once your standards are revised they become your new comfort zone.

Overcoming Resistance to Change

If change is so difficult for most people, how do you sustain positive change in your own life and in your organization? Simply put, in spite of our tendency to hold on to the status quo, change doesn't have to be a big struggle. It may never become your favorite thing, but with patience, practice, and some adjustments in your comfort zone it doesn't have to be overly difficult.

As a manager you're responsible for helping your team deal with change – and even thrive – in today's volatile environment. So what can you do to help create successful change? Here are a few ideas you might find useful:

- Explain & educate

- Involve people in the process

- Tie in rewards

- Listen!

- Empathize

- Observe & support
- Reframe

Explain & Educate

Often the major reason for resistance is a simple lack of information. Once people understand the situation that makes the change necessary, they may be more receptive. If the new way of doing things also means acquiring new skills or behaviors, a focused training course may be required.

Involve People in the Process

We must be the change we wish to see in the world.

Mohandas K. Gandhi

Involving your team in the entire process of change goes a long way toward dispelling resistance to change. It's hard for someone to object to and fight change if they've been involved in the process from Day One. And even if they haven't been heavily involved from the beginning, including them in planning for and implementing the change will substantially reduce their resistance.

Tie in Rewards

When employees can see how the proposed change will benefit the organization, the team, and them personally, they're much less likely to resist. What will the payoff be to each of them in terms of the way they do their job? Will they get to learn new and interesting skills? Will they have an opportunity to step up and develop their leadership abilities? Is there the potential for a more tangible reward if they get the change installed successfully?

Listen!

People often resist change because they feel they haven't been paid attention to; they feel their objections and concerns are ignored or undervalued. So listen carefully. Deep listening involves not only what they're saying but also paying attention to their emotions, fears, hopes, and concerns. Use your questioning skills to draw out the underlying reasons for resistance. In many situations that person simply wants to be heard.

Empathize

It pays to follow Stephen Covey's advice: "Seek first to understand, then to be understood." You can show your caring for another person and their point of view without necessarily agreeing with them. The key is to truly listen and then demonstrate your understanding of their issues/concerns about the change. Often you'll find that listening with empathy and caring melts resistance.

Observe & Support

Remember that people have a number of different natural reactions when change is happening. Once you understand the form their resistance takes, you'll be better equipped to effectively counter it. Helping others understand the change process – and our natural reactions to it – can go a long way toward getting them on board.

Reframe

Reframing is an effective conflict resolution technique. You restate what the other person has said in a way that causes less resistance and increases the chances they'll see more than their own point of view. This is clearly helpful when a team member perceives a change as having a cost or negative result for them personally.

Resistance to change is a natural human condition. Effective managers understand that reality and use a variety of techniques to help create successful change with their team.

> Become a student of change. It is the only thing that will remain constant.
>
> *Anthony D'Angelo*

Chapter 28
Change: Large and Small

When it comes to both personal and organizational change, the magnitude and complexity of the change affect the change process. Large-scale change requires a big-picture or strategic focus, while small-scale change is more gradual, incremental, and ground-level.

Large-Scale Change

Large-scale change tends to be driven by significant strategic challenges. In organizations this shows up in response to major competitive changes, technological watersheds, major industry developments, mergers and acquisitions, or significant reorganizations. This holds true for all sizes of organizations. If you own a small grocery store in a town of 25,000, an announcement that Wal-Mart is going to build a store three miles from yours is going to result in some large-scale change for you. If your doctor says you must lose 50 pounds or die, you're going to have a large-scale experience in change. This type of change usually has three characteristics:

- It involves revolution vs. evolution.

- It's driven by mission, vision, and values.

- It's led from the top.

Involves Revolution vs. Evolution

Rather than gradually shifting and adjusting, large-scale change requires major effort. The environmental drivers for large-scale change are often viewed as potentially catastrophic; failing to successfully adapt and change may imperil the very existence of the organization. Examples include aerospace companies that must shift from military to civilian projects, automakers that must switch from selling large SUVs to more fuel-efficient hybrids, and

If you don't like the way the world is, you change it. You have an obligation to change it. You just do it one step at a time.

Marion Wright Edelman

Great spirits have always encountered violent opposition from mediocre minds.

Albert Einstein

nonprofit organizations that have achieved their original mission and must find a new one.

Large-scale change isn't found only in threatening situations; it can come in the form of opportunities as well. Examples include the small-business owner whose main competitor retires or sells out, and downsized pharmaceutical scientists who refuse their employer's offer to move and instead start their own company.

In essence, the organization or the external environment reaches what Malcolm Gladwell calls a *tipping point* – a point at which an emerging trend or changing situation accelerates rapidly to become the norm rather than a rarity.

> Micro change is when "I" must change; organizational change is when "we" must change; macro change is when "everyone" must change.
>
> *Daryl Conner*

Bruce's Tipping Point

Individually, we also experience large-scale change. For instance, Bruce had always eaten whatever he wanted. As he neared his 50s his weight started to get above 250 pounds. He worked a lot, which meant that he was "too busy" to exercise. His blood pressure average had gone up too, and he no longer had the energy he had when he was in his 30s.

His doctor had been telling him that he needed to exercise more, change his diet, and lose weight. Bruce had heard that mantra for the past five years but had pretty much ignored it. Then one day, when his latest blood work came back from the lab, his doctor told him, "Bruce, you are borderline diabetic. You have two choices. You can change how you live or you can die. You decide." Bruce was faced with a personal tipping point – immediate, large-scale change whichever path he chose!

Driven by Mission, Vision & Values

Because large-scale change is often wrenching, it's critical to keep everyone focused on the mission of the organization and the vision of what the future will look like. When its mission and vision are unclear and poorly communicated, an organization will tend to founder. People imagine the worst and resistance to change grows. In organizations where the mission and vision are clear at all levels, change is viewed as an opportunity. Because everyone knows where the organization is heading, the *how* to get there becomes much clearer and less confusing.

As Collins and Porras have noted in their book "Built To Last," organizations that are successful over the long haul are those that know what their core values are and stick to them for a long time. Values provide the framework, the backbone of the organization, helping to anchor it in the midst of rapid change. This doesn't mean the changing environment has no effect on the organization. Rather, it means the mission, vision, and values serve as a navigational guide through large-scale change.

Led From the Top

Large-scale change isn't going to turn out well unless senior management is out in front of the troops. It's up to the top levels of the organization to lead the change, describe the vision, and reconnect everyone to the mission. When change is imposed on the organization from the outside, there's bound to be disagreement and confusion. So having senior management highly visible is a prerequisite for success.

> We must remember that one determined person can make a significant difference, and that a small group of determined people can change the course of history.
>
> *Sonia Johnson*

During major organizational change, the amount and frequency of communication from the change leaders is critically important. In most organizations the rumor mill runs well most of the time. In high-change situations the rumor mill cranks into overdrive and feeds off generalized fear about the future. Much of the communication "static" generated during major change moves at warp speed through an organization. And, of course, most of what the rumor mill produces is wrong. The only way to keep all of this from creating additional problems is to increase the communication flow from the top of the organization. Senior management needs to communicate more lavishly for three reasons:

- To provide guidance to the organization during the change process. This helps move the organization through the change in a more planned, orderly fashion.

- To reassure employees, customers, and other key stakeholders (bankers, advisors, other owners, etc.) about the progress of the change initiative and how it will affect them.

- To support those in the organization who are going through the brunt of the change process, particularly if there are negative consequences such as layoffs and plant closings.

> Change will not come if we wait for some other person or some other time. We are the ones we've been waiting for. We are the change that we seek.
>
> *Barack Obama*

When this essential communication piece is handled poorly, the change process becomes more difficult, more time-consuming, and less successful. When it's ignored, the result is often disaster.

The Main Challenge

When a large-scale change initiative is underway, senior management needs to avoid the tendency to control and micro-manage the process. Often senior leaders will over-control without intending to, telling themselves they're just doing what they can to support the process throughout the organization.

Frequently the senior team has studied the central strategic issues for some time while other levels in the organization – particularly people and facilities remote from the center of power – may not even be aware of the challenge. Lower-level staff, who aren't privy to the senior team's deliberations, often don't react to install the new approach as quickly as senior management would like. Then, to help move the process forward, the senior team focuses more on the daily business of their respective sub-units. This steals initiative from the staff and short-circuits the natural flow of change. A lack of patience and understanding about how the change process works can result in senior leaders giving up on a large-scale change initiative at precisely the time the front-line troops finally say, "Ah-ha! *Now* we understand what we need to do!"

There's an essential messiness to change, especially large-scale change. Unless you understand that this messiness is natural and allow it to occur to some degree, the change process will be short-circuited. The results will almost always be less than you hoped for.

Small-Scale Change

Small-scale change is more likely to directly involve front-line supervision and middle management. It's often made up of components or subsets falling out of large-scale change. Changing a work team's focus as part of a new product roll-out . . . altering a reporting relationship . . . refocusing a department after a restructuring . . . switching to new cash management software . . . all are examples of small-scale change that are part of some larger initiative. This type of change is usually characterized by:

- Incremental, short-term focus

- Frequent check-in with upper management

> You don't have to be afraid of change. You don't have to worry about what's been taken away. Just look to see what's been added.
>
> *Jackie Greer*

Incremental, Short-Term Focus

The magnitude of the change and the timeline involved are both shorter in this type of change. It is more evolutionary than revolutionary, and it operates at a lower level in the organization. As an individual supervisor or manager, you may understand how your particular unit or operation is affected by a large-scale change initiative, but you're going to be focused on making incremental changes over a period of weeks or months. You'll share responsibility for the change with your individual team members and with other teams working on their particular set of change initiatives.

Frequent Check-in With Upper Management

In small-scale change, front-line personnel need to frequently update higher levels of the organization about how their particular pieces of the process are doing. It's a matter of saying, "Here's where we are right now with our projects and initiatives; here's what we think needs to happen next. Does that seem to match what you're looking for? Any advice or course corrections you see us needing to make?" When it works well this communication process is continuous, back and forth, up and down, and across the organization.

Small-Scale Change in Smaller Settings

In smaller organizations or in units within a larger organization, you may need to make changes that are incremental or not part of a larger change initiative. It's not unusual to make adjustments in the way the work is done to improve quality, productivity, or customer satisfaction. The psychology of small-scale change is somewhat different in these situations.

The key attitudes are a willingness to be flexible and a commitment to continuous improvement. Most organizations operate in an environment that is fluid and dynamic, so adaptability and a willingness to meet changing demands are required for success. (Customers whose needs go unmet will cease to be *your* customers; they'll become somebody else's customers!) As you contemplate and then execute these small-scale internal changes, make sure you consider how they will affect those upstream and downstream from your team. Neglecting to consult with your peers usually results in unintended consequences, which are rarely positive.

> Changes are not only possible and predictable, but to deny them is to be an accomplice to one's own unnecessary vegetation.
>
> *Gail Sheehy*

The Challenge in Change

The challenge for you as a supervisor or manager is to move your own particular piece of any size or type of change along, while coordinating with other parts of the organization. At the same time, you need to keep an eye on the larger goal or the context you're operating in. This requires a bi-directional focus that isn't easy to sustain. While you're taking care of daily business you also need to make sure what you're doing fits in to the mission and vision of the organization. A tall order for any supervisor.

When your organization faces change, all levels – from the CEO to front-line supervisors – need to exhibit effective leadership skills. Handle change well, and your people are motivated and energized. Handle change poorly, and you'll watch them become less engaged, more negative, and perhaps even walk out the door. After all, if *you* don't believe in the importance and value of the change why should they?

Managing the challenge of change within today's fast-paced, chaotic environment will call upon all of your abilities to effectively solve problems and make decisions. That's the subject of *Skill 6*.

Unless you are prepared to give up something valuable you will never be able to truly change at all, because you'll forever be in the control of the things you can't give up.

Andy Law

The dogmas of the quiet past are inadequate to the stormy present. The occasion is piled high with difficulty, and we must rise with the occasion. As our case is new, so we must think anew and act anew.

Abraham Lincoln

Skill 6

SOLVING PROBLEMS AND MAKING DECISIONS

"Energy and persistence conquer all things."

Benjamin Franklin

Skill 6 – Solving Problems and Making Decisions

Supervisors and managers make decisions – lots of decisions – every day. Most of the time those decisions are made more or less automatically; we make choices almost without thinking.

That's fine for many routine issues that lie within your span of control – situations you know you can handle easily and successfully. But other decisions require careful thought because they carry the potential for far-reaching consequences. You need to consider alternative approaches, weigh the options, and then make the decision carefully.

Problems crop up every day. Some can be solved based on your previous experience. You look at the problem, conclude it's "just like" other issues that have come up before, and choose to do what you've done before. Other problems aren't routine, but they're fairly simple and the correct solution is obvious based on common sense. Still others are simple, there are several workable solutions, and the alternative you select really doesn't matter much. In that case, you pick one alternative and go with it.

But as your responsibilities increase, you'll face complex problems that require more sophisticated problem-solving and decision-making skills. In addition to the more objective, logical techniques and skills typically associated with problem solving, you'll need to use your intuition – your "gut feel" for what the best choice might be in any given situation. If you want to be truly successful as a supervisor and manager, you must develop and practice your problem-solving and decision-making skills.

Imagination is more important than knowledge.

Albert Einstein

We live in an epoch in which the solid ground of our preconceived ideas shakes daily under our certain feet.

Barbara Ward

Chapter 29
What's the Problem with Problems?

Problems exist in every organization. Simply stated, a problem represents a difference or gap between what is supposed to happen and what actually happens. Solving the problem removes the difference or closes the gap.

Problems are only opportunities in work clothes.

Henry J. Kaiser

Consequences of Unresolved Problems

When problems go unsolved there are negative consequences, such as:

- Lower staff morale

- Higher turnover

- Wasted resources

- Decreased capacity for change

- Lack of success

Lower Staff Morale

Even when it isn't stated openly, employees know when you aren't willing or able to deal with problems and successfully resolve them. As a result, they become less willing to raise issues that prevent them from being productive. "They don't handle problems when we bring them up, so why bother?" Your team may give up on you as a problem-solver and go about their business as best they can. This creates unmotivated, frustrated, disengaged employees; some of them may be so frustrated or angry that they even sabotage your efforts.

If you want real, significant, sustainable change, you need talented, committed local line leaders.

Peter Senge

Higher Turnover

Highly talented staff may leave, seeking an environment or a manager that handles issues effectively. Talented people usually don't have trouble finding a new opportunity somewhere else. Highly skilled people with proven track records in their field are able to move much more easily than average employees, regardless of the economy. If your approach to issues and problems is to ignore or avoid them, more proactive managers may recruit your talented folks away from you. You've probably heard that people don't leave organizations; they leave managers who don't meet their needs. This is particularly true during difficult economic times. If you're an effective manager, your talented staff will tend to prefer the security of the known (that's you) to the uncertainty of the unknown.

Wasted Resources

Quality means doing it right when no one is looking.

Henry Ford

Failing to solve problems and address issues has real, bottom-line costs. People are less productive than they could be, and that means output is less than it could be. Errors and mistakes that are not corrected or prevented from recurring are costly. In his book "Quality Without Tears," Philip Crosby asserts that mistakes cost you three times as much as doing it right the first time:

- The initial cost to do the job incorrectly the first time

- The cost to correct the mistake, and

- The opportunity cost of what you *could* have been doing while you were correcting the mistake

Decreased Capacity for Change

In today's dynamic environment the ability to adapt quickly is mission-critical. When problems or issues aren't addressed or resolved, your organization's change and growth may slow or even grind to a halt. Or the organization might grow or change unevenly, with some units forging ahead to meet changing needs while other units (yours?) lag behind because problems aren't being handled. The goal of continuous improvement becomes much harder to meet when this happens. For example, manufacturing may have increased its capacity, but the purchasing department's limitations means there aren't enough raw materials to run at the higher capacity.

Lack of Success

When you ignore, avoid, or put off dealing with problems and making decisions, your boss is going to notice. This is particularly true when the problems or decisions are within your span of control. If your approach is to avoid handling the issues within your control, you won't be given the opportunity to "graduate" or take on new, more challenging tasks and responsibilities. As a front-line supervisor or mid-level manager, you're *expected* to handle problems as they occur and you're *expected* to make decisions about issues that are appropriate for your position and level. When you don't, you aren't doing your job. Your boss and even their boss are looking to you to handle those issues. Delegating upward because you don't want the hassle is a career-breaking move.

Types of Problems

Most problems fall into two general categories: (1) system or process problems, and (2) people problems. How much of each category you deal with depends on your organization, role, and specific job responsibilities. However, most supervisors and managers deal with at least some of both types.

In real life this is an artificial distinction because most problems contain both system/process *and* people problems. Sometimes a problem is more of one type than the other, but usually both system and people issues need to be resolved. What's important to understand is that the *methods* used to solve system or process problems may be different from those used to solve people problems.

Be bold. If you're going to make an error, make it a doozy, and don't be afraid to hit the ball.

Billie Jean King

If you find a path with no obstacles, it probably doesn't lead anywhere.

Frank Clark

System & Process Problems

Every organization uses systems and processes to make sure things happen when and how they should. Those systems may be automated, manual, or a combination of both. Usually the expectation is that everyone will use those systems every time. That, of course, doesn't happen as often as we'd like. Systems are designed by people, people make mistakes, and sometimes those mistakes show up as systems that don't work very well.

In some cases, systems may be flawed from the very beginning. For instance, a system might have been designed without input from the people who use it, or the designer's understanding of the problem might have been incorrect. In any event, the system or process simply doesn't work well. It may be fixable, but that typically won't be easy.

Sometimes an individual manager thinks the system is wrong, unworkable, or just plain stupid. When that happens the best you'll see is malicious compliance and half-hearted implementation. It's as if that manager *wants* the system to fail.

Occasionally, a system that has worked well in the past may begin to fail. Perhaps conditions have changed, new technology has been acquired, or the original reasons for the system no longer apply. Too often, large organizations add new systems or processes without eliminating the old ones, which can lead to duplication of effort. Sometimes two similar systems in different parts of an organization cannot communicate with one another. An example of this occurred on September 11, 2001, when two of the World Trade Center's towers in New York City were attacked. City, state, and federal agencies and responders were unable to communicate with one another due to incompatible radio systems.

Systems problems are often *process* problems writ large. You can have a system that generally works well but a process within that

> If what we know about our processes cannot be expressed in numbers, we don't know much about them. If we don't know much about them, we can't control them. If we can't control them, we can't compete.
>
> *Excerpted from Motorola Co's. Quality Policy*

system doesn't function properly. Process problems frequently require specialized knowledge or technical expertise, and they often make up parts of larger systems.

Sometimes a process that works well simply becomes overwhelmed by an increase in workload or demand until it breaks down. Or a change made in one process causes problems with another because people don't understand how intertwined those processes have become. In the aftermath of the attack in New York City, the lack of ability to communicate among jurisdictions was a *system* problem; the lack of a preplanned method for dealing with those different systems was a *process* problem. Whether a problem is a system issue or a process issue is largely a matter of scale. But regardless of the scope, system and process problems can usually be solved by applying logic, statistical analysis, and/or process improvement techniques.

There's one additional thing worth noting here. In larger, distributed organizations there's a tendency to apply systems and processes too broadly in the name of standardization. What works well in one area or location might not work as well in others. If a large organization has grown by acquisition or merger (or if it's a multinational corporation), upper management may forget that the remote sites have different cultures, processes, and work forces. If communication from headquarters to remote locations is vague or ambiguous, the way a decision, system, or policy is interpreted can vary a lot.

> Today, if you're not confused, you are not thinking clearly.
>
> *Irene Peter*

People Problems

While you may have examples of system and process problems in your own organization, most of the issues you'll face as a supervisor or manager are likely to involve people. Solving people problems requires a different set of skills and attitudes than process improvement or statistical analysis techniques. People don't necessarily respond logically. Each person's hardwiring (e.g., personality preferences, information processing preferences, talents) helps to make them an individual. And those different individuals may have wildly different ideas about what's happening as part of your team. Factor in their emotions, your own emotions, and the emotions of others, and you have a lot of potential reactions and misunderstandings to deal with.

In the New York City 9/11 example, the incompatibility of the various communications systems had been known for some time prior to the WTC attack. The fact that this particular issue had not been resolved prior to 9/11 was also – and perhaps primarily – a *people* problem.

When it comes to people problems, you'll want to think it through carefully before you do anything. Try to clarify the nature of the problem, perhaps by asking yourself the following questions:

- Is this a "fit" issue? Is the employee simply not well suited for what their job requires?

- Is this an attitude issue? Does the employee seem to be a glass-half-empty or highly negative type of person?

- Is this a training/retraining issue? Could the employee benefit from a different approach to learning the task? Do you need to have a conversation about expectations and outcomes?

- Is this a human resources issue? Do you need to discuss this issue with someone in your HR unit? (Their advice and perspective will not only be valuable right now, but it may help you avoid spending time in court later.)

- Is this a personality conflict between the employee and you or someone else in the unit? Does it make sense to use a conflict-resolution process to address and possibly resolve the issue?

Good management is the art of making problems so interesting and their solutions so constructive that everyone wants to get to work and deal with them.

Paul Hawken

- Is this a personal issue for the employee? Is there something going on in their personal life (e.g., illness, divorce, legal problems) that's affecting their work?

- Are there other issues that need to be addressed as part of the process? If so, what might they be?

System or People?

As you compare the following list of problems to your own situation, think about whether they are *primarily* system/process or people problems:

- Workflow and project coordination have suddenly been disrupted.

- Equipment or machinery is breaking down.

- A new product or service has been launched and customers are complaining.

- An excellent performer is turning into a problem employee.

- Problems in the supply chain are causing production delays.

> No one can defeat us unless we first defeat ourselves.
>
> *Dwight Eisenhower*

While each of these examples is primarily one type of problem or the other, they *all* contain substantial *people* issues and *system* or *process* issues.

What's *Your* Attitude?

Many of us operate as if the existence of problems to solve is a burden or we think, "This would be a great place to work if it weren't for all these problems." But problems to be solved are a part of life. They give you a chance to stretch your brain, try out new ideas, analyze, debate, and then solve them so you can go on and solve more tomorrow.

Since most days are likely to present you with problems to solve and decisions to make, it may improve your results if you take a look at your own attitude. Making decisions that successfully solve problems requires a certain mind set. Here are three helpful attitudes to consider.

View Problems as Opportunities

Your problem solving and decision making will be more effective if you believe that problems are an *opportunity* to make a difference and help your team, your customers, and your organization become more successful. Of course, when an employee brings you a problem that needs to be solved or a decision that needs to be made, this may not be your initial reaction. You might feel your jaw tighten, feel a bit frustrated, and/or view the decision or problem (as well as the problem-bringer) as an unwanted interruption in your otherwise carefully planned day.

> Success is simply a matter of luck. Ask any failure.
>
> *Earl Wilson*

Instead, practice viewing the problem you're facing as another great opportunity to satisfy a customer. Whether that customer is someone who's buying your product or service, an employee, or a co-worker, this is a chance for you to create a "win" for your customer and for your team. This isn't blue-sky, Pollyanna-ish thinking. As we've discussed already, your attitude and beliefs directly affect how you approach a problem, how creative you'll be, and the decisions you'll ultimately make.

Be Willing to Change What You Do

> Never doubt that a small group of thoughtful, dedicated people can change the world. Indeed, it is the only thing that ever has.
>
> *Margaret Mead*

You need to be willing to continually change what you do as specific problems occur. If you're going to be successful at solving the wide variety of problems you'll face, you need to be flexible and do things differently than "the way we've always done it around here." Humans tend to try to fit new problems into standardized or familiar solutions: "This problem is a lot like the XYZ situation; just do what we did to solve that one." But that won't always work, so being willing to adjust your approach and look for new ideas or methods is important to your success.

Be Willing to Learn

The attitude that might bring you the greatest return is a willingness to learn what is necessary to successfully implement change. Changing things often involves learning new behaviors, perhaps even a new way of thinking. And as you know from *Chapter 26*, the process of change can be somewhat messy, complete with false starts and backsliding. As you dig into a problem you may discover that what appears at first to be a straightforward problem is actually far from simple. You may even end up feeling that you've bitten off more than you can chew. To be an effective and successful problem-solver and decision-maker, you'll be learning all the time. The mindset that seems to work best is to simply view this learning as a lifelong process. Enjoy it!

> How you win is as important as whether you win.
>
> *Kay Yow*

It's All About Context

Problems don't happen in isolation. Solving problems and making decisions always occurs in a *context* – the systems, processes, and relationships that make up the organizational culture. The higher you go in an organization, the more complex and inter-related the issues you deal with are likely to be. Often the relationships between individuals and functional units will push your decisions in one direction or another, depending on organizational politics, previous decisions, and your previous dealings with others.

> Failure is only the opportunity to begin again more intelligently.
>
> *Henry Ford*

Some of the contextual issues that will influence your decisions include:

- Decisions made by the person who previously held your position

- The level of risk tolerance – yours, your boss's, and the organization's

- Formal or informal constraints or requirements for approvals

- Previous experience (especially negative outcomes) with the results of similar problems or issues

- Your own demonstrated previous success in handling similar issues

- The degree of freedom you have to make and implement decisions on your own – the width of your span of control and sphere of influence

There are, of course, all kinds of other factors that influence the context within which you make decisions. Keep in mind Nordstrom's caveat, "Use your own best judgment at all times." In many ways, good decision making, regardless of the context, will reflect your own personal values and the organizational culture you operate in. You are part of the context.

Chapter 30
Solving Real Problems, Every Day

What kinds of problems do *you* have as a supervisor or manager? Are there certain kinds of issues that seem to keep showing up regularly? This chapter explores some of the types of problems you might face and provides some suggestions for how to go about solving them.

So What's the Problem?

Think about a typical day on the job in terms of problems you face that need to be solved. As you read the following list, see if any of these situations sound similar to anything you've faced in the past year:

- Workflow and project coordination difficulties with another unit have been uncovered.

- Old equipment or machinery is starting to fail.

- Team or workload scheduling is scrambled due to a key employee's sudden illness.

- Individual or team results are failing to meet expectations.

- Promised information, supplies, or materials are not being delivered on time, causing unanticipated delays.

- Breakdowns or under-performance in a process or system are causing bottlenecks, missed deadlines, and other operational problems.

- Equipment is missing; nobody seems to know where it went.

- A new product/service with a number of "bugs" has been launched; customers are upset.

- Two employees do not get along and are constantly bickering.

> Everything you need to know about handling mistakes you learned in nursery school: acknowledge your error, fix it immediately, and say you're sorry. Odds are your customers, like your mom and dad, will forgive you.
>
> *Carl Sewell*

- Some employees have a lot of family problems and are having difficulty focusing on work.

- An employee has lodged a sexual harassment complaint against a manager, causing major uproar in the organization.

- An employee who lost his temper has punched a hole in the wall.

- A recent promotion decision is being questioned by another employee who applied for the job.

Probably more than one of these sounds familiar to you. These are typical examples of the kinds of problems you'll deal with in your career as a supervisor or manager. In these situations, making an off-the-cuff, seat-of-the-pants decision isn't appropriate. You might get lucky once in awhile, but neglecting to use a proven problem-solving process will almost certainly come back to bite you later.

> When you come to the end of your rope, tie a knot and hang on.
>
> *Franklin D. Roosevelt*

Becoming successful at solving these kinds of problems is a learning process, but it *can be* learned. When you get good at solving complex problems or making good decisions about complex issues, you usually get promoted to take on bigger issues at a higher level in your organization. Or you become a good candidate to be recruited by another organization. Either way, you win.

So There *IS* a Problem

> The best way out of a difficulty is through it.
>
> *Will Rogers*

When you begin to think about how to solve a problem, what you'll want to look at first is the gap. Something is causing a gap between what you wanted to see – your expectations – and what's actually happening – the results. It sounds simple, but most problems really are about expectations and results. When they don't match there are problems to solve and decisions to make.

The majority of managers are Extraverts and Judgers. They have a strong preference for action: see a problem, fix it fast, and move on to the next. But complex problems don't necessarily lend themselves to that approach, no matter how much a manager may enjoy the adrenalin rush that comes with it. And since many managers are also Sensors and Thinkers, they tend to focus on the details and use the resulting concrete information to make logic-driven decisions.

Unfortunately, this style of decision making often deals with the *effects* of a problem rather than its actual *causes*. You may end up treating the symptoms instead of the disease, and that means you'll deal with the same issues again and again. You might feel driven to develop and implement a standard way of doing certain things – to create a procedure for handling similar issues. Sometimes this works, but usually you need to step back, look for the root cause of the problem, and find a way to eliminate that cause. As you become more successful at using your long-term, big-picture focus, many of the larger systemic issues you face will get dealt with more effectively.

> In the middle of difficulty lies opportunity.
>
> *Albert Einstein*

A Basic Model for Solving Problems

Even though many problems can be solved and decisions made without much conscious thought or structure, there will always be a number of issues that come up that need more than a quick, off-the-cuff answer.

For example, you might need to rearrange one or more shift assignments due to a problem between two employees. Your boss may toss a new, unfamiliar project in your lap. An important piece of equipment might fail, requiring an unbudgeted replacement. Or the organization may be faced with a mandated layoff of 10 percent of the work force, and you have to come up with recommendations from your group. These are all routine tasks for supervisors and managers.

There's no one best approach to making important decisions. There are lots of models, theories, and even software that claim to show you how to consistently make great decisions. Over the years I've tried a number of them, mostly with mixed results. Perhaps this comes from a lifetime of solving problems and making decisions, but the problem-solving process seems to come down to these five steps:

1. Describe the situation.

2. Generate alternatives.

3. Decide what to do.

4. Implement the decision.

5. Evaluate the results.

Step #1: Describe the Situation

What's going on that needs to be different? Is this a decision that needs to be made or a problem that needs to be solved? What would a successful resolution look like?

> We are all entitled to our own opinions but not our own facts.
>
> *Daniel Patrick Moynihan*

With fairly straightforward issues or decisions a brief statement may be enough. "One of our team members will be off for six weeks on medical leave, and we need to make sure the team can still get the work done while they're gone." For more complex situations the description will be more involved, possibly calling for discussion of the issue within your team to gather input and promote buy-in. The key is to describe the present situation completely enough so that you have a clear understanding of what's going on.

Once you understand the nature of the situation and can clearly describe it to those who'll be involved in solving the problem or issue, you're ready to move to the next phase of the process.

Step #2: Generate Alternatives

Now is the time to develop a variety of potential approaches to solving the problem or making the decision. At this stage in the process the key is to come up with ideas and alternative approaches. It's important that your focus is on *generating* ideas, not *evaluating* them. This isn't the place for any type of decision making. You're simply in the creative development, imagining, blue-sky, right-brain mode. The goal is to come up with as many alternatives as possible, even if some of them seem a little wild, silly, off-beat, or unworkable at first.

Some issues are clearly solo decisions where you don't need or want the team involved. Others call for the involvement and input of a group. For issues that could benefit from group input, you may want to generate some alternatives on your own *before* involving your team in a brainstorming session. For instance, in the case of the team member about to go on medical leave, you might think about the people who work closely with that person. Who can do that individual's work? What career opportunities does this offer others on the team? What basic tasks can be pooled and assigned to a temporary, entry-level person, freeing the team members to take on other responsibilities? Are there any cross-training opportunities?

> If everyone is thinking alike then somebody isn't thinking.
>
> *George S. Patton*

Handling this part of the process well pays significant dividends in improved morale; greater buy-in for finding new ways to work; fewer brushfires to put out; and a more focused, engaged, and motivated work force. Your people have good ideas and are closest to the front line. Your job as their manager is to liberate those good ideas and give your staff a chance to show what they can do. That's how everybody wins.

Step #3: Decide What to Do

After you've generated several alternatives, you need to decide which one seems to be the best solution. Questions you might ask yourself or the team at this point include:

- Does one alternative clearly get us closest to the results we're seeking?

- Would a combination of features from several alternatives give us better results?

- What kinds of issues might emerge from each alternative?

- Are there any possible unintended consequences that might be generated by the preferred solution? (Admittedly, a difficult question to answer!)

- What will each alternative cost, and what resources will each use?

This is the time to weigh the various alternatives, discuss the potential down sides of each, and otherwise refine your alternatives. One solution *might* stand out above the rest, or you might decide to go with another choice because of potential implementation issues with your first choice. For instance, your preferred solution might involve significant resistance from another unit in the organization. This might be enough to make another approach more successful in the long run.

> I used to be indecisive . . . but now I'm not so sure.
> *Unknown*

Step #4: Implement the Decision

Now that you've determined which alternative or combination of ideas seems to be the best solution, what's the process for implementing the decision? Keeping in mind the various stakeholders involved, how will you communicate the decision to them? If you anticipate resistance from outside the team, what's the best way to handle that? (See more about implementing decisions in *Chapter 31*.)

Step #5: Evaluate the Results

After you've implemented the decision, you'll want to evaluate the results. After all, you can almost always learn something from examining the outcome of your decisions. Ask a few basic questions, such as:

- How well did the decision meet the need?

- Did we get the result we were looking for?

- Is there anything we would do differently now?

- Is there anything we've learned from this situation that would be useful the next time we face a similar problem/situation?

You may want to involve the team in this post-implementation review process or simply do it on your own. The important thing is to include this evaluation process as part of the normal course of events. If the issue or problem is important enough for you to devote your time and energy to finding a solution, conducting even a brief post-mortem can have great benefits. And if the issue is important enough to involve other team members, closing this loop yields even greater benefit. If nothing else, it lets the team know that you place a high value on continually trying to improve how you get the work done. It also helps motivate team members to perform well because they know there will be a post-event discussion of results. (See the *Post-Decision Checklist* in the *Appendix* for an example).

> Life isn't fair. The reality is that people everywhere have hard choices to make.
>
> *Joyce Podziba*

Issues & Considerations

Making decisions and solving problems is not a completely objective process; there are other issues and considerations to take into account. For example:

- Your intuition

- Your mental model

- Your ability to prioritize
- Your ability to gather "just enough" information

Your Intuition

You probably noticed that the simple problem-solving model discussed above is a fairly logical process. While many problems can be solved using rational, logical, measurable means, that doesn't mean that *all* problems can be solved through logic. There are plenty of issues that involve listening to your gut – your intuitive take on a situation based on your experience. Sometimes your intuition will say one thing even though the numbers and logic say something very different. It's important to learn to trust your instincts and your experience. That "still, small voice" that nags at you as you make your decision is an inner voice that needs to be involved in the decision. Often that nagging feeling is an internal red flag that involves some type of ethical, moral, or values concern. If your logical thinking results in a choice that just doesn't seem quite right, for goodness sake pay attention!

Your Mental Model

Just as your *mental model* affects how you deal with change (see *Chapter 26*), the way you view yourself, your work, and your organization influences how you solve problems and make decisions. At the most basic level, your beliefs about what *is* a problem will influence your perceptions about whether a given situation is a problem to be solved or simply "the way things are." At a deeper level, when you see something as a problem to solve or a decision to be made, you may limit the kinds of alternatives you're willing to consider. Some potential solutions may be too strange, different, unworkable, or downright weird to warrant serious consideration.

Consider, for instance, how we view the world. Most of us over the age of 35 probably have the Mercator Projection map of the world

> Creativity is not a solitary occurrence. It's very much a collaborative effort.
>
> *Andy Stefanovich*

> It is no sin to attempt and fail. The only sin is not to make the attempt.
>
> *SuEllen Fried*

as our mental model of the size and position of the continents. Since that's the way we've been taught to picture the world, that's how we look at most global issues. However, the Mercator Projection map was developed in the mid-1500s. It does show the continents' *shapes* quite accurately, and it works pretty well if your objective is to show the round earth on a flat surface. But if your objective is to accurately depict the *size* of the continents in relation to one another, the Mercator Projection map is wildly inaccurate. In fact, the farther away from the equator you move, the more "off" or distorted the relative sizes of the continents become.

Map of the World - Mercator Projection

Notice that Greenland and Africa are shaded. They appear to be quite similar in shape and size. Remember that image.

The Peters Projection (developed in the mid-1970s) and other similar maps are *equal area* depictions of the globe. As such, they show the various land masses as they truly are relative to size. The shapes of the continents may be somewhat different than what we expect, but the relative size of the continents is *really* different. Now

If a man does not know to what port he is steering, no wind is favorable to him.

Seneca

let's take a look at Greenland and Africa again, this time based on their actual *size*.

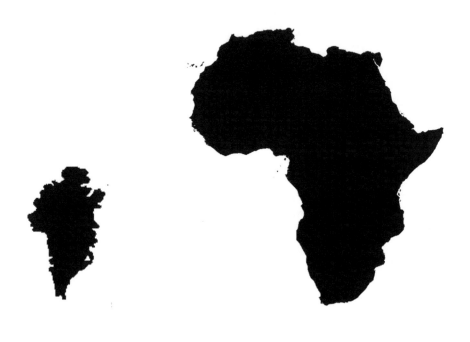

| **Greenland** | **Africa** |
| 2,175,600 sq. mi. | 11,608,161 sq. mi. |

Quite different, aren't they? Greenland is actually less than 20 percent the size of Africa. Stated another way, Africa is more than five times the size of Greenland.

The lesson is simple: the images we see help to shape our perceptions of the world around us. And it is useful to realize that there are many different ways of looking at issues, situations, problems, and potential solutions. Don't let your preconceived ideas (your mental models) about what is real be controlled by the limitations of your own point of view. That way you'll be able to give ideas and suggestions that seem odd and unworkable a bit more consideration when solving problems and making decisions.

Your Ability to Prioritize

You may report to one of those managers whose basic approach is "Everything is a #1 priority." Or your boss may constantly change priorities on you, with the latest issue or idea becoming the new first priority.

As a supervisor or manager, you should be able to determine the half-dozen or so significant projects, problems, or issues you're working on that contribute most to the organization's mission. In the majority of cases, an avalanche of *"This* is top priority" assignments is caused by having a boss who is:

- Unfocused or oblivious to what is really, truly important

- Unorganized, scattered, and feeling out of control in their own job

- Getting a lot of pressure from their own manager to produce

- Unaware of the scope and magnitude of the issues and projects on your plate

When this occurs, it's time for *you* to step back and take a look at everything you're trying to deal with. Decide what you think the most important issues and projects are. Then have a discussion with your boss to clarify the relative importance of everything on your plate. You need to reach agreement about those items that *really* are the most important few.

In most cases, your boss will understand that making everything a top priority is not realistic. You should be able to negotiate an agreement about where you and your team need to concentrate your efforts. Frankly, bosses who are unfocused and out of control are likely to appreciate efforts to keep things on track and focused on results. And if you go to them with a well-thought-out set of priorities, their reaction is likely to be, "Great! I'm glad someone around here knows what they need to do!"

> Life's hard. But it's harder if you're stupid.
>
> *John Wayne*
> *"The Sands of Iwo Jima"*

> Keep focused on the substantive issues. To make a decision means having to go through one door and closing all others.
>
> *Abraham Zaleznik*

Your Ability to Gather "Just Enough" Information

How long do you go on gathering information before making a decision? How much data do you *really* need in order to decide what to do?

While many decisions can be delayed until more information is available, most of the time we have to make decisions with less information than we'd like to have. (By some estimates, most decisions are made with no more than about 25-40 percent of the information desired.) Making decisions without having crucial data is risky because we may fail to take into account an essential piece of information. At the same time, delaying a decision until we have *all* the data frequently means an opportunity passes us by.

> Mistakes are part of the dues one pays for a full life.
>
> *Sophia Loren*

This is where your experience and intuition will help you know when it's time to decide and move on. If you're new to the organization, new to your position, or new to the team, you may need to gather more information and input because your instincts and experience aren't finely honed enough to make a good decision. But after you have a bit more experience under your belt, you should be able to sense what you need to do and you can make a firm decision earlier in the process. Clearly, this is a place where you have to know yourself, know your capabilities, and trust your instincts. Learn to listen to that still, small voice inside you that tells you when it's time to make a decision and move on.

Pareto's Principle: The 80/20 Rule

The Pareto Principle was developed in 1906 by Vilfredo Pareto, an Italian economist, who made this observation: 20 percent of the people owned 80 percent of the land in Italy. Little did he know that this statement was nearly always true in relation to most statistical processes. Studies have shown that this principle even is true when a problem occurs; 20 percent of something is almost always responsible for 80 percent of the results. Here are some other observations:

- About 80 percent of sales come from 20 percent of the customers (and usually from 20 percent of the total products or services offered).

- Approximately 80 percent of health care costs are incurred by 20 percent of the population.

- About 20 percent of your employees will cause 80 percent of the performance problems.

- Truly great performance will be achieved by a few easily identifiable individuals (about 20 percent); the rest of your employees are likely to be good, solid, average performers.

Unconsciously perhaps, organizations often give their most highly skilled workers the toughest work, even though concentrating their skills on problem-free jobs could allow them to produce significantly more than their less-skilled colleagues. The most talented people are often assigned to the most challenging problems which, even when resolved, may contribute little additional revenue.

Pareto's Principle is a daily reminder to focus most of your time and energy on the things that really matter. This means paying attention to really important, mission-critical issues instead of trivial problems that contribute little to overall success but are easy to deal with. Identify which problems are the most important and focus on them. This is what is really meant by the admonition to "work smarter." Working smarter is concentrating the bulk of your effort on the right things – those issues, projects, and tasks that will produce the greatest results for you and the organization.

> Opportunity rarely knocks on your door. Knock rather on opportunity's door if you ardently wish to enter.
>
> *B. C. Forbes*

Decision Making in Crisis

Every job includes problems to solve and decisions to make that you cannot plan for. Emergencies, crises, fires to put out (sometimes literally), fast-breaking opportunities – all of these are in the realm of the unexpected.

You can, however, anticipate some situations that *might* occur. You can even plan for and practice how you and your team will handle things if those situations come up. For instance, have you thought about how you'd handle any of the following events?

- An employee has a heart attack at work.

- An accident involving a piece of machinery leads to an injury, requiring a call to 911.

- An employee has just been notified that a family member has been in an auto accident.

- A serious fire breaks out in a manufacturing plant, leading to an evacuation and heavy damage to a major facility.

- A food product your company processes is linked to the poisoning of people in several states.

- A major competitor has just gone out of business, leaving their customers unsupported.

Some of these examples are life threatening or involve serious injury and need to be dealt with immediately and competently. In these situations people will usually respond to whoever steps up and takes command. Emergencies, particularly those where the risk is visible and significant, tend to produce more followers than leaders. In many situations our natural instinct is to freeze; we're physiologically wired for a deer-in-the-headlights approach to danger. But this instinct must be overcome. Someone has to step up, make decisions, and solve the problems.

Energy and persistence conquer all things.

Benjamin Franklin

From a personality preference standpoint, people who are Sensors and Perceivers are more likely to respond immediately and well in emergencies. They value the immediacy of the situation and the need for a response. In fact, Sensing Perceivers seem to gravitate toward occupations or fields that offer the opportunity to respond to rapidly changing situations. They're over-represented in occupations such as emergency medicine, firefighting, law enforcement, and the front-line military. All of these fields offer a lot of variety and a chance to respond to high-adrenalin situations. Because they involve rapid response to a constantly changing environment, these occupations tend to create, practice, and perfect individual and team procedures for effectively coping with emergencies. This sort of training and practice was the primary reason for the January 15, 2009, successful landing of US Airways Flight 1549 on New York City's Hudson River.

High Achievers
- make no small plans.
- are willing to do what they fear.
- are willing to prepare.
- are willing to risk failure.
- are teachable.
- have heart.

John Noe

Other situations may not be immediately life threatening but may have far-reaching implications. Over the years there have been a number of examples. The classic case of how Johnson & Johnson handled a Tylenol poisoning scare in 1982 demonstrated the wisdom of basic planning for the unknown. While there's no way to anticipate every possible future event, it certainly is possible to develop and practice a process for dealing with emergencies per se. The ineffective handling of various food poisoning outbreaks by both government agencies and the private sector has demonstrated what happens when you *don't* have a well-practiced process in place for handling crisis.

Concentration is the secret of strengths in politics, in war, in trade, in short in all management of human affairs.

Ralph Waldo Emerson

For a new supervisor or manager, an early to-do might be to meet with your team for some crisis planning. It would be especially helpful to know if you have any Sensing Perceivers among your employees and have them in this meeting. Ask questions like:

- What kinds of emergencies have occurred in the past couple of years?

- How did we respond?

- What were the results?

- What is our current process for handling crises or emergencies when they occur?

- What do we need to do differently?

- What best practices are being used in other fields or organizations that we could learn from?

Whatever happens, you need to be able to immediately identify the scope and scale of the situation and use all of your skills to respond appropriately. Practicing a bit and thinking through how you might respond in unusual, fast-developing, and challenging situations just makes good sense.

Useful Problem-Solving Tools

Complex problems or thorny decisions respond better when you use the right tools. While there are all kinds of tools available (some of them quite sophisticated and technical), some fairly simple techniques deserve a place in your toolkit. The following brief list of some of these tools is supplemented by additional information and examples in the *Appendix*. Frequently used tools include:

- *Flow Chart* – a method to graphically depict a process or system

- *Fishbone Diagram* – a method to organize a problem

- *The 5 "Whys" Method* – a simple approach to finding the root cause of an issue

- *The Phoenix Checklist* – a series of questions to look at an issue from all angles

You've got to go out on a limb sometimes because that's where the fruit is.

Will Rogers

Implementation Chart

The Implementation Chart is a way to give objective ratings to various components of one or more alternative decisions. It can be a good way to look at one or several alternatives as you approach your final decision.

Score each possible solution on a scale of 1 (least desirable) to 5 (most desirable) in each of the five categories.

Possible Solution	Ease of Implementation	Cost	Receptivity	Longevity

Chapter 31
Creativity: From Decision to Implementation

> The significant problems we face cannot be solved at the same level of thinking we were at when we created them.
>
> *Albert Einstein*

Einstein knew what he was talking about. Difficult decisions and complex problems are part of the job and part of life. Tough issues cannot be solved with "business as usual" thinking. So you have to get creative and look for new answers and new ways of thinking. If you don't try new approaches to difficult problems, they won't get solved. And if they were easy, they would have been solved before now.

Although some people seem to be born with exceptional creativity, creative problem solving and decision making can be learned and practiced. It involves a few basic steps or behaviors – things we all did well as children but probably have stopped doing.

Good leaders are very curious, and they spend a lot of time trying to learn things.

Jeffrey Immelt

Brainstorming

A favorite technique to jump-start creativity in many organizations is group brainstorming. This is the process of taking an issue, problem, challenge, or opportunity and asking a group or team to generate ideas and suggestions together.

While it may work in some situations, the fact is that group brainstorming really doesn't work all that well. A group of people will almost always generate *fewer* ideas than the same number of people doing so *alone*. In a group setting individuals feel subtle (and often not so subtle) pressure to conform and please the boss. At best, underlying powerful messages are in the room: fit in, be cautious, don't appear foolish, be serious, don't make a mistake.

This all combines to chill the creative juices that are inside each of us. At worst, people are allowed to evaluate ideas as they come up, disrupting the entire process.

The Idea Killer

One former CEO (we'll call him Henry) used to toss a major issue or problem to his senior staff and ask for "great ideas." When a team member would say, "Well, we could do A," Henry often responded with, "That's one of the dumbest ideas I've ever heard! Now, who has a good idea?" Of course, the room would immediately go quiet. Everyone was thinking, "Man, I saw what happened to her. I'm not saying anything." Henry constantly complained that his VPs weren't very creative and depended on him to come up with most of upper management's ideas.

What would you attempt to do if you knew you could not fail?

Robert Schuller

If you're looking for fresh ideas, out-of-the-box thinking, and those "Eureka!" moments, you're better off asking people to do some thinking on their own *before* bringing them together in a group. Make sure they know that what you'd like is *lots* of ideas, no matter how off-the-wall some of them may seem. Then you can pull the individuals into a group session to look at all the ideas. When the ideas surface, it's important to capture them in writing *without* evaluating them in any way.

This is definitely a case where quantity matters. If you want to have a great idea, the best place to start is with lots of ideas. At some point in the group process it will appear that everyone is tapped out; ideas will stop coming. Rather than wrapping up the session at that point and working with what has been generated, take a short break and then come at it from a different angle. You'll be amazed! In one study a group brainstormed for 36 minutes straight while another group brainstormed for the same length of time but took a six-minute break halfway through the session. The group that took a break came up with *two-thirds more* ideas than the group that didn't take a break. And many of their best ideas came *after* the break.

Practical Creativity

If you're like most people you'll have to practice being creative before you can successfully tackle the tough issues. Learning how to use the various problem-solving tools mentioned in *Chapter 30* with more routine issues will help prepare you to take on more difficult situations. As you get adept at problem solving, you can focus more attention on the bigger challenges. And by involving your team in problem-solving discussions, you can delegate some tasks so you can take on bigger projects.

Even if you currently don't see yourself as a creative person, there's no reason for your mindset to stay that way. You *can* change your mind and increase your creativity! Here are some other tips:

- Set an idea quota for yourself.

- Write down your ideas as they occur to you.

- Immerse yourself in the problem you want to solve.

- Look for connections to other issues and ideas on a broad front.

- Let ideas incubate, simmer, grow, and mutate over time.

- Be willing to wait for "it."

Set an Idea Quota

Decide that you will come up with, say, four ideas every day. The first day or two may be challenging, but your first few ideas are likely to generate other related ideas. Keep at it, no matter how far-fetched or goofy your ideas seem.

> When people feel phenomenally valued and respected, their creative passion and energy can erupt all over. That energy is infectious.
>
> *Charlie Kouns*

The key to creativity is to have lots of ideas, not evaluate their utility. Thomas Edison held nearly 1,100 patents. His personal quota was a minor invention every 10 days and a major invention every six months. He just kept generating ideas, week after week, month after month, year after year.

Write Down Your Ideas

Regardless of whether you have a "good" idea or simply an interesting notion, grab it and get it down on paper immediately. Brain researchers have found that we're only able to retain six to 10 pieces of information in our mind at a time. New information tends to push older information out of our conscious mind before our brain can prepare the older information for long-term memory. Writing down the idea, even if you have no intention of doing anything specific with it later, helps to send the idea into your long-term memory.

Immerse Yourself in the Problem

Look at the problem from as many angles and perspectives as possible. What does this situation look like? How would you describe it to someone who is unfamiliar with the issue? What do you think the root cause is? What immediate and downstream effects is it creating?

Look For Connections

Also look at the problem in relation to things you've experienced before or have been taught. Ask yourself lots of questions:

- Does this issue sound, look, or feel like something else you've dealt with before? If so, how is it the same? How is it different? What did you do before? How would you need to change what you did before to solve this problem?

Adventure is worthwhile in itself.

Amelia Earhart

When in doubt, make a fool of yourself. There is a microscopically thin line between being brilliantly creative and acting like the most gigantic idiot on earth. So what the hell, leap.

Cynthia Heimel

- What do other organizations do? What do other units in your organization do? If you were a manager or leader you really admire (a mentor perhaps), what would you do?

- Are there people inside your unit you should brainstorm with? People outside your unit? Whose perspectives would be useful? Are there really sharp people whose opinion and/or advice you value that you could ask to join in?

Let Ideas Incubate

Keeping a log or journal of your ideas and then reviewing, revising, and adding to those ideas can turn what seems at first like an unworkable idea into a major project that benefits you, your unit, and your organization. Set up a simple set of categories and evaluate your ideas as they percolate:

- Excellent – has strong potential for success

- Good – needs some refinement

- Possible – needs improvement

- Unlikely – hold for future review

Be Willing To Wait For "It"

Breakthroughs often occur when you're relaxed or focused on something else. This is why you're able to solve a problem while you're in the shower. Your focus is elsewhere, you're relaxed, and ideas can more readily surface out of your subconscious into your conscious mind.

Whether you perceive yourself as a creative person or not, the process of thinking in new and creative ways is a learned skill. Practice, practice, and more practice may be required, but your reward will be the ability to be practically creative when faced with problems to solve and decisions to make.

> Imagination will often carry us to worlds that never were. But without it we go nowhere.
>
> *Carl Sagan*

Case: You're as Creative as You Think You Are

Several years ago, the CEO of a large publishing company (we'll call her Vicky), was concerned about the lack of creativity in some of her editorial and marketing staff employees. She retained a group of psychologists to find out the difference between the creative employees and those who weren't particularly creative.

After studying the staff for a year, the psychologists discovered there was only one difference between the two groups: the creative people believed that they were creative; the less creative people believed that they weren't. The individuals' perception of reality was different between the two groups. So the psychologists recommended that the company install a fairly simple process to help people change their beliefs about their own creativity. It had two components:

1. Training in how affirmations affected their perceptions of what is true and real. (See the section in *Chapter 11* about "Talking to Ourselves.") This included each person creating an inventory of all their positive qualities, attributes, successes, and strengths, and then adding to and reviewing the list regularly.
2. Having each person develop and use affirmative statements to reinforce the belief that they were creative. For instance, "I have a real gift for coming up with creative ideas." "I have new ideas every single day."

After implementing the process and having the staff work on their "self-talk" every day for several months, the publishing company experienced significant increases in the creativity exhibited by the editorial and marketing staff members. During the following year Vicky saw a major jump in the number of blockbuster books developed and marketed by the group.

Implementing Your Decisions

Creativity won't get you much of anywhere unless you're also good at implementation – i.e., figuring out what needs to be done and actually getting it done. This is where the rubber really hits the road in problem solving and decision making.

Creating some kind of written implementation plan will help you develop a specific strategy to implement a decision. Here are some of the steps you might use.

Step #1

Determine what the major steps (or bullet points) need to be to get the problem solved or the decision implemented. There will usually be several, perhaps a half-dozen or so. Watch for the tendency to put in too much detail at this point; individual action steps will come later.

For example, you have a problem with several pieces of equipment breaking down too often. Looking things over, you've discovered a pair of root causes:

- One of the machines is well beyond the end of its useful life, is fully depreciated, and has been superseded several times over by newer technology.

- The other machines have lots of expected life left, but they're breaking down because the preventive maintenance schedule hasn't been followed regularly.

The first cause is a system or process problem. Either there was no process in place to examine downtime data against expected equipment lifespan, or the process in place wasn't followed properly. The second cause could well be a training issue; we hope it isn't an employee engagement issue.

I find that the harder I work, the more luck I seem to have.

Thomas Jefferson

CREATIVITY: FROM DECISION TO IMPLEMENTATION

As a result, your implementation path becomes clear:

- Run a cost/benefit analysis comparing the benefit of replacing the outdated machine. If that shows the benefits outweigh the cost, the equipment needs to be replaced. Then, of course, you'll have to ask yourself if *that* decision is within your span of control or more within your sphere of influence. If it's within your sphere, you'll need to devise a plan for gaining the approval of the appropriate person.

- Review the preventive maintenance schedule with the maintenance staff to figure out how to make sure the schedule gets followed in the future.

Step #2

Determine the accountabilities involved:

- *Who.* Who is going to be responsible for which phases of the implementation process? In the above example, one of your team might volunteer to get competitive test data comparing your current machine with a new unit. Meanwhile, you can contact your purchasing unit to request a price quote on a replacement machine. Then you discuss it with your boss before proceeding.

- *When.* What are the deadlines/completion date targets? Continuing our example, it would be reasonable to ask that the various parties get back to you within two weeks. You should track the requested price quote on your calendar so you can follow up if the quote doesn't show up on time. And you should track your teammates' commitment to gather the test data.

- *How.* How will the responsible (and accountable) party do their work? This should be stated in broad terms, providing overall direction and guidance, not step-by-step instructions. So you might suggest certain specified sources to your staff researcher. Or you could specify that the new machine needs to be installed and operational within a certain timeframe after placing the order.

Step #3

Develop the communication, feedback, and progress processes needed to keep everyone in the loop; gather information about progress; and determine how well the solution, decision, or project is being implemented. In this case, you might establish some guidelines about how you want your team member to update you regarding progress or hurdles they run into. If you're leaning toward purchasing the new machine you'll need to bring the physical plant personnel into the loop, just in case the new unit requires a change in infrastructure such as wiring, hydraulics, air-handling, or site preparation.

As you go about your daily work as a supervisor or manager, your ability to identify issues, solve problems, and make decisions has everything to do with your success. Practice is more than important; it's mandatory. Learning to use a variety of creative problem-solving methods puts more tools in your toolbox, and you'll find opportunities to use them all at one time or another.

Problems come in all shapes, sizes, and complexities. They're simply part of life. Being adept at handling and solving them, then moving ahead to implement changes, helps provide the juice that makes our professional lives rewarding and our personal lives interesting.

Outstanding people have one thing in common: an absolute sense of mission.

Zig Ziglar

Skill 7

LEADING AND EMPOWERING

"The best form of leadership is to be conscious of the leadership potential with the followers and to let them unleash this potential in a spontaneous way. When a great leader accomplishes this task with effortless ease, the followers say, 'We did it ourselves.'"

Lao Tzu

Skill 7 – Leading and Empowering

No matter where you work or what you do, to effectively manage your team and get the job done, you'll need to be a *leader*. If managing yourself (*Skill 1*) is the foundational skill that begins your path to success, then *leadership* helps you continue the journey throughout your career. Becoming a leader gives you the chance to dramatically widen your sphere of influence. (See *Chapter 10*.)

Leadership is a complex, much-discussed topic. It's all over the Web, and blogs abound. A Google search for the term "leadership" recently produced 153 million hits. A similar search for "leadership books" produced nearly 19,000 hits in Amazon.com's online store. To say the least, leadership is a hot topic!

Our focus is on understanding what leadership means and how you can improve your success as a leader. You may be a front-line supervisor or middle manager in a large organization, or you may be running a business or nonprofit with 10, 25, 100, or even 1,500 employees. Regardless of the size or complexity of your organization, once you start supervising the work of others, *Skill 7* becomes increasingly important.

Fifty years ago, a substantial number of people believed that leaders were born rather than made. And certainly there are numerous examples of people who are viewed as natural leaders who seem to just instinctively know how to lead. People like Steve Jobs; Frances Hesselbein; Colin Powell; Winston Churchill; Martin Luther King, Jr.; Margaret Sanger; Ronald Reagan; Margaret Thatcher; Estee Lauder; Ray Croc . . . the list goes on and on. Their individual hardwiring certainly contributed to the path they followed to leadership. However, it's what they did and how they behaved that earned them recognition as leaders.

> I'm an idealist. I don't know where I'm going, but I'm on my way.
>
> *Carl Sandburg*

> Leadership is not something mystical and ethereal that cannot be understood by ordinary people. It is an observable, learnable set of practices.
>
> *James Kouzes & Barry Posner*

Both leadership and management involve acquiring and developing knowledge, skills, attitudes, and behaviors. Once you're reasonably adept at *Skills 1* through 6, you'll be ready for *Skill 7 – Leadership*.

> Do not wait for leaders; do it alone, person to person.
>
> *Mother Teresa*

But What If . . .

What if you've reached this point in the book and have been thinking to yourself, "If I need to be good at all of this stuff and now you tell me there's more . . . I'm frankly not sure I *want* to be a supervisor or manager." Whatever the reason, if that's what you're thinking, then deciding not to become a manager and/or finding another job may be the best decision you'll ever make in your career. After all, you don't have to actually supervise others in the formal sense to be an effective leader. True leadership is not so much about your position or title as it is about:

Attitude. The way you approach your work and other people

Impact. The way you influence how others do their work and interact with each other

While leadership and position often do go together, the flattening of organizations and the shift to project teams has led to the need for a lot more leaders and a lot fewer managers at all levels. The role of the project team member, individual contributor, or outside contractor has substantially expanded. People often serve on several project teams, taking on different roles on different teams – sometimes as the project leader. In each case, they deliver their value-added service to the team based on the needs of the specific project. Once the project is completed, the team members move on to other project assignments.

The thing to keep in mind is this: leadership is about who you are (your attitudes, beliefs, and character) *and* how you behave (your personal style, the way you interact with other people, and your success at getting others to follow your lead). Leadership is, in the final analysis, a personal choice. You can *choose* to lead or not, regardless of your position or job title. It's up to you.

Chapter 32
Leaders and Leadership

Having studied, taught, and coached leaders for nearly four decades, I can say with confidence that leaders are *made* much more often than they're born. Research about leadership during the past 25 years suggests that you must both manage *and* lead to effectively get things done and to help other people get things done.

Management is about *getting things done right*; *leadership* is about *getting the right things done*. There is a critical difference between the two. *Leadership* is about setting the direction; communicating the mission, vision, values, and strategy; and helping the team move in the right direction. *Management* is about maintaining an established direction, taking care of resources, and keeping an eye on getting things done in the correct way.

Organizations need leaders at all levels – people who (1) understand what needs to be accomplished, (2) are able to help create positive change, and (3) can successfully get the job done by influencing other people. Leadership doesn't come with a position or title; it's granted by those who are being led. It's given *to* you 1because people want to follow you. They want to go where you're going, they buy into your vision of the future, and they want to have that vision become real.

Having great leadership at the top of an organization is certainly helpful, perhaps critical. But a great CEO, or even a handful of outstanding leaders at the top, *will not* ensure success. For an organization to be successful over the long haul, it must have *leaders at all levels* – people who provide solid leadership within their teams, their departments, and their divisions.

> The first responsibility of a leader is to define reality. The last is to say thank you. In between, the leader is a servant.
>
> *Max DePree*

> Leaders are visionaries with a poorly developed sense of fear and no concept of the odds against them.
>
> *Robert Jarvik*

What Leaders Do

There are so many different organizations, different sizes, different missions, and different industries. Yet what leaders actually *do* seems to be remarkably similar regardless of the setting. There are plenty of individual differences in *how* each leader goes about leading, but the set of overall behaviors is quite similar.

Warren Bennis has done considerable research about leaders and leadership. His original and best-known work, "Leaders: The Strategies for Taking Charge," was based on individual discussions with 90 of the most effective, successful leaders in the United States. It defines, better than most, what leadership is.

Bennis said, "For awhile I sensed much more diversity than commonality among them. The group included both left-brain and right-brain thinkers; . . . well-spoken, articulate leaders and laconic, inarticulate ones; . . . ." On the surface at least, he found that leaders come in all shapes, sizes, persuasions, and demeanors.

So if people who are successful leaders have little in common when it comes to background, what is it that they *do* have in common? What do they *do* that creates their success?

> Leaders rock the boat. Leaders are up-front. Leaders change things - the woods are full of good managers who are not good leaders because they are afraid to risk failure.
>
> *Warren Bennis*

- *Leaders Manage Focus.* They have the ability to draw others to them because they have a vision for the future and they consistently demonstrate their commitment to achieving that vision.

- *Leaders Manage Understanding.* They're able to communicate their vision in such a way that others "get it" and want to go to a place they haven't been before.

- *Leaders Live Their Values.* They know what they stand for, and their daily actions match their beliefs and values. (When you know what you stand for and what you don't, life becomes a lot clearer.)

- ***Leaders Manage Themselves.*** They know themselves. They know what they're good at, and they have a realistic perception of themselves. They enhance and nurture their strengths, surround themselves with people who can fill in the gaps in their own skills, and then deploy the team's assets effectively.

At some point you've probably worked in a group that had outstanding leadership. That may be in your current position (lucky you!), working for an effective manager/leader. Or it may have been in your past – in a sports team, a volunteer organization, or a church group perhaps. When you think about good leaders you've worked with, you probably remember feeling the positive energy and "juice" they gave to the team or the group. Organizations with good leadership *at all levels* are vibrant, exciting, engaging, satisfying places to work.

> Leadership: the art of getting someone else to do something you want done because he wants to do it.
>
> *Dwight Eisenhower*

When You Have Good Leadership . . .

Does good leadership really matter? Does it make a difference to the employees on the front line? Yes, absolutely, it does. When you have good leadership:

- ***People are Engaged.*** People feel that what they do is important and meaningful. They believe they can make a difference, deliver a great product or service, and be part of something special. There's a feeling of community – a sense of "We're all in this together."

> The price of greatness is responsibility.
>
> *Winston Churchill*

- ***High Performance is Expected.*** There are high expectations for performance, quality, and customer service throughout the organization. There is a strong commitment to continuous improvement, so learning and professional growth are simply part of "the way we do things here." Mistakes and false starts are viewed as opportunities to learn and improve rather than as failures requiring someone to blame.

- *People are Enthusiastic.* Work is exciting and it pulls people toward a mission, vision, or goal. As a result, employees are happy, more productive, and proud to be part of the team. And good people want to join up and help the organization succeed.

> Nothing great was ever achieved without enthusiasm.
> *Ralph Waldo Emerson*

Things to Remember

Here are some ideas to keep in mind as you read about *Skill 7*:

- *Leadership Can be Learned.* Leadership is simply a word or a label for skills, beliefs, attitudes, and knowledge that can be learned by virtually anyone. By paying attention to the attributes shared by leaders, you *can* teach yourself to be a leader.

- *Use Whatever Makes Sense & Appeals to You.* There are so many different ideas and suggestions to choose from when it comes to leadership. Keep your eyes open for new ideas, and then use the ones that make sense to you. There's no one right way to be a leader.

- *When You Lead, Others Will Follow.* If you consistently apply what you learn about leadership, people will follow you. Most people would rather follow a good leader than try to be a leader themselves.

> It isn't polls or public opinion of the moment that counts. It's right and wrong and leadership.
> *Harry Truman*

- *Your Leadership is in What You Do* As you practice leadership skills, people will follow you because of what you do much more than what you say. What you *do* represents who you *are* every day. When a person is deciding if they respect you as a leader, they observe what you *do* to understand who you *are*. They use their observations to decide if you're an honorable, trusted leader or a self-serving person who misuses authority to look good and get promoted. People follow leaders; they may simply obey managers. This might seem like a subtle difference, but it is real. Would you rather be obeyed or followed?

A Matter of Semantics?

One of the difficulties with writing about leadership and management is that the two terms are often used interchangeably. Whether you're a front-line supervisor in a 10-person shop or the CEO of a Fortune 100 company, *you'll be both a manager <u>and</u> a leader.* It's simply a matter of degree. Some of the time you'll be managing, and some of the time you'll be leading. They're two different sides of the same coin. CEOs tend to devote most of their workweek to leading, while supervisors devote most of their time to managing.

In trying to explain the difference between managing and leading, it is tempting to use the wonderful quote from Admiral Grace Murray Hooper (the founder of computing in the military): "You don't manage people; you manage things. You lead people." That gets the essential difference across, but it isn't quite enough. Some of what you do with the people you supervise is *management*, such as providing them with detailed feedback about their performance. However, when you engage them in a discussion about their long-term career goals, the overall scope of their job, or where you see the department heading in the next several years, that's a *leadership* function. It may seem like hair-splitting to some degree, but leading is a different mindset than managing. And, as we've said before, to be effective in your job, you must become proficient at *both* managing *and* leading.

As a supervisor or manager, how do you become more of a leader? The next chapter explores the traits, skills, and styles of leadership.

> Management is efficiency in climbing the ladder of success; leadership determines whether the ladder is leaning against the right wall.
>
> *Stephen Covey*

Chapter 33
Leadership Traits, Skills, and Styles

During the early 1900s, many people believed that management's goal was to design the most efficient way to accomplish a task and then teach workers the specific steps needed to complete the job. The same process . . . done the same way . . . every time. Back then, people were viewed pretty much as a mechanical asset, like equipment or facilities. Scientific Management – as advocated by Fredrick Taylor, Lillian Gilbreth, and others – was seen as the best way to build standardized, long-run, assembly-line products at the time. Since then, we've learned a few things about how to run our organizations more effectively and humanely.

Leadership Traits

In any discussion of leadership it's important to begin by looking at the traits of those who have been successful leaders. Every leadership book, it seems, has its own list of traits exhibited by excellent leaders. But once you review all the different lists, the following five traits seem to emerge in one form or another:

- **Intelligence.** How smart you are in both cognitive ability (IQ) and emotional intelligence (EQ)

- **Self-Confidence.** Your belief in your own competence and skills

- **Determination.** An unwavering desire to get the job done

- **Integrity.** Being (and being perceived as) honest and trustworthy

- **Social-ability.** How easily you connect with others

If you're going to be a leader, these traits are core qualities or attributes. What you choose to do with these traits, and your individual ability to exhibit them consistently, is entirely up to you.

Don't compromise yourself. You are all you've got.

       Janis Joplin

It's useful to pay attention to your own approach to leading and empowering your team. Self-analysis and reflection will help you determine your individual strengths and weaknesses (i.e., opportunities for improvement). If you have the chance to use a 360° feedback instrument, it will help you understand how others perceive you. Also, tools like the Myers-Briggs Type Indicator and the StrengthsFinder will provide data for analysis and increased self-knowledge. All of these will help you answer questions such as:

- Do I have the qualities needed to move up in the organization?

- Who am I as a leader, and where do I fit in the organization?

- How do others perceive me as a leader?

- Where do I need to grow/change to increase my impact?

Unfortunately, the main limitation of studying only leadership traits is that they focus on the *leader.* They don't take into account the *followers* OR the *situation* in which a group operates.

Leadership Skills

To deal with this limitation, the study of leadership as a set of skills or personal characteristics influenced management and leadership thought during the 1960s and 1970s. Leadership came to be seen as a set of *skills* that could be learned and developed. This was markedly different from the trait approach, which was more oriented toward a "leaders are born" perspective.

The leadership skills that emerged from this new perspective included:

- ***Technical Skills.*** Having specialized knowledge and expertise in a specific type of work or activity, often with things such as equipment, budgets, products/services, etc.

> If one advances confidently in the direction of his dreams and endeavors to live the life which he has imagined, he will meet with a success unexpected in common hours.
>
> *Henry David Thoreau*

- *Human Skills.* Understanding and being able to work effectively with people – understanding human nature, dealing with others as individuals, communicating effectively, etc.

- *Conceptual Skills.* Having the ability to work with ideas and concepts – developing and articulating a vision, strategic thinking, practicing innovation, etc.

How the various parts of this skills model are weighted depends on the organizational level of the leader. For front-line supervisors, technical and human skills are most important. For mid-level managers, all three skill areas – technical, human, and conceptual – are important. For upper-level managers/leaders, human and conceptual skills are most important. Note that human skills are expected in all levels of responsibility. If you can't understand and work effectively with others, your ability to grow and lead in an organization will be severely limited.

> Good leaders are scarce; so I'm following myself.
>
> *Dale Carnegie*

The basic notion of the skills model is simple: if people learn from their experiences, they'll be able to develop their leadership abilities whether they're born leaders or not.

Leadership Styles

The study of leadership as a set of *behaviors* leading to a "style" gained traction with separate research at Ohio State University and the University of Michigan at about the same time in the late 1940s to mid-1950s.

As a result, effective leadership began to be seen as a set of behaviors dealing with two major factors: *people* and *tasks*. Effective leaders focused on getting the job done – the tasks on their plates – but *also* focused on relationship-oriented behaviors. They usually did *not* do the same kind of work as their direct reports. Their tasks were different, including planning and scheduling, coordinating activities, and providing the team with necessary resources. They also spent time helping their employees set task goals that were both challenging and achievable. They were more considerate, helpful, and supportive of employees than in an earlier era. They also provided recognition for the efforts of their team members.

Overall, under this model, effective leaders preferred a more hands-off style of supervision rather than exercising tight control over their employees. They set goals and provided guidelines, but then gave their direct reports plenty of leeway about how those goals were achieved. However, there are other approaches or styles that are effective, depending on the specific organization, unit, manager, and work team.

> Forget past mistakes. Forget failures. Forget everything except what you're going to do now and do it.
>
> *William Durant*

Lessons in Leadership: The Third Shift Paint Line

Some years ago I conducted a 360° assessment for the management team at a manufacturer in the steel-bending business. They made high-quality file cabinets, shelving, and supermarket checkout stands using rolled steel. We gathered data for about 40 managers and executives, including the supervisor of the third shift paint line, a guy we'll call Jack.

Jack had quite a background. His first career was as an MP in the Marines, while his second career was as a sheriff's deputy on road patrol and in county jail posts. When I reviewed his feedback, I saw that he was viewed as very directive and definitely not participative in his approach to his employees. (At the time I believed that a highly participative style was the most effective way to manage people.)

I talked to the CEO about Jack's style. He suggested I take a look at Jack's team firsthand. So I went into the plant at 11 p.m., 1 a.m., and 3 a.m. over the course of a week and hung out with the team. I learned a lot. I learned that the third shift paint line was the "dumping ground" for the rest of the plant. If a worker didn't get along with people, Jack's unit was the last chance before being fired. I discovered that about two-thirds of the dozen people on the team had criminal records, with a history of being problem employees. One of Jack's employees told me, "Hey, we can get out of hand sometimes and Jack has to take us out behind the building and smack us around a bit, but we get the job done."

Frankly, I was confused. I expected Jack's employees to be sullen, resentful, and unproductive. They weren't. I expected them to dislike Jack as a supervisor. They didn't. More research revealed that Jack's turnover record was substantially better than other third shift units and even better than most of the first and second shift units. His productivity and quality numbers were better than the second shift's and nearly as good as the first shift's.

Lessons Learned

As I considered all of this, I realized I had learned a major lesson in leadership:

- *Leaders use different styles. The style that you and I would use in the same situation might be different.*

- *A style that works well in one situation won't work everywhere.*

- *If turnover isn't excessive, and productivity and quality results are up to standard, then the style being used may be appropriate.*

Jack turned out to be a pretty good supervisor. He wouldn't be my cup of tea if I worked for him, but the team he led did a good job, had jelled pretty well as a team, and generally thought Jack was a good guy.

So here's the question. Is the leadership style you're using getting you the results you need?

Participative Leadership

Some leaders have found using a highly *participative* style works well in their situations. Participative leaders ask for employee input, suggestions, and ideas. Then they use that input to change the way they or the team get the work done. Participative leaders frequently involve their employees in the goal-setting process and are open to different ways of getting the job accomplished. The effect of participative leadership is to build a cohesive team that works together rather than a set of individuals working on their own.

Situational Leadership

The idea that a leader should use different styles depending on the individual person being managed has come to be called *situational leadership*. It's closely identified with Paul Hersey and Ken Blanchard. The co-author with Spencer Johnson of "The One Minute Manager" and a host of other books, Blanchard is probably better known than Hersey. However, the two of them were the original creators of Situational Leadership Theory. Using the results of the Ohio State and University of Michigan leadership studies as a beginning point, they developed a leadership model that took into account individual differences among employees. Their landmark book "Management of Organizational Behavior" is now in its ninth edition and continues to be one of the best and most comprehensive books available on management and leadership.

Their approach asks the leader to use a leadership style appropriate to the needs of the situation. It has proved popular with managers over the years because it's simple to understand and it works in most environments for most people. A good situational leader is one who can quickly change leadership styles as the situation changes. According to Hersey and Blanchard, a leader's style should be based on the *ability* and *willingness* of their followers to perform well. There's no single best or optimum style. Effective leaders are

> It marks a big step in your development when you come to realize that other people can help you do a better job than you could do alone.
>
> *Andrew Carnegie*

> Judge yourself by two standards: where you are today compared with last week and where you want to be next week.
>
> *Yoheved Kaplinsky*

flexible and adapt themselves to the situation, which is driven by the level of the individual follower's readiness to perform well.

Lessons in Leadership: Carolyn & Sally

Sally was a solid, knowledgeable, results-oriented employee with good skills, extensive experience, and a positive attitude. She had worked in several administrative support positions during her 20-year career. Carolyn was an office manager, leading six people in the largest branch office of a state government agency. Her team was highly productive, consistently delivering outstanding results. When Sally joined Carolyn's team, she continued to be a reliable, hard-working employee.

Although the agency required only one annual performance appraisal, Carolyn had regular informal performance discussions with each of her staff. As she prepared for her first meeting with Sally, she remembered what had occurred with two major new projects. When she had approached Sally about managing them, Sally hesitated and became unusually tentative. She subtly resisted having the tasks delegated to her and postponed starting the new assignments, claiming she didn't have the time in her workload. In situational leadership terms, Sally was "able and willing" to perform well and did so except when she was responsible for taking on a new project.

Carolyn quickly realized that something about the project assignments were outside of Sally's comfort zone. She understood that Sally either lacked the ability to perform well or she lacked the willingness to take on the projects. As Carolyn thought about how to approach Sally, she came up with three initial options:

- *Find another employee who knew how to do the new project assignments, and have them act as a resource or mentor for Sally.*

- *Carve out pieces of the new projects related to Sally's current workload so she could have a small "win" to build her confidence.*

Continued on Next Page

> - *Reinforce her confidence in Sally's abilities, and find opportunities to support her as the projects proceeded.*
>
> Using the situational leadership approach, Carolyn knew she needed to match her leadership style to Sally's readiness level. It was Carolyn's responsibility to adapt to Sally's current behavior – not the other way around.
>
> In this case, Carolyn decided to simply discuss the two new project assignments with Sally in behavioral terms. Carolyn's approach was non-confrontational. She basically said, "Here's what I see; let's talk about what occurred and see if we can figure out what's going on." During that meeting Carolyn learned that Sally saw the two projects as overwhelming. She was confident in her ability to get things done when somebody else figured out what needed to be done, how to do it, and then handed off the tasks to her. But Sally had never planned and implemented a big project on her own, and she felt insecure about doing it.
>
> ### Lessons Learned
>
> After discussing the situation, Carolyn and Sally decided that she needed some training in project planning and a bit of hand-holding on the first of the two projects to get things rolling. Ultimately, they discovered that Sally had a talent for project management and actually enjoyed taking on new projects.

So what does this all mean? Simply put, there are many different ways to look at, discuss, or debate the notion of leadership. The basic fact is this: regardless of your approach to managing and leading your team, it's the results you achieve that determine how effective you are. If your team is performing well, *and* you don't have a lot of turnover and/or absenteeism, *and* you're developing your people to increase their value to the organization, you're much more likely to be viewed as an effective leader.

The Vision Thing

Having a vision for the future direction of your organization is essential, whether your organization is three, 300, or 300,000 people. Without a vision for the future, you won't be an effective leader for long. And if you're managing a team of, say, 15 people in a 3,000-employee organization, you need to clearly understand how your team fits into the larger vision of the whole organization.

That leadership skill can be hard to master, particularly when it comes to seeking information and asking serious questions of higher-level leaders. In some "dinosaur" organizations, asking senior management, "Where is the organization going in the next five years and what trends will we be responding to?" may be viewed as inappropriate. But having the answers to questions like these makes it easier to lead your team. And if senior management doesn't know the answers, you'll have learned something very important about future job security; the chances are good that the organization will be out of business within five years.

Why is having a vision of the future so important to leadership? If you don't have a clear vision of the environment your team or organization will face and how you'll operate within it, you can be sure your team will be reactive. Reactive teams are less successful. A proactive team requires a well-communicated vision.

> Mission starts with determining what you really care about and want to accomplish and committing yourself to it. You can always develop expertise. First discover your preference.
>
> *Charles Garfield*

The clear direction supplied by a well-articulated vision is a huge boost to the productivity, focus, attitude, confidence, and optimism of an organization. When your employees hear you say, "Here's where we're going, here are the challenges I foresee, and here's how we'll get the job done," your team can get to work making your vision a reality. You provide the goal or target and point the way; your employees help make it real. And, of course, as a leader you roll up your sleeves, pitch in, and work alongside them.

> Nothing happens unless first we dream.
>
> *Carl Sandburg*

Try it, do it, and keep doing it. That's leadership too.

Chapter 34
Empowering Your Employees

One of the most common criticisms employees have about management and leadership in general is, "I don't get enough information to do my job properly. The communication around here is lousy."

Employees typically want and need information about a wide variety of issues and concerns – usually a lot more than upper management thinks they do! How well you're able to meet these needs has a major effect on your team's ability to get their job done. It also demonstrates how effective you are in your job and what kind of leader you are. Good communication (*Skill 2*) and good leadership are intertwined. You simply can't be a good leader if you aren't a good communicator.

> One's mind, once stretched by a new idea, never regains its original dimensions.
>
> *Oliver Wendell Holmes, Jr.*

Employees generally want and need information about three major areas:

- The organization (including their own unit)

- Their specific job

- Policies and procedures that affect them

The table on the next page provides examples of the kinds of information employees want.

Employee Information Needs Chart

The Organization & Unit/Team	Their Specific Job	Policies & Procedures
What are the mission, vision, goals, and objectives of the organization? Of my team?	How does my job fit into the overall mission, vision, values, goals, and objectives?	What are the rules that govern how I do my job?
Who are our major stakeholders? (For organization; also team)	How does what I do contribute to our ability to meet our customers' needs?	What policy/procedure changes are expected and why are they taking place?
What products and/or services do we provide to our customers?	Are there any changes in the works that will affect how I do my job in the future?	How much leeway do I have in interpreting policies and procedures?
Who are our major customers?	What does the organization expect of me as an employee?	How much leeway do you, as my boss, have in interpreting policies and procedures?
Who are our major competitors? Who are the major players in our industry?	What do you, as my manager, expect of me?	How do I go about suggesting changes in policies and procedures?
What marketplace do we serve as an organization? As a team?	What is your definition of success for me in my job?	Is a policy handbook available?
How do our customers use our products and/or services?	How will I be held accountable for producing the expected results?	How are policy and procedure changes communicated?
What benefits do our customers get from using our products/services?	How will I be rewarded for doing a good job?	If I discover a policy has been violated, what should I do?
What is the overall financial status of our organization?	How much freedom do I have to produce the expected results?	If a procedure has not been followed, what should I do?

What Employees Need to Know: The Organization

When employees believe communication is adequate, timely, and useful, they're much more likely to "own" their job and their responsibilities. They're also much more empowered to do their job well – to make appropriate decisions and to understand when they need to seek information, approval, or advice.

Your team members have friends, neighbors, and relatives who've been laid off, outsourced, restructured, or merged into the unemployment line. They may have experienced this themselves before they came to work for you. In any event, the notion, "If I work hard, produce good results, and am loyal my job is pretty safe," no longer holds true. Industries consolidate. Productivity improvements and new technologies make job skills obsolete almost overnight. Job security is something that was true for your employees' parents or grandparents, but it isn't something they can count on for themselves.

Perseverance and audacity generally win.

Dorothee DeLuzy

As a manager or supervisor, you can't assume you'll get a clear commitment from your employees unless they understand a lot about who you are, what you do, and what stake they have in the organization's collective success. It's amazing how many times employees find out about layoffs or a major new contract by reading their local newspaper, watching the evening news, scanning a Web site, or following a Facebook or Twitter entry. The loyalty and commitment of your employees is not a given, and this kind of internal communications failure can destroy that overnight. Their trust must be earned and renewed every day.

Many employees need fairly detailed information about expectations and outcomes. When provided with enough detail, they'll typically work very hard to provide you and the organization with those results. But if they don't get these details, you shouldn't be surprised if results look much different than you anticipated. In most situations, once your team clearly understands the desired outcome and your expectations about results, you can back off and let them run with the ball.

What Employees Need to Know: Their Specific Job

Most employees show up at the beginning of their workday wanting to do a good job. When mistakes occur it's usually the result of something going wrong in the system or unclear expectations.

Even when employees seem to be indifferent to doing a good job, it's unlikely they showed up that way on Day One. If your hiring practices are reasonably effective, lazy, unmotivated bozos with bad attitudes seldom get hired. The screening process weeds them out. So if an employee is a poor performer now, were they always that way? If so, then you made a mistake hiring them in the first place (or you inherited them when you were promoted), and you didn't correct that error immediately when you discovered the mistake. If not, then what has happened to turn them into a poor performer? Something in the way they've been managed? An illness or accident? Or perhaps something outside of work, such as a personal problem at home?

As I've conducted management assessments for thousands of individual managers during the past 25 years, I've found that most employees would like to get a *lot* more feedback about how they're performing. The annual written performance appraisal process is not enough, and it really has very little to do with managing employees' performance. What employees really want and need is day-to-day coaching and feedback from you – the ongoing conversations that help them grow and develop in their job. (See *Chapter 25.*)

> Learning is not attained by chance, it must be sought for with ardor and attended to with diligence.
>
> *Abigail Adams*

What Employees Need to Know: Policies & Procedures

How many times have you learned about a change in policies or procedures from someone who's thrilled to tell you why the change is a dumb idea and won't work here? It happens all the time. As a supervisor or manager who's also a leader, it's your job to be on top of changes and be prepared to help your people understand how the new policy or procedure is going to affect them and their jobs. From *Skill 5 – Managing Change*, you know that people have some natural reactions to change and those reactions are seldom, "Wow! What a great idea!"

Your responsibility is to understand current policies and procedures well enough to be able to explain "why we do things the way we do them around here." You also need to keep up to speed with changes as they develop. Particularly in larger organizations, there's a tendency to create policies and procedures that make sense and work well for *most* of the organization. However, those policies might not work equally well in *all* parts of the organization. So procedures are likely to be announced, implemented, and then modified based on input from units and individuals. That's the nature of policy and procedure development. Helping your team understand that this type of adjustment and course correction is natural is part of your job as a leader.

Employees' need and desire for information is much stronger than you might think. When they don't receive the information they need through official channels, they'll get their information through other sources. Naturally, the information they get is likely to be less than accurate (and sometimes wildly inaccurate). You can easily spot organizations with inadequate internal communications; most employees hear about what is happening through the rumor mill rather than from their immediate supervisor.

When hiring key employees, there are only two qualities to look for: judgment and taste. Almost everything else can be bought by the yard.

John W. Gardner

Rumor Mills, Intranets & You

The traditional worksite rumor mill has been fundamentally changed by the use of intranets. These computer networks help speed information flow inside large or geographically dispersed organizations while maintaining internal security. Most of the time, they're a great tool for transferring information, keeping people up to speed, and managing top-down communication about policy changes.

As a manager or supervisor, it doesn't matter what your team's purpose is. You *must* be comfortable with your organization's intranet and use it daily, or you'll risk being seen as out of the loop by your teammates. In most cases, your employees are going to look to you for accurate information about what's going on: policy and procedure changes, events in other units, and any relevant news. In other words, your employees will see you as the go-to person for answers about the organization, their job, and what they need to be doing.

When you know what's going on . . . keep up to speed on changes coming down the pike . . . and keep your people up to date with useful information . . . they may dismiss the rumor mill as irrelevant. When employees get accurate, timely information about their jobs, they don't seem to spend a lot of time and energy spreading rumors or speculating about how they're going to get shafted by someone. But when you don't keep up with what's on the company intranet . . . when you're out of the loop . . . when you don't have the information employees want . . . they'll get their information from other sources, usually the rumor mill.

The bottom line? To lead, you need to keep up to speed. You need to communicate upward and downward and across boundaries in your organization. You need to proactively find the right information when you don't know the answers to employees' questions. The intranet (not to mention the Internet) can help you with all this. Often the content won't be perfect, but it's an information pipeline that efficiently moves information around your organization. Ignore it at your own peril.

Empowering Your Team

There are many ways you can lead and empower your team. Some of the following ideas might strike a chord with you. If you spot something that does, give it a try and see what happens. If it works, great! If it doesn't, try something else.

- Follow up consistently.

- Clarify who is responsible.

- Encourage employees and others to express themselves.

- Empower purposefully.

Follow Up

Simply tracking commitments and following up to determine progress and results will go a long way toward determining your own and your unit's success.

How many times has somebody said to you, "Sure, I can have that information to you by Friday"? When Friday rolls around, did they keep their commitment? If not, did you check with them to see what the problem was? Did they forget? Did they run into a roadblock? Did someone else they were relying on for data not come through?

Tracking the commitments of others and following up when they're due is critical if you want others to keep their commitments. If I make a commitment to you to do something and report back to you . . . and if I see you make notes about that commitment . . . and if I know from past experience that you'll follow up with me about that commitment . . . then I'll do my very best to ensure my commitment is kept. And I'm likely to keep my commitment to you before I do a task assigned by someone who doesn't track and follow up.

> Hire people who are better than you are, then leave them to get on with it . . . ; Look for people who will aim for the remarkable, who will not settle for the routine.
>
> *David Ogilvy*

Clarify Responsibilities

Determining the general responsibilities for each position within the team is important. To use a popular metaphor, it's a matter of getting the right people "on the bus" (the selection or talent-acquisition process) and then making sure you have people "in the right seats" (the task assignment process) on that bus.

The Gallup Organization suggests that a person's *talents* – their innate, hardwired abilities – have a lot to do with determining what seat on the bus a person is best prepared to occupy. Many leaders attempt to determine what people's weaknesses are and then "fix" them. There's an underlying assumption that all managers and supervisors need to become equally adept at the same things. But this doesn't take advantage of individual strengths and talents. You'll see this frequently in development programs based on competencies – where an effort is made to identify a set of attributes, attitudes, and skills that all employees at a certain level should possess. While it makes sense to determine what those competencies are, it doesn't make sense to believe that each of us needs to (or can) become adept at all of them. (See *Chapter 8*.)

Encourage Expression

If you're a manager who expects your employees to agree with you all the time, you're kidding yourself. You might feel you have to be right all the time and have the definitive perspective on the one, true answer to every question to be an effective, respected leader. But this is impossible, and trying to lead this way will quickly wear you out or lead to "perfection paralysis."

Do not be too timid and squeamish about your actions. All life is an experiment.

Ralph Waldo Emerson

This attitude will also rob your team members of the ability to think on their own, to exercise initiative, and to be self-starters in identifying and resolving problems. So ask questions. Ask for your employees' and colleagues' opinions and ideas. Do you *really* know how your employees feel and what they think about how to get the best results . . . accomplish the unit's goals . . . improve methods and procedures . . . respond to new challenges . . . and get the job done? If not, ask them. It will empower them and make things a lot easier on you!

Empower Purposefully

The idea of empowering employees to think and act on their own has been around for years. And a good idea it is. But not everyone is equally ready or able to be empowered. Leadership in this arena involves much more than just saying, "Go forth and be wonderful."

Too often people are aimlessly empowered. They're told they should own their jobs, and then they're left to figure things out for themselves. As a manager or supervisor, you need to think through the empowerment process from several angles, including each employee's level of experience, commitment, and willingness to operate independently. How much leeway can each person handle effectively? It won't be the same for everyone on your team. Empowerment is a good idea; it just shouldn't be applied universally and without thought.

Staff Development

To a great extent your success as a supervisor, manager, and leader will be determined by the performance of those you lead. Successful managers hire people who are sharp, focused, and committed to achieving results. Poor managers tend to hire people who aren't so sharp, often because the manager feels threatened by people who are smart, savvy, and successful. When I was managing large numbers of people, I always wanted to surround myself with the brightest people I could find. They were smarter than I am, but they made me look really smart because of the results they produced!

Once you get past a certain point in your career, your success will be directly linked to how successful you are in developing yourself

> I believe the real difference between success and failure in a corporation can be very often traced to the question of how well the organization brings out the great energies and talents of its people.
>
> *Thomas J. Watson, Jr.*

and your team. Helping your staff to grow and develop will let you take on new assignments, expand your sphere of influence, and leverage your skills and abilities as a leader. That might sound like a lot of work. But making staff development a top priority can pay huge dividends for you and your entire organization.

An Ongoing Effort

Developing your staff requires ongoing effort from both you and your employees. Helping your people to grow and develop, teaching them new skills, and providing opportunities for them to take on new responsibilities will help your team adapt to a rapidly changing environment. This doesn't mean, however, that all you have to do is send your employees off to a seminar or two each year. This "training as reward" approach simply won't get the job done. Instead, you need to look at each of your employees as individuals and work as a partner with them to determine their developmental needs and help guide their progress.

Will all of your employees be at the same level of readiness for development? Of course not. You're likely to have a few employees who are ready and eager right now for promotion or a new assignment. Others will need further training, development, and experience in their current roles before they're truly ready for a new challenge. And still others may appear to have little or no interest in, or potential for, future promotion. That's part of the reality of managing a unit or team. Instead of agonizing about those at the farthest end of the development continuum who will take the most work, begin by focusing on the other two groups.

Who's Ready Now?

Team members who are ready right now for a new assignment should be your first concern, because great employees leave when they don't see opportunities for advancement. And even if they

> It's not whether you get knocked down; it's whether you get up.
>
> *Vince Lombardi*

don't leave the organization, their attitude and productivity may slide if they don't see much of a chance for new challenges.

If promotion into a new role isn't possible right now, you'd better figure out how to use these high-potential employees in other ways. One approach is to do some development-in-place with your sharpest people by giving them new responsibilities. For example, they could mentor a new teammate or become the resident expert on certain processes and systems. Another approach is to help them shift to another part of the organization that can use their skills. Ultimately, this is a win-win-win – for them, for the organization, and for you because you've shown your leadership savvy.

> Always recognize that human individuals are ends, and do not use them as means to *your* end.
>
> *Immanuel Kant*

Who Has Future Potential?

The middle group on the continuum is likely to be the largest. These are employees who have solid potential but need development. Individual employees in this group will be at different stages in their knowledge, skills, and interest in professional growth, but they all will be "not quite ready for advancement." Group training and development programs are useful. But those need to be combined with individually focused action plans and careful coaching.

With this group you definitely need to lead by example. If you haven't bothered to develop yourself, these folks won't see you as *really* being committed to developing your team. But when you're actively involved in your own growth and development, they'll notice, and most of them will be more willing to participate in the development process.

> I have always had a dread of becoming a passenger in life.
>
> *Queen Margaret of Denmark*

Who Needs the Most Help?

The third group – those who don't appear to have much potential for growth and advancement – takes special attention and planning. You need to start by understanding what makes them tick when it comes to professional development. They tend to fall into one of four types:

- The currently competent, content employee
- The currently competent, maxed out employee
- The marginal, uninterested employee
- The marginal, interested employee

In some cases you're dealing with employees who are well-suited to their current roles and perform them competently. They're content, happy where they are, and they simply have no interest in taking on new tasks or assignments.

> Study as if you are going to live forever; live as if you were going to die tomorrow.
>
> *Marion Mitchell*

Other employees are currently doing okay, but they lack the ability or skills to take on any new tasks. For whatever reason (e.g., they may be close to retirement or have a limiting disability of some kind), they've maxed out and they're unlikely to increase their value to the team or the organization.

Neither of these types of employees should be written off as "losers." Having steady, reliable, solid performers on your team is very valuable, even if they have no current interest in further professional growth.

Then there are the marginal employees – those who really aren't even competent in their current job. There can be a huge difference between marginal performers who are uninterested in professional development and those who want to grow and learn. In both situations the real issue is the individual employee's *attitude* and *mindset*.

Marginal, uninterested employees are unlikely to seek or accept opportunities to grow. They aren't engaged in their job *or* their own development. In fact, they might actively resist anything you do to help them. They probably need to move on, and your HR personnel can help you help them to do that. They're a living example of the statement, "Everyone needs to be someplace, but sometimes that place isn't *here*."

On the other hand, marginal but interested employees are more likely to embrace opportunities when they're offered *and* improve their performance as a result. They'll see the opportunity to grow and develop as a benefit. They have at least the possibility of changing their potential value to the team.

If you're new to supervising a particular team, you may discover that your initial perceptions about each individual's potential were inadequate or simply wrong. You don't know what has caused each person to be a star performer, a disengaged robot, or something in between. You can't assume that a lack of interest in professional development is part of someone's basic makeup. Today's marginal, uninterested employee may surprise you when they see others on the team learning new skills and taking on new challenges. The bottom line is this: each of your employees is an individual and their professional development needs to be managed individually.

Nurturing Leadership Potential

How does an organization create effective leaders at all levels? As an individual supervisor or manager, what can *you* do?

One of the best ways to start nurturing leadership potential in others is to get a handle on your own leadership abilities. You can do that by gathering feedback from those who work with you most closely. Often that feedback is gathered through some sort of survey process, such as a 360° feedback tool. Over the years we've used these sorts of assessments with managers at all levels in a wide variety of organizations.

Using a proven 360° feedback tool will give you solid baseline data that you can use for your own professional development. When you use an instrument like this you'll usually see a fair amount of consistency in the responses, so you can have a high degree of confidence in the results.

Most of the time, when you get this kind of feedback you can quickly determine which factors and specific behaviors you're seen as doing frequently. (Those might match up with your greatest talents in the StrengthsFinder.) At the same time, you might clearly see items that you appear to be doing rather infrequently. Once you have this information, you can make decisions about adding to your current strengths and/or improving something you'd like to do better. In any event, once you know how your boss, your employees, and your peers perceive you, it gives you a great place to begin applying *Skill 8 – Growing Yourself.* (See *Chapters 35-36.*)

In 20 years of using 360° tools and other assessments to help grow, develop, and manage supervisors and leaders in all kinds of organizations, certain issues have come up with remarkable frequency. Very few organizations excel at staff development. Most managers and many leaders spend little time helping their employees prepare for future responsibilities. Instead, they tend to focus on maximizing productivity and predictability rather than innovation and growth. Newly promoted supervisors and managers often hang on to their old responsibilities, either by choice or due to insufficient bench strength. Regardless of the reason, an opportunity to delegate and promote employee growth is lost.

Peter Drucker often claimed that many duties were being performed at least one level higher in the organization than they should be. While I don't know how to validate that, it seems to make sense, like many of his ideas. The bottom line is simple: how we develop our people is how each of us is judged as a leader. Truly

> Because a thing seems difficult for you, do not think it impossible for anyone to accomplish.
>
> *Marcus Aurelius*

successful leaders focus a substantial amount of their time on staff development, nurturing leadership in others.

Lessons in Leadership: The Staff Development Champ

Jane has built a highly successful treasury management client services operation for a large multi-state bank. One of her core values is staff development. After new hires have developed their basic skills, they have opportunities to serve on task forces, take on new project assignments, help develop new products and services, and suggest and make improvements – i.e., they get to really grow professionally. Employees with the interest and potential have plenty of opportunities to take on new and more challenging tasks.

Not only are employees encouraged to grow and advance, but Jane and her staff supervisors remind employees to "think résumé." When an employee picks up a new skill, participates on a project team, or receives an accolade, it gets added to their résumé. If a higher-level position becomes available and an employee expresses interest, Jane or one of her supervisors will review the posting and the employee's résumé with them. They will even help the employee practice in a mock-interview setting. The results?

- *Employees throughout the bank see Jane's department as a place where they will be supported and encouraged to advance.*

- *The department has a significantly lower turnover rate than other departments.*

- *When employees leave, they're usually headed for a promotion that takes advantage of their skill set.*

- *Jane has former employees working in virtually every area in the company, so she knows who to call when an inter-unit issue arises.*

Continued on Next Page

> ### *Lessons Learned*
>
> This kind of leadership creates several winners: (1) the bank, because it has intensely loyal employees who aren't interested in leaving the organization just to get a promotion; (2) the employees, because they see they have a future within the organization; (3) the bank's customers, because they deal daily with well-motivated, positive individuals who see the organization as really caring about them; and (4) the department's management, because they don't have a revolving door when it comes to finding and retaining employees. Everybody wins!

Now it's time to move to the final of the *8 Essential Skills,* the one that takes everything you've learned and turns it into reality. *Skill 8* is *Growing Yourself.*

Skill 8

GROWING YOURSELF

"Believe deep down in your heart that
you will do great things."

Joe Paterno

Skill 8 – Growing Yourself

When many baby boomers began their careers, developing management talent was usually the responsibility of the organization. Today's world is vastly different in many ways, including who bears responsibility for talent development. Even in the largest talent-focused organizations, much of the responsibility has shifted to the individual. Each employee must be an active partner in their own development, whether the organization is involved in the process or not.

The half-life of any skill set is now measured in months, and continual learning is not optional. In fact, lifelong learning and a strong focus on self-development is mandatory for survival. After all, you may be doing a great job and have an excellent team, but if your office/plant/business is acquired, merged, defunded, or otherwise put out of business, you may well be looking for work. If that happens, your skills, talents, and experience are all you have to sell. So you'd better keep sharpening that skill set!

> Life is what we make it, always has been, always will be.
>
> *Grandma Moses*

When a team or work group within an organization has common developmental opportunities, those can often be addressed through formal training or other group activities. But individual opportunities should be handled through the development of personal/professional Action Plans. Expecting to grow and improve professionally or personally without some sort of organized approach is, frankly, not very realistic.

All of us have some ideas about how we'd like to grow and improve. You might want to get better at providing performance feedback and coaching your employees. Or you may want to improve some aspect of your communications skills. Perhaps you want to improve your organizational, personal productivity, and decision-making skills. Or you might have your eye on more "big picture" areas, such as strategy, teamwork, or project management.

Whatever your initial thoughts are about your professional development, it's a good time to get some of them down on paper. As you think about your current job, are there areas that could stand some improvement? What kind of job would you like to do next? What skills do you need to acquire to be ready if the opportunity comes along? Whatever your current situation is, start thinking and behaving like your growth and development is your responsibility. Because it is.

> We cannot become what we need to be by remaining what we are.
>
> *Max DePree*

If you seriously want to improve as a manager and leader, you *need* some type of developmental Action Plan. Look at this Action Plan for your own growth the same way you would any other business or project plan. The same components will be needed: clearly defined goals; specific steps; necessary resources (people, money, time); and some sort of timeline. Your particular organization may have a process like this already in place. If so, that format may work well for you. What's important is to find or create a format that reflects the way *you* plan and work – and then actually use it!

One approach that we use (the *Developmental Action Plan Form*) is included in the *Appendix*, along with a completed sample. But this is just to get you started and give you some ideas to help you develop your own approach. Feel free to use all of it, parts of it, or create something else entirely.

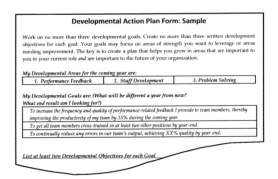

Developmental Action Plan Form: Sample

Work on no more than three developmental goals. Create no more than three written development objectives for each goal. Your goals may focus on areas of strength you want to leverage or areas needing improvement. The key is to create a plan that helps you grow in areas that are important to you in your current role *and* are important to the future of your organization.

My Developmental Areas for the coming year are:

1. Performance Feedback	2. Staff Development	3. Problem Solving

My Developmental Goals are: (What will be different a year from now? What end result am I looking for?)

To increase the frequency and quality of performance-related feedback I provide to team members, thereby improving the productivity of my team by 15% during the coming year.
To get all team members cross-trained in at least two other positions by year-end.
To continually reduce any errors in our team's output, achieving XX% quality by year-end.

List at least two Developmental Objectives for each Goal

Chapter 35
Setting Developmental Goals

If you really want to grow and develop professionally, it's important to establish some developmental goals for yourself. Then, once you've set those goals, the next step is to craft and implement a personal Action Plan.

> Already have a professional development goal-setting process that works well for you and your team? Skim the rest of this chapter; then turn to Chapter 36 to learn about creating and using Action Plans.

Goal Setting: An Overview

Setting goals and objectives is a good idea. Sure, you've heard that before! In fact, it's true. In general, people who set goals for themselves, write them down, and regularly review them for progress are substantially more successful and happy in life than those who don't (regardless of how you define "success").

We always get what we pray for, like it or not. Who we want most to be, we are.

Richard Bach

Whether you buy that notion or not, setting goals is much more likely to get you the results you want than just drifting professionally – as long as those goals are clear, specific, challenging, and in line with your organization's expectations. You'll find you seem to do a better job when the goals and purpose behind it all are clear and relevant. Just as setting production, service, and quality goals helps move an organization in the desired direction, setting individual development goals helps move you toward *your* desired outcomes.

Management by objectives works if you first think through your objectives. Ninety percent of the time you haven't.

Peter Drucker

Ideally, goal setting is a joint effort between you and your boss. But whether they're actively involved or not, you'll need to set your own goals and develop your own Action Plan. To do this, work with your boss, your HR department, a mentor, and/or whoever else would be appropriate and useful. The key is to *do something*, not just think about it or put it off until you "have time."

Once you've developed your goals and Action Plan, you'll need to put your own monitoring or progress-tracking process into place. If you set goals, develop your plan, and start working on action items in your plan, but then fail to track if you're achieving anything, all you're doing is setting yourself up for frustration. A goal may reflect your desired end result, but if you don't regularly assess your progress, you won't have the chance to identify and implement course corrections along the way.

How often you check your progress depends on your situation. If you have a lot of balls in the air, you may need to take stock monthly or even weekly. For longer-term or strategic goals, a quarterly review might work best. The key is to assess progress as often as you need to and make adjustments when it makes sense.

If setting professional development goals and measuring your progress is new to you, start by setting short-term goals and measuring your progress daily and weekly until you're used to the process. Small initial wins will help to instill the habits and patterns you need to tackle larger, longer-term goals such as advanced degrees, certifications, or career shifts.

Where to Begin?

If you're like most people there are certain aspects of your job that you do very well. In some other roles you're solidly competent, while still others could use some improvement. More than likely, the things you do well play to your strengths. As we saw in *Chapter 8*, your innate talents can become strengths, and your strengths are a major factor in your success.

> There is no achievement without goals.
> *Robert McKain*

> You are free to choose, but the choices you make today will determine what you will have, be, and do in the tomorrow of your life.
> *Zig Ziglar*

But what about your weaknesses? You do have them, of course, and how you deal with them is an important consideration in setting your development goals and crafting your Action Plan. The key differences between those who are successful and those who aren't is this: successful people . . .

- Leverage and build upon their strengths, *and*

- Make sure their weaknesses don't hold them back, *and*

- Know where the gaps are between their current abilities and the needs of the organization.

You probably have some sense of what your strengths and weaknesses are, but how do you know the needs of the organization? If you report to someone who communicates clearly and regularly about the organization's expectations, plans, mission, and values, that's wonderful. At least you have some solid information to work with. But what do you do if your boss isn't a great communicator? Then you have to be proactive and ask. Ask your manager, your peers, the owner, and/or the CEO. The idea is to get as clear a picture as you can of where the organization is going and how you can contribute to its progress while advancing your own professional journey.

When you're setting your professional development goals, you might want to think about using the S.M.A.R.T. concept. Goals that fit this acronym are:

<u>S</u>pecific   <u>M</u>easurable   <u>A</u>greed Upon   <u>R</u>ealistic   <u>T</u>imely

Specific

What do you need to accomplish? What do you want your end result to look like? The more specifically you can describe your goals and what they will do for you, your team, and the organization, the more likely it is you'll reach them.

> People grow through experience if they meet life honestly and courageously. This is how character is built.
>
> *Eleanor Roosevelt*

We don't receive wisdom; we must discover it for ourselves after a journey that no one can take for us or spare us.

Marcel Proust

Measurable

How will you know whether you've accomplished a goal? How will you measure your progress? Are there interim benchmarks or project components that will help you keep things on track as you move ahead?

Agreed Upon

Unless you're operating totally on your own, you'll want to get your manager's agreement that your goals are in sync with the goals of the organization. In most cases your boss will be pleased that your self-improvement efforts are taking into account how you can add value to the organization. And when your goals are aligned with the bigger picture, you're more likely to be encouraged and supported along the way.

Realistic

Almost by definition, when it comes to professional development you'll want your goals to be a "stretch." Achieving them should help you grow; they should be challenging, but not impossible. Setting up small, consistent wins for yourself will lead to better results than setting the bar too high.

Timely

When would you like specific professional development goals to be accomplished? What deadlines are you working with? Short-term objectives will provide in-process waypoints to gauge your progress toward accomplishing a larger goal. Major multi-year goals (e.g., "obtain advanced degree" or "get first book published") need to contain smaller, interim goals to keep you focused on getting the job done. So "obtain advanced degree" might include an interim goal such as "complete two courses in first year of study with at least a 3.5 overall GPA."

By the way, you can use this same S.M.A.R.T. concept when you're working on goals related to your team members' professional development. (See *Chapter 34* for more information about staff development.)

As we mentioned above, after you've developed your initial take on your professional development goals, you should review your goals with your manager. There are three major payoffs to having that kind of discussion:

- It gives you an opportunity to gain your manager's involvement, approval, and support for your professional development.

- It demonstrates to them that you're serious about your career and the contribution you can make to the organization's future.

- It can increase your sphere of influence; your manager may start looking for ways to provide you with the developmental assignments you're seeking.

You can expect to adjust, alter, and refine this process as you proceed. Wherever you are in your own professional journey, reading this book and putting some of these suggestions into practice means you're already taking the kinds of steps necessary to grow and develop yourself. And it doesn't matter what you've done before. The important thing at this point is to set some goals and take those next steps in your professional development journey.

> I never intended to become a run-of-the-mill person.
>
> *Barbara Jordan*

Chapter 36

Creating and Using Action Plans

A developmental Action Plan is an outline of the specific steps you'll take to meet goals for your own professional development during a defined period of time. It's a living document that's updated periodically as your career progresses and you gain new skills.

How to Create Your Action Plan

Your Action Plan will be most effective if you develop it yourself. If you're like most people, you're more likely to follow through on a plan you create for yourself than one that's prescribed for you or created by others. Even if your organization has a formal process, you'll want to create your own working plan to make sure you're growing in the right direction. If you're fortunate enough to work for a manager who's strongly committed to staff development, you may get some excellent ideas, recommendations, and suggestions from them. Most of us, though, have to figure it out on our own. Here's a step-by-step approach.

Creating an Action Plan includes the following steps:

1. Identify your focus.

2. Establish your goals.

3. Create developmental objectives.

4. Identify next actions.

5. Put it in writing.

> The indispensable first step to getting the things you want out of life is this: decide what you want.
>
> *Ben Stein*

Step 1: Identify Your Focus

First, identify your current strengths and opportunities for improvement (i.e., weaknesses) so you can decide on the overall focus for your plan. Use your own intuition, feedback from others,

> Decide upon your major definite purpose in life and then organize all your activities around it.
>
> *Brian Tracy*

performance reviews, and other sources to help you determine where to concentrate your development efforts. Think about which skills, behaviors, and attitudes are truly important to your current job, your team members, your manager, and/or the organization as a whole.

Using the *8 Essential Skills* outlined in this book as your starting point, what weaknesses would you like to improve, and what strengths would you like to develop further?

		Skill	**Chapters**	Improvement Needed?
Skill 1		Managing Yourself	6 – 11	
Skill 2		Communicating for Results	12 – 18	
Skill 3		Building Successful Relationships	19 – 21	
Skill 4		Managing Others	22 – 25	
Skill 5		Managing Change	26 – 28	
Skill 6		Solving Problems & Making Decisions	29 – 31	
Skill 7		Leading & Empowering	32 – 34	
Skill 8		Growing Yourself	35 - 36	

Once you've decided where you want to grow and develop, you need to set some goals that will help move you in that direction.

Step 2: Establish Your Goals

Next, create two or three broad professional development goals that relate to your focus. Decide what you want to accomplish during the next few months. Think about what specific behaviors will change, what those new behaviors will look like, and how you'll know when you've reached each goal.

> Whatever we wrap away in thought is opened for us, one day, in experience.
>
> *Richard Bach*

Step 3: Create Developmental Objectives

Now you're ready to create two or three objectives for each goal. Be specific. What measurable actions can you take that will move you toward your goal? As you can see in the *Developmental Action Plan Form* sample in the *Appendix*, if your *goal* is to increase the frequency and quality of performance-related feedback, one of your *objectives* might be to hold a weekly performance discussion with each team member.

Goals vs. Objectives: What's the Difference?

There are a number of different approaches to the process of setting individual and/or group goals. For the sake of simplicity, here's how we approach it:

- *A Goal is a long-term target or aspiration you're committed to. Typically it will take several months to several years to accomplish the goal, and the process will consist of successfully completing several projects and/or tasks.*

- *An Objective is either a short-term or mid-term target that supports the accomplishment of a longer-term goal. Or it can be a standalone target unrelated to a specific goal. In this book we refer to objectives as the interim steps needed to accomplish a goal.*

So a goal is supported by one or more objectives, and those objectives serve as waypoints or interim steps on the path to accomplishing a goal.

Everyone has an opportunity to be great because everyone has an opportunity to serve.

Martin Luther King, Jr.

Never, never, never, never . . . give up.

Winston Churchill

Step 4: Identify Next Actions

This is the most detailed step. Now you need to identify the specific next steps, next actions, or next activities you need to do to accomplish your objectives (and ultimately your goals). As you figure out each task, action, or step, determine who is involved; what resources, knowledge, data, skills, priority changes, or approvals you need; and what the timeframe is. You don't necessarily need to plan out every step in the process right now, but you at least need to know what the next few steps are for each of your objectives. Again, the sample in the *Appendix* is a good reference for what goes into this part of the process.

Step 5: Put It in Writing

You've probably been taking notes along the way, but now it's time to create the Action Plan document – either on paper or in an electronic worksheet. Writing it down in some sort of organized fashion will greatly increase the chances that you'll actually follow through and do what you say you want to do. (Feel free to make copies of the blank *Developmental Action Plan Form* in the *Appendix* if you like that approach.) Once you've written down your plan, pay attention to it, review it regularly, modify it as you get closer to your goals, and keep "tossing out the rock" as time goes by.

Tips & Suggestions for Success

Once your Action Plan is created, how do you implement it and get the results you seek?

- Show your action plan document to your boss and get their feedback. Most managers are happy to help and proud (even if they don't say so) to be part of their employees' growth and development. When it comes to handing out new assignments or challenges, managers are more likely to select someone who's actively engaged in self-improvement, so why not have that person be *you*?

- Transfer each activity from your Action Plan document to the appropriate place in your professional calendar or time/project management system.

- Do the activities you've defined, refining them and performing course corrections as you proceed.

- At least once a week, review your Action Plan document and check off items you've completed.

> It's better to be a lion for a day than a sheep all your life.
> *Sister Elizabeth Kenny*

- Conduct a regular (weekly or monthly) follow-up with yourself to make sure you're moving forward on your development plan. The first couple of weeks are absolutely critical to your success. Don't avoid doing your follow-up; check in with yourself no matter what else is going on in your life. Create the habit of working on small chunks of your development plan and going on to a next action. This will create a pattern of success and keep you focused on moving ahead.

- As you check in, keep revising your Action Plan. There's real power in course correction, so revise your Action Plan as you see what best promotes your professional development.

- Hold periodic (perhaps quarterly) update discussions with your boss to review your progress, seek feedback, and make any adjustments needed to continue your development.

- Share your plan with a key peer or a mentor as well as your boss. Ask for feedback regularly about how you're doing compared to the plan. Remember to compare your actual results with the Action Plan. How are you doing in specific, concrete terms?

- Don't be afraid to shift gears and change the focus of your plan as circumstances shift. Self-development Action Plans are meant to help you make productive changes, not lock you into something that doesn't work. The more you test and work with your Action Plan, and the more you make it part of the way you operate daily, the better your results will be.

- *Do something* every day that helps you move your plan forward. It doesn't need to be a major task; just make sure you keep the process moving. If one thing doesn't work, try something else. Don't forget to pat yourself on the back when you make some progress with your plan. Set yourself

> Do not let what you cannot do interfere with what you can do.
>
> *John Wooden*

up for success by acknowledging small wins, and reward yourself for your accomplishments.

- Take your own personality preferences into account when selecting specific actions. Make sure your initial steps don't take you too far out of your comfort zone. Especially at first, small steps are better than attempting big change all at once.

- Stay positive! It's important to believe that you'll succeed in making the ideas in your Action Plan a reality.

The key is to get started now with an Action Plan for one or two goals and see how this works for you. You don't need to focus just on your weaknesses. You often get the best payoff by finding ways to capitalize on your strengths and natural talents. In either case, you'll gain the most by working on the areas that are most critical to your position. If you're unsure about what is most important, it's time for a talk with your boss to get their input.

Using Feedback

You'll have noticed by now that gathering and using feedback is a critical part of professional development. Making good use of feedback is essential to creating an effective Action Plan. More feedback is usually better than less. With more feedback you can select the most useful, relevant information that helps you move forward.

There are basically two types of feedback you should pay attention to: (1) *external feedback* from others, and (2) *self-feedback*, which emerges from introspection and tracking progress. Let's start with self-feedback.

It's important to notice the results you're getting from your professional development efforts – to track your progress as you implement your Action Plan and make up your own mind about

If you can't live through adversity, you'll never be good at what you do. You have to live through the unfair things, and you have to develop the hide to not let it bother you and keep your eyes focused on what you have to do.

Maurice "Hank" Greenberg

You may have to fight a battle more than once to win it.

Margaret Thatcher

how you think things are going. You don't want to ignore subtle clues or information that might lead you to rethink your approach. So, as we've said, it makes sense to regularly take a few minutes to check in with yourself. You'll want to practice tracking your results, assessing your progress, and making adjustments to your Action Plan based on self-reflection. This kind of introspection is a key skill for anyone truly interested in self-development.

The most important and useful external feedback is going to come from those you work with most closely – your manager, peers, employees, and customers. Their opinions, perceptions, and observations will – if they're truthful – have enormous value in the long run. When you first ask these key people for feedback, they might not have a lot of useful suggestions. But the fact that you're seeking their advice is a great deposit in your emotional bank account with them. And once you've solicited their feedback a few times, they'll see that you're serious and give you some useful information. After all, the purpose of asking for feedback is to get information that can help you grow and improve. (By the way, don't expect that you'll get only positive feedback. In fact, if you don't get ideas to help you improve, you're not getting truly useful feedback!)

> The only happy people I know are the ones who are working well at something they consider important.
>
> *Abraham Maslow*

Case: Learning to Love Being Audited

In one of my first management positions I learned the value of having objective outside feedback. Each year a team of outside auditors would descend upon the organization. Since I was in charge of one of the largest departments, we saw quite a bit of the audit team. At first, I was worried that they would discover something we'd done wrong and that this would reflect poorly on my department and on me personally. A much more experienced manager told me, "We are so deeply inside of what we do on a daily basis that the only way we'll ever really make substantial improvements is to have the auditors point out the problems for us."

It turned out to be true. From then on I told the auditors on the front end, "If you can't find at least a half-dozen things we could do better, you haven't done a thorough audit."

Lessons Learned

Over the course of several years we were able to significantly increase our efficiencies, reduce waste, and improve compliance by welcoming feedback from these outside experts. And I learned another lesson. When it comes to getting feedback on your performance as a manager or supervisor, the more feedback you can get, the more likely you'll be to make great strides in your own development.

Action Plans – Some Final Thoughts

Accept Responsibility

> I do the very best I know how - the very best I can; and I mean to keep on doing so until the end.
>
> *Abraham Lincoln*

Nobody else is responsible for your professional and personal development. You're the only one who can initiate change in the way you do your job and live your life. You have many strengths, but you also have room for improvement and growth. Take ownership of where you are right now in your own development and then *decide to grow and develop further*. Accept this as part of your responsibility as a supervisor and manager.

Be Persistent

Maintaining your focus on your own professional development is part of having a long-term commitment to the entire process of individual growth and development. As we know from *Skill 5 – Managing Change*, the process of personal growth and change is often a matter of two steps forward and one step back. It's easy to get distracted by all the stuff you have to deal with each day and push your own development to the back burner because of other commitments. So persistence is a master-key trait when you're engaged in self-development. If you're serious about mastering *Skill 8*, you'll have to be truly committed to personal growth and self-improvement.

Be Resilient

Maintaining a strong commitment to growing yourself is only half the battle; you also need to be resilient in the face of change and challenge. Your initial Action Plan will need frequent adjustments and course corrections, particularly during the first weeks and months. So don't be alarmed if your initial foray into self-improvement proves to be off-target. You're embarking on a different way of viewing yourself, your skills, and your knowledge.

Involve Your Employees

Once you've made some initial progress on your own Action Plan, it's time to start your employees on the same process. They'll appreciate the attention and concern you show for their careers, and they'll want to copy the improvement they see in your development. Of course, not everyone will enthusiastically jump on the bandwagon immediately, but your growth will become a powerful motivator for most of the team. If you demonstrate a willingness to adjust, persist, and take setbacks in stride, it's more likely that your employees will too. Your confidence in your own ability to improve – and your expressions of confidence, enthusiasm, and support – will help increase their confidence. Everybody wins when everyone is growing.

Get Moving Now!

As you've read this book you probably had ideas or spotted suggestions that might be useful in your particular situation. Chances are you've thought of one or more areas in your job that could stand some development or improvement. If you're unsure where to begin, select one major goal from one of the other *8 Essential Skills* and list each activity you'll do to develop yourself in that area.

You can focus on just one goal at a time or you can go through the same steps for a second goal. The process is always the same, no matter how many goals you set for yourself. Set a goal, identify some objectives, and define specific activities that will help you meet those objectives – all written down in some sort of Action Plan. You can use this Action Plan approach to guide your professional development for the rest of your career.

What's the next step now? Turn to the final chapter, *Putting It All Together,* for some thoughts about implementing *The 8 Essential Skills for Supervisors & Managers.*

> When one door of happiness closes, another opens; but often we look so long at the closed door that we do not see the one which has opened for us.
>
> *Helen Keller*

Resources to Help Build Your Action Plan

There are lots of resources to help you develop and implement your Action Plan. Here are a few:

This Book. Use the information in this book as a personal guide and source of ideas. If nothing else, it will help you start thinking about how you can grow yourself. It contains useful information such as:

- Checklists and self-scored surveys
- Lists of tips and suggestions
- Reading list suggestions (see *Appendix*)

Readings & Resource Materials. Explore other books, videos, audiotapes, trade journals, general business publications, podcasts, the Internet, and offerings in your organization's training department.

Your Network, Mentor & Manager. Talk with colleagues inside and outside of your organization, friends in other fields who seem to be on top of things, peers in other parts of the organization who seem to be succeeding, your manager and their manager, and others.

Other Tools.

- Recent performance reviews and feedback from your current work
- Data from a 360° feedback survey
- Informal conversations with your boss and your co-workers

PUTTING IT ALL TOGETHER

"It's easy to make a buck. It's a lot tougher to make a difference."

Tom Brokaw

THE **8** ESSENTIAL SKILLS

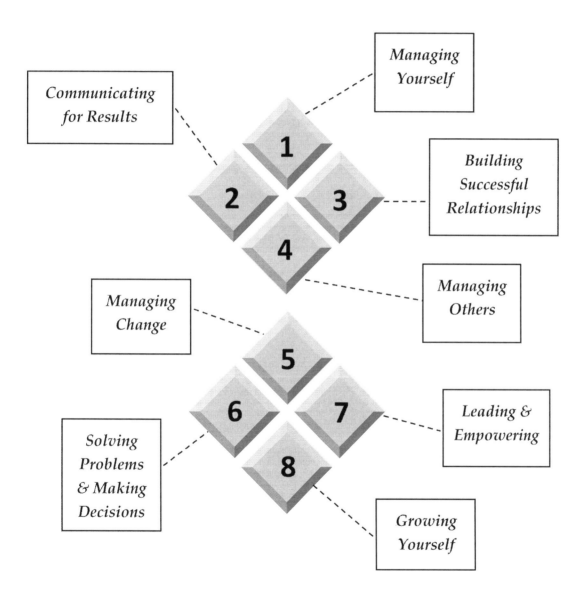

Managing Yourself

Communicating for Results

1

2

3

Building Successful Relationships

4

Managing Others

Managing Change

5

6

7

Leading & Empowering

Solving Problems & Making Decisions

8

Growing Yourself

Chapter 37
Putting It All Together

Now that you've reached this point in *The 8 Essential Skills*, you're much better equipped to be successful as a supervisor or manager. We've covered a lot of ground in these pages and given you plenty to think about. You might have a better idea of who you are as a manager, what you're good at, and what needs more work. If you've created and started working on your own developmental Action Plan, so much the better.

In many ways, though, you're just beginning your journey to managerial excellence. Why just beginning? Because developing yourself and becoming expert at the *8 Essential Skills* is a life-long process. So let's think a bit about what you've learned within these pages.

The Job of the Manager

Before learning about the individual *Skills*, you learned what the work of a supervisor and manager includes. Unless you're relatively experienced at the business of managing, you probably thought that the first section of this book seemed a little overwhelming. Supervising and managing successfully means keeping lots of projects, tasks, programs, products, services, and personalities moving forward. It's no wonder some people compare managing a team to herding grasshoppers! It's all about understanding and successfully meeting the wide variety of expectations held by different stakeholders who somehow relate to you in your job. And then there are your own expectations layered on top of theirs. It's a tough job, a challenging job, and not everyone's ideal job, but it's a tremendously rewarding job too.

> Laughter is inner jogging.
> *Norman Cousins*

Managing Yourself

It's no wonder that self-management is *Skill 1*. It's almost impossible to be successful at managing and supervising others unless you can effectively manage yourself. And managing yourself is only possible if you understand who you are: your personality preferences, your learning style, the kinds of information you prefer to work with, and your skills, all combining to make you the unique person you are. Once you know yourself and understand what drives you, more intelligent and informed choices open for you and you learn to focus on the truly important issues.

Communicating for Results

There's no way you (or anybody else) are going to successfully manage other people without good communication skills. Communication is so critical that it's *Skill 2*, second only to self-management. The four communication components (verbal, nonverbal, written, and listening) combine to form a set of core skills that every successful manager must master. No doubt you'll be better at some aspects of communication than others, but striving to become a more effective communicator is likely to be an important part of your ongoing plan for self-development.

Building Successful Relationships

Skill 3 is at the heart of your success as a manager. When work relationships are healthy, open, and cooperative, the entire organization benefits from a smoother flow of information, improved collaboration and teamwork, mutual respect, and a willingness to help each other succeed. Organizations with solid relationships are simply a lot more rewarding places to work in. Divisive organizational politics is reduced, there's a shared feeling of common mission, and the atmosphere is focused on "win-win."

Managing Others

The work of a manager is different from the work of their team. The manager provides direction, information, and support to the team members, helping *them* to do the work. Whatever approach to supervising and managing seems to make the most sense to you, you'll need to learn a variety of techniques to get the results you want. And since very few teams are comprised of only star players, you know you'll be managing people with different skills, experience, education/training, attitudes, and intelligence. By now you've also discovered that effectively managing your boss is part of your job as a supervisor or manager. Learning how to utilize *Skill 4* is a major milestone on your professional road to success.

Managing Change

Regardless of the kind or size of organization you work in, you're going to be operating in an ever-changing environment. Even if policies and procedures don't change a lot where you are, the external environment shifts and changes constantly. *Skill 5* helps you understand the process of change and how to help your employees and colleagues embrace the reality of change. It's an advanced skill for supervisors and managers.

Solving Problems and Making Decisions

Skill 6 helps equip you to see problems as simply part of the daily ebb and flow of life and work. The kinds of problems *you* need to solve are not so different from those faced by most supervisors and managers. And think about it; if there were no problems, why would the organization need you? Having a variety of tools and techniques to use for solving problems and making decisions just adds to your professional toolkit.

Leading and Empowering

Skill 7 is about leadership – and about the difference between *leading* and *managing*. Leaders manage and managers lead; your organization needs you to be *both* a leader and a manager. Don't panic. Leadership is a skill that can be learned by nearly anyone. Of course, leading a team involves empowering your employees. But empowering them effectively requires a lot more than just turning them loose and letting them figure things out on their own.

Growing Yourself

Skill 8 gives you the opportunity to take the knowledge you acquired in *Skills 1-7* and use that to create your personal developmental Action Plan. Your willingness to *practice* the *8 Essential Skills* and your commitment to growing and developing your abilities as a manager has a lot to do with how successful you'll be. When all is said and done, personal and professional growth is not an option; it's a basic requirement for success in work as in life.

> Success doesn't come to you . . . you go to it.
> *Marva Collins*

When you've mastered the *8 Essential Skills*, you'll be significantly more effective as a supervisor, manager, and human being. Helping you to grow, develop, and become the best you can be is, after all, the purpose of this book.

Best wishes for the future!

Paul Knudstrup

APPENDIX

Appendix

Table of Contents

About the Author   357

Reference List   358

Other Recommended Readings and Resources   359

Colleagues and Associates   361

Management Skills Self-Assessment   364

Distribution of MBTI Types: Females and Males   367

Hemispheric Preference Exercise   368

Information Processing Preferences Exercise   370

Flow Chart   371

Post-Decision Checklist   372

Fishbone Diagram   374

The 5 "Whys" Method   375

The Phoenix Checklist   376

Developmental Action Plan Form: Sample   378

Developmental Action Plan Form: Blank   380

About the Author

Paul Knudstrup is president of Midwest Consulting Group, Inc. (www.midwgroup.com), based in Kalamazoo, Mich. He has been involved in the training and development field for more than 30 years. In addition to consulting with a wide variety of corporate and nonprofit clients, Paul has designed and delivered training programs for more than 100 organizations from across the globe. He has also served as a guest faculty member, speaker, and workshop leader at a number of universities.

Paul's professional areas of interest and expertise include organizational strategy, leadership, personal productivity, management development, action planning, nonprofit fund development, and executive coaching. With his extensive knowledge of organizations, management, and leadership – and decades of actual management experience – he has a wealth of practical experience to draw from.

Paul's academic background includes bachelor's and master's degrees and doctoral work at Western Michigan University. A native of central Michigan, he is married with one daughter and granddaughter. In his spare time he is a private pilot, plays jazz flute for fun, and includes vintage auto racing among his many interests.

Reference List

Allen, D. (2001). *Getting Things Done: The Art of Stress-Free Productivity.* Viking.

Bennis, W., & Nanus, B. (1985). *Leaders: The Strategies for Taking Charge.* Harper & Row.

Blakely, M. (2000). *Why Not You? Understanding Why You Do What You Do.* Azuray Learning, Inc.

Blanchard, K., & Johnson, S. (1982). *The One Minute Manager.* William Morrow.

Buckingham, M., & Clifton, D. (2001). *Now, Discover Your Strengths: How to Develop Your Unique Talents and Strengths.* Free Press.

Collins, J., & Porras, J. (1994). *Built To Last: Successful Habits of Visionary Companies.* Harper Collins.

Covey, S. (1989). *The 7 Habits of Highly Effective People: Powerful Lessons in Personal Change.* Simon & Schuster.

Crosby, P. (1984). *Quality without Tears: The Art of Hassle-Free Management.* McGraw-Hill.

DePree, M. (1992). *Leadership Jazz.* Currency Doubleday.

Gladwell, M. (2000). *The Tipping Point.* Little Brown & Co.

Helmstetter, S. (1989). *Choices: Manage Your Choices and You Will Manage Your Life.* Pocket Books.

Hersey, P., Blanchard, K., & Johnson, D. (2001). *Management of Organizational Behavior: Leading Human Resources.* Prentice Hall.

Juran, J. (1988). *Juran on Planning For Quality.* Free Press.

Koneya, M., & Barbour, A. (1976). *Louder Than Words: Nonverbal Communication.* Charles E. Merrill Publishing.

Laney, M. (2002). *The Introvert Advantage: How to Thrive in an Extrovert World.* Workman.

Leslie, J., & Van Velsor, E. (1996). *A Look at Derailment Today: North America and Europe.* Center for Creative Leadership Press.

MBTI Manual. (1998). *A Guide to the Development and Use of the Myers-Briggs Type Indicator* (3rd ed.). Consulting Psychologists Press, Inc.

McGregor, D. (2005). *The Human Side of Enterprise* (Annotated ed.) McGraw-Hill.

Mintzburg, H. (1980). *The Nature of Managerial Work.* Prentice Hall.

Other Recommended Readings and Resources

Albrecht, K. (1980). *Brain Power: Learn to Improve Your Thinking Skills.* Prentice Hall Press.

Allen, D. (2008). *Making It All Work: Winning at the Game of Work and the Business of Life.* Viking.

Allen, D. (2003). *Ready for Anything: 52 Productivity Principles for Work & Life.* Viking.

Association for Psychological Type International [APTi]. www.aptinternational.org. APT International, 9650 Rockville Pike, Bethesda, MD 20814-3998.

Bandler, R. (1989). *Using Your Brain For A Change.* Real People Press.

Benfari, R. (1999). *Understanding and Changing Your Management Style.* Jossey-Bass.

Block, P. (1987). *Empowered Manager: Positive Political Skills at Work.* Jossey-Bass.

Bly, R., & Booth, W. (1988). *A Little Book on the Human Shadow.* Harper San Francisco.

Buckingham, M., & Coffman, C. (1999). *First, Break all the Rules: What the World's Greatest Managers do Differently.* Simon & Schuster.

Buzan, T. (1983). *Use Both Sides of Your Brain: New Techniques to Help You Read Efficiently.* Dutton.

Clifton, D. (1992). *Soar with your Strengths.* Dell.

Covey, S., Merrill, R., et al. (1994). *First Things First.* Simon & Schuster.

Covey, S. (1990). *Principle-Centered Leadership.* Summit Books.

David Allen Co. www.davidco.com. 407-F Bryant Circle, Ojai, CA 93023

DeGeus, A. (2002). *Living Company: Habits for Survival in a Turbulent Business Environment.* Havard Business School Press.

Drucker, P. (1995). *Managing in a Time of Great Change.* Dutton.

Drucker, P. (1982). *Practice of Management.* Perennial Library.

Drucker, P. (1977). *People and Performance.* Harper's College Press.

Garfield, C. (1992). *Second to None: How Our Smartest Companies Put People First.* Irwin.

Gilley, J., & Boughton, N. (1996). *Stop Managing, Start Coaching: How Performance Coaching Can Enhance Commitment and Improve Productivity.* Irwin.

Harvey, J. (1988). *The Abilene Paradox: And Other Meditations on Management.* Lexington Books/ University Associates.

Helmstetter, S. (1989). *Choices: Manage Your Choices and You will Manage Your Life.* Pocket Books.

Iacocca, L. (2007). *Where Have All the Leaders Gone?* Scribner.

Kanter, R., Stein, B., et al. (1992). *The Challenge of Organizational Change: How Companies Experience It and Leaders Guide It.* Free Press.

Katzenbach, J. (2000). *Peak Performance: Aligning the Hearts and Minds of Your Employees.* Harvard Business School Press.

Kotter, J. (1999). *What Leaders Really Do.* Harvard Business School Press.

Kriegel, R., & Brandt, D. (1996). *Sacred Cows Make the Best Burgers: Developing Change-Ready People and Organizations.* Warner Books.

Kroeger, O., & Thuesen, J. (1992). *Type Talk At Work.* Delecorte Press.

Kroeger, O., & Thuesen, J. (1988). *Type Talk: Or How to Determine Your Personality Type and Change Your Life.* Delacorte Press.

Lencioni, P. (2002). *Five Dysfunctions of a Team: A Leadership Fable.* Jossey-Bass.

Loehr, J. (2003). *Power of Full Engagement: Managing Energy, Not Time, Is the Key to High Performance and Personal Renewal.* Free Press.

Lundin, W. (1993). *Healing Manager: How to Build Quality Relationships & Productive Cultures at Work.* Berrett Koehler.

Matejka, K., & Dunsing, R. (1995). *Manager's Guide to the Millennium.* AMACOM.

Maxwell, J. (1993). *Developing the Leader Within You.* Thomas Nelson.

Michalko, M. (1991). *Thinkertoys: A Handbook of Business Creativity for the 90s.* 10 Speed Press.

Northouse, P. (2004). *Leadership: Theory and Practice.* Sage.

Rath, T. (2007). *StrengthsFinder 2.0.* Gallup Press.

Rosenthal, R., & Jacobson, L. (1968). *Pygmalion in the Classroom.* Holt, Rinehart & Winston.

Sinetar, M. (1989). *Do What You Love, The Money Will Follow: Discovering Your Right Livelihood.* Dell.

Smith, P. (1988). *Taking Charge: Making the Right Choices.* Avery.

Stone, D., Patton, B., et al. (1999). *Difficult Conversations: How to Discuss What Matters Most.* Viking Penguin Group.

Colleagues and Associates

Paul Knudstrup

Paul is the president and founder of Midwest Consulting Group, Inc. He focuses his consulting work on strategic planning, management team development, succession planning, management selection, performance management, and personal productivity. He also assists nonprofit organizations with fund development strategy. See "About the Author" for more information.

PaulK@MidwGroup.com   www.MidwGroup.com   8essentialskills.wordpress.com

Janet Andersen

Jan is the owner of Beyond Words, Inc. She specializes in organizational communications, general and technical writing and editing, grant/proposal development, and book editing. She has a niche expertise in helping faculty members and other professionals prepare articles for submission to peer-reviewed journals, and coaches/consults with authors. Jan works primarily with health care, higher education, and nonprofit organizations. janbeyond@earthlink.net   www.janbeyond.com

Mary Jo Asmus

Mary Jo is the owner of Aspire Collaborative Services. She is an executive coach who works with senior leaders and their teams, facilitating leadership assessment, development, and team building. She specializes in helping senior leaders become every bit as strategic about their relationships as they are about achieving business results. Mary.Jo.Asmus@aspire-cs.com   www.aspire-cs.com

Michael Busch

The owner of Busch + Company, Mike's expertise is in coaching, leadership development, managing work conversations, high-performance team development, and strategic business communication systems. In addition to his work with clients, Mike is an adjunct professor at Jones International University. He has published several articles, has been featured in "Training" magazine, and was cited by the Tom Peters Group for his innovations in management and leadership development. MBuschphd@gmail.com

Chris Christensen

Chris is the owner of Christensen Consulting Group and teaches in Marquette University's Executive M.B.A. Program. He also develops and presents business seminars. Chris is an expert in manufacturing management, with more than 25 years of experience in a variety of business positions. His focus is in lean manufacturing, operations management, supply chain management, logistics, and materials management Chris has had more than 70 articles published in professional and trade magazines. He is also the co-author or contributing author to two books. Rchristensen1958@wi.rr.com

Joan Dzuro

Joan is president and CEO of Dzuro and Associates, a firm specializing in HR consulting. She has held HR positions during a 30-year career in the aerospace, oil, newspaper publishing, manufacturing, high-tech, insurance, and medical industries. Her firm assists clients by training newly promoted HR professionals, creating and maintaining new HR departments, training teams in effective management skills, and conducting HR audits, as well as updating policy manuals, handbooks, and safety manuals. JDzuro@msn.com www.dzuroandassociates.com

John Greenhoe

John is a fundraising expert with more than 20 years of nonprofit leadership experience working in higher education and grassroots organizational settings. Placing a strong emphasis on relationship-building strategies, John is a seasoned trainer of beginning, mid-level, and advanced development teams and has served as an adjunct faculty member in fundraising for Western Michigan University and Grand Valley State University. John has expertise in annual giving, major gifts, and foundation and corporate fundraising. Greenhoe@hotmail.com.

Gretchen Johnson

Gretchen is the founder and principal of WordPlay Marketing Communications, a boutique marketing agency that helps individuals and organizations develop and tell powerful stories. Her more than 20 years of experience includes a range of client-side roles in marketing, sales communications, and advertising. She specializes in building marketing programs from the ground up and has managed large and small campaigns, including multi-million dollar global branding initiatives. Gretchen@virtualwordplay.com www.virtualwordplay.com

Gail Lutey

Gail has held a variety of HR management positions within companies both large and small. She started her career with General Motors and Unisys Corporation, developing college recruiting programs and managing extensive direct hiring activities. During over 20 years in HR she has worked for and with GM, Unisys, several IT services companies, and a variety of small business owners, providing strategic planning and human resource services. She provides clients with the entire spectrum of HR services. GLutey146169MI@comcast.net

Vicky Scherff

Vicky manages the MCG office and helps us keep all the balls in the air. She has worked in the public accounting, telecommunications, banking, and financial services industries. She has assisted a wide variety of clients with office organization and workflow consulting services and has designed administrative systems that help improve productivity, efficiency, and space utilization. VickyS@MidwGroup.com

Holly Office Dog

Holly is our office dog. She enjoys working with us in the office, provides comic relief, chases off any vicious squirrels, and consults on any projects involving dog treats. She is an expert in eating, sleeping, begging, and hanging out. She doesn't do E-mail.

Management Skills Self-Assessment

What is your *current* level of success in the *8 Essential Skills*?
Assess yourself using a 1-5 scale (5 = highest)

Skill 1 - **Managing Yourself**

	1 - 5
1. How you use time	
2. Your approach to accomplishing the goals and objectives of your unit and organization	
3. How you recognize and deal with the really important issues	
4. How open and approachable you are to your employees and others	
5. Your willingness to keep up to date technically	
6. Your level of self-confidence and ego maturity	
7. Your willingness and ability to make decisions	

Skill 2 - **Communicating for Results**

1. How openly, candidly, and frequently you communicate	
2. How straightforward you are dealing with employees' performance	
3. How effectively you conduct team meetings	
4. How willing your employees are to bring up problems and issues	
5. How well you write	
6. How well you listen	
7. How effectively you scan the environment	
8. How well you present information to others	

Skill 3 – **Building Successful Relationships**

1. How supportive and helpful you are to employees	
2. How effectively you resolve conflicts	
3. How willing you are to confront tough issues	
4. Your willingness to involve employees in setting their own goals	
5. How well you promote teamwork	
6. Your willingness to create and sustain an atmosphere of trust with your people	

Skill 4 - **Managing Others**   1 - 5

1. How well you set challenging objectives with and for your employees	
2. How well you appropriately plan and coordinate the work of the team	
3. How clearly you define specific performance standards for each employee	
4. Your willingness to meet regularly with your employees to discuss their performance	
5. Your willingness to help your employees achieve high performance levels	
6. Your willingness to discuss performance problems with employees and seek their suggestions for improvement	
7. How effectively you use recognition and praise to reward excellent performance	
8. How consistently you recognize good performance more often than criticizing	
9. How committed you are to developing your staff	

Skill 5 - **Managing Change**

1. How well you understand and support change in your organization	
2. How willing you are to look for opportunities to improve your team's results	
3. How quickly and successfully you let people know when plans and goals change	
4. How you go about facilitating the change process within your group	
5. The ease with which you implement changes in direction, priorities, or projects	
6. The level of resistance you exhibit toward imposed or mandated changes	
7. Your willingness to seek out information about why changes are needed	

Skill 6 - **Solving Problems and Making Decisions**

1. Your willingness to make clear-cut decisions when needed	
2. Your willingness to involve employees and others in generating ideas, suggestions, and alternatives to complex problems	
3. Your willingness to consider new information, differing opinions, or viewpoints contrary to your own	

Skill 6 – Solving Problems and Making Decisions, *continued*   1 - 5

4. Your ability to solve problems and make decisions with less information than you would prefer	
5. Your ability to understand the financial implications of your decisions	
6. Your ability to use critical thinking skills to weigh alternatives	
7. Your ability to provide guidance, support, and encouragement to others	

Skill 7 - Leading and Empowering

1. Your ability to follow up on important issues and actions	
2. Your willingness to clarify who is responsible for what within the group	
3. Your willingness to be open and encourage people to express their feelings and viewpoints, including when they disagree with you	
4. Your ability to empower individuals in a purposeful manner	
5. Your ability to keep a positive focus in front of the team	
6. Your willingness to help others overcome roadblocks and resistance to moving toward goals	
7. Your commitment to staff and team development	

Skill 8 - Growing Yourself

1. Your ability to understand your own strengths, weaknesses, and opportunities for improvement	
2. Your willingness to request and utilize honest feedback from others	
3. Your willingness to create and effectively use a personal development action plan	
4. Your commitment to lifelong learning and personal growth as an evolving standard	
5. Your persistence and willingness to try again and again until you achieve your goals	
6. Your resilience in the face of change and challenge	
7. Your willingness to actively encourage the same behaviors in your employees and colleagues	

Distribution of MBTI Types

ISTJ 6.9%	ISFJ 19.4%	INFJ 1.6%	INTJ 0.8%
ISTP 2.4%	ISFP 9.9%	INFP 4.6%	INTP 1.8%
ESTP 3.0%	ESFP 10.1%	ENFP 9.7%	ENTP 2.4%
ESTJ 6.3%	ESFJ 16.9%	ENFJ 3.3%	ENTJ 0.9%

E	52.5%
I	47.5%
S	74.9%
N	25.1%

FEMALES
GENERAL U.S. POPULATION
Percentage Distribution

T	24.5%
F	75.5%
J	56.2%
P	43.8%

SOURCE: (MBTI MANUAL, 1998)

ISTJ 16.4%	ISFJ 8.1%	INFJ 1.3%	INTJ 3.3%
ISTP 8.5%	ISFP 7.6%	INFP 4.1%	INTP 4.8%
ESTP 5.6%	ESFP 6.9%	ENFP 6.4%	ENTP 4.0%
ESTJ 11.2%	ESFJ 7.5%	ENFJ 1.6%	ENTJ 2.7%

E	45.9%
I	54.1%
S	71.7%
N	28.3%

MALES
GENERAL U.S. POPULATION
Percentage Distribution

T	56.5%
F	43.5%
J	52.0%
P	48.0%

SOURCE: (MBTI MANUAL, 1998)

Hemispheric Preference Exercise

Mark the one statement from each pair that best describes you. If you're unsure about an item, your initial gut reaction is usually the most accurate.

A   B

_____ You like studying with a group.
_____ You like studying by yourself.

_____ You ignore the instructions and just begin a task.
_____ You read the instructions before beginning a task.

_____ You often have several tasks you are working on at the same time.
_____ You usually finish each task before moving on to the next.

_____ You will begin a task without waiting to see how other people are doing it.
_____ You like to see how other people are doing a task before you begin.

_____ You remember the main ideas better than the details when you read.
_____ You remember the details better than the main ideas when you read.

_____ You prefer essay tests where you can explain your answer.
_____ You prefer tests that are multiple choice or true/false.

_____ Your workspace often gets cluttered.
_____ Your workspace is usually fairly organized.

_____ You like team competition rather than individual competition.
_____ You like individual competition rather than team competition.

_____ You like to choose how to perform a task.
_____ You like to know exactly how a task is to be performed.

A   *B*

_____   You want to see the results of your tests, but don't care about correcting answers.

_____   You want to go over your tests and correct any mistakes.

_____   You have difficulty ignoring distractions while you are studying or working.

_____   You can easily ignore distractions while you are studying or working.

_____   You want to know the whole assignment before working on the details.

_____   You prefer to break down an assignment into parts and work on the details.

_____   You ask other people for input in making decisions.

_____   You like to come to decisions by thinking them through by yourself.

_____   You tend to organize papers and documents into piles.

_____   You like to have a detailed filing system for sorting papers.

_____   You are more motivated to read a book that includes pictures and diagrams.

_____   You are more motivated to read a book because of its title and cover, even if it doesn't include pictures.

_____   Total Marks in Each Column

Source: (Blakely, 2000)
Used by Permission

Add the total number of marks in each column and enter them on the line above. The column with the higher number *may* indicate your hemispheric preference. Column **A** indicates a right-brain preference; Column **B** indicates a left-brain preference.

Information Processing Preferences Exercise

Sensory Checklist

Mark all of the following statements that you feel strongly describe yourself. You may have several items checked in a section, only a couple, or none at all.

Kinesthetic

☐ You learn best when you can perform a task.
☐ You have trouble paying attention if you sit still for a long time.
☐ You often slouch in your chair or fidget if you sit still too long.
☐ You feel like you always have to be moving some part of your body.
☐ Movies or books must be full of action to keep your attention.

Auditory

☐ You talk out loud to yourself to solve problems or vent anger.
☐ You need to hear yourself say things in order to remember them.
☐ To memorize information, you need to repeat it aloud or to yourself.
☐ You would rather listen to a description of something than read about it.
☐ You can easily remember information put to a beat or music.

Visual

☐ You learn best if you can see the information you need to learn.
☐ You like to see charts and pictures, in addition to text, when studying.
☐ You are drawn to bright, colorful objects.
☐ You often visualize situations in your head as you think about them.
☐ You remember something better if you see it in writing.

Source : (Blakely, 2000)
Used by Permission

Count the number of boxes you checked in each section. The section with the most marks is probably your dominant or conscious sense. The section with the second highest number of marks is likely your support or subconscious sense. The section with the fewest marks is probably your weakest or unconscious sense.

Flow Chart

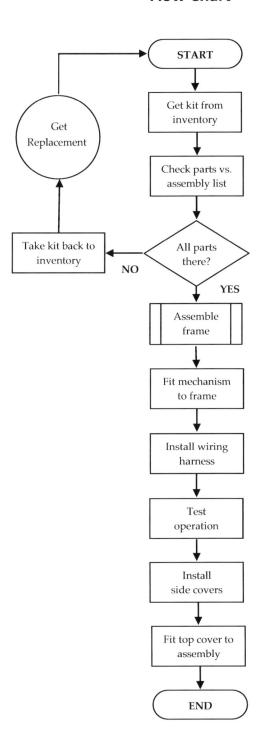

Post-Decision Checklist

Some problems and decisions are mission-critical or have far-reaching implications for your unit or the entire organization. When the issue is important, the stakes for you professionally, your team, and perhaps your organization may be high. Even when you've used a good process, balancing your analytical left brain with your creative, intuitive right brain, you can still make a poor decision due to factors you might not have anticipated.

So once you've made a decision – or when you think you're close to committing to a particular course of action – ask yourself a series of questions *before* actually implementing the decision. The following checklist may be helpful:

☐ Are there additional risks growing out of your selected alternative that haven't already been addressed? What are they? Is the level of risk acceptable? If not, is there another alternative that carries less risk?

☐ How will you communicate the solution/decision to those who are involved? Who will be negatively affected by the decision? How do you plan to deal with their potentially negative reaction? Is there any information that they should have before the decision is announced or implemented?

☐ Is there anyone else you want (or need) to consult with before moving ahead? Do you know who *all* the important stakeholders are and how your preferred solution will be viewed by them?

☐ How serious are the political consequences of this alternative?

☐ Are there any ethical or values-system consequences to this alternative that could prevent you from succeeding? How does this decision and its likely results feel to you?

☐ Do you have the systems in place to make this decision work successfully?

☐ If you read about this decision on the front page of the (*insert the name of your local paper*) and it was accurately reported, would you feel comfortable with that?

(Continued on next page)

☐ What might be the second- and third-order effects of this alternative that you haven't thought about? Will the recommended choice affect how someone downstream (e.g., other units or your customers) does *their* work? If so, have you involved them in the decision-making process?

☐ Are there any potential negative AND important consequences you haven't thought of yet? Any unintended consequences that you haven't thought through that *could* occur?

☐ Will this decision enhance the reputation of this organization and its leadership?

Obviously, you won't use this checklist for routine daily decisions or minor problems. However, when the stakes are high and the decision has far-reaching implications, walking yourself and/or your team through the checklist might save you from making a major mistake. At that point, if you get pushback from important stakeholders, you'll be more confident that you have made the correct decision.

Fishbone Diagram

A Fishbone Diagram or Cause-and-Effect Diagram can reveal the relationship between a given outcome and all of the factors that influence that outcome. The diagram helps to show the relationship of the parts to the whole by:

- Determining the factors that cause a certain outcome (or effect)

- Focusing on a specific issue without resorting to complaints and irrelevant discussion

- Determining the root causes of a given effect

- Identifying areas where there's a lack of data

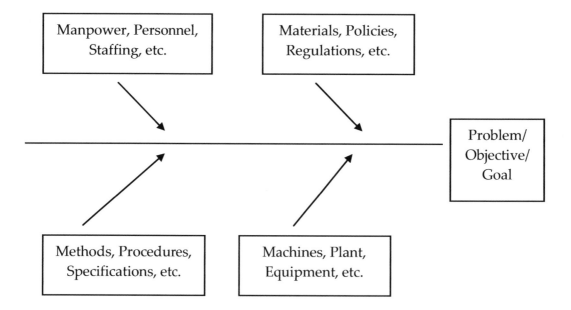

This technique works well whether you're trying to accomplish an objective (a positive effect) or solve a problem (a negative effect). Focusing on problems can produce finger pointing, while focusing on desired outcomes fosters pride and ownership over productive areas. The resulting positive atmosphere often enhances the group's creativity.

The "5 Whys" Method

The "5 Whys" is a question-asking tool used to analyze the relationship of cause and effect in a problem. The goal of the "5 Whys" method is to determine a root cause of the defect or problem.

Example:

PROBLEM STATEMENT
My car will not start.
    WHY?
The battery is dead.
    WHY?
The alternator is not functioning.
    WHY?
The alternator belt has broken.
    WHY?
The alternator belt was well beyond its useful service life and has never been replaced.
    WHY?
I have not been maintaining my car according to the recommended service schedule.
    ROOT CAUSE

While asking "Why?" five times is generally sufficient to get to a root cause, additional levels of "Why?" may be needed in certain situations. The point is to encourage the individual or team to avoid assumptions by tracing the problem directly through the layers until the *real* root cause is discovered. The "5 Whys" is more "quick and dirty" than other methods, but it's useful for a rapid, general approach to determining a root cause.

The Phoenix Checklist

The Problem

When you have a challenge in front of you, knowing what questions to ask can make the difference between doing something extraordinary and doing the same old thing. This checklist was developed by the CIA to help their agents successfully deal with complex problems and issues.

- Why is it necessary to solve the problem?
- What benefits will you receive by solving the problem?
- What is the unknown?
- What is it you don't yet understand?
- What is the information you have?
- What isn't the problem?
- Is the information you have sufficient? Or is it insufficient? Or redundant? Or contradictory?
- Should you draw a diagram of the problem? A figure?
- Where are the boundaries of the problem?
- Can you separate the various parts of the problem? Can you write them down? What are the relationships of the parts of the problem?
- What are the constants (i.e., things that can't be changed) of the problem?
- Have you seen this problem before?
- Have you seen this problem in a slightly different form?
- Do you know of a related problem?
- Can you think of a familiar problem having the same or a similar unknown?
- Suppose you find a problem related to yours that has already been solved. Can you use it? Can you use its method?
- Can you restate your problem? How many different ways can you restate it? More general? More specific? Can the rules be changed?
- What are the best, worst, and most probable cases you can imagine?

The Plan

- Can you solve the whole problem? Part of the problem?

- What would you like the resolution to be? Can you picture it?

- How much of the unknown can you determine?

- Can you derive something useful from the information you have?

- Have you used all the information you have?

- Have you taken into account all essential notions in the problem?

- Can you separate the steps in the problem-solving process? Can you determine the correctness of each step?

- What creative thinking techniques can you use to generate ideas? How many different techniques?

- Can you see the results? How many different kinds of results can you see?

- How many different ways have you tried to solve the problem?

- What have others done?

- Can you intuit the solution? Can you check the result?

- What should be done? How should it be done?

- Where should it be done?

- When should it be done?

- Who should do it?

- What do you need to do at this time?

- Who will be responsible for what?

- Can you use this problem to solve some other problem?

- What is the unique set of qualities that makes this problem what it is and like none other?

Developmental Action Plan Form: Sample

Work on no more than three developmental goals. Create no more than three written development objectives for each goal. Your goals may focus on areas of strength you want to leverage or areas needing improvement. The key is to create a plan that helps you grow in areas that are important to you in your current role *and* the future of your organization.

My Developmental Areas for the coming year are:

1. Performance Feedback	2. Staff Development	3. Problem Solving

My Developmental Goals are: (What will be different a year from now? What end result am I looking for?)

1.	To increase the frequency & quality of performance-related feedback I provide to team members, improving the productivity of my team by 15% during the coming year.
2.	To get all team members cross-trained in at least two other positions by year-end.
3.	To continually reduce any errors in our team's output, achieving XX% quality by year-end.

List at least two Developmental Objectives for each Goal

Goal 1	Goal 2	Goal 3
Hold weekly performance discussion with each team member	Involve team members in cross-training decision choices	Improve accuracy of quality data for comparison purposes
Establish performance improvement targets with each team member	Create & manage the cross-training process in cooperation with Human Resources	Find, select, and complete a Quality Improvement course.

Action Plan Components – Goal #1 (Performance Feedback)

Projects/Tasks	Who is Involved?	Resources Needed	Timing / Timeframe	Done
Review last year's performance data	Mgr./HR	Performance reviews	Week One	
Schedule 1st round of meetings with team members to gather their perspectives	Assistant	Calendar (mine & team)	Week Two	
Meet with each team member re data	Me + Team	Clarify expectations	Weeks Three/Four	
Create tool to track performance results	HR	Hr's sign-off on format	Week Five	
Establish performance targets with each team member	Individual team members	Current standards & historical output data	Week Six	
Have informal weekly 5-10 minute feedback discussion	Individual team members	Track observations	Week Six - Ongoing	

Action Plan Components – Goal #2 (Staff Development)

Projects/Tasks	Who is Involved?	Resources Needed	Timing / Timeframe	Done
Discuss developmental needs/wants with each team member in 1-on-1 sessions	Individual team members	Discuss resources available with HR	Week Three	
Schedule team meeting to discuss cross-training project & gather input	Entire team	None – schedule meeting	Week Five	
Create rotating cross-training plan	Mgr's Input	Timeframe needed to cross-train on each position	Week Ten	
Devise method to evaluate cross-training progress and make adjustments	Mgr., HR, Team	Approval for evaluation & test protocols	Week Twelve	
Plan & hold quarterly team meetings to review progress and make adjustments	Entire team	None – schedule meeting	Ongoing	

Action Plan Components – Goal #3 (Problem Solving)

Projects/Tasks	Who is Involved?	Resources Needed	Timing/ Timeframe	Done
Review QI data & discuss w/ QI Manager	QI Mgr.	QI data for past 24 months	Week Two	
Research available QI courses locally and online	Assistant	My time and mindshare	Week Four	
Set meeting w/ QI Manager to pick their brain	QI Mgr.	Research results	Week Six	

Use additional paper as needed. Review your plan with your supervisor or manager, discuss any differences, and obtain their agreement with your plan. Sign and date below.

_____   _____
      Action Plan Originator   **Supervisor/Manager**

Date: _____   **Date:** _____

Developmental Action Plan Form: Blank

Work on no more than three developmental goals. Create no more than three written development objectives for each goal. Your goals may focus on areas of strength you want to leverage or areas needing improvement. The key is to create a plan that helps you grow in areas that are important to you in your current role *and* the future of your organization.

My Developmental Areas for the coming year are:

1.	2.	3.

My Developmental Goals are: (What will be different a year from now? What end result am I looking for?)

1
2.
3.

List at least two Developmental Objectives for each Goal

Goal 1	Goal 2	Goal 3

Action Plan Components – Goal #1

Projects/Tasks	Who is Involved?	Resources Needed	Timing / Timeframe	Done

Action Plan Components – Goal #2

Projects/Tasks	Who is Involved?	Resources Needed	Timing / Timeframe	Done

Action Plan Components – Goal #3

Projects/Tasks	Who is Involved?	Resources Needed	Timing/ Timeframe	Done

Use additional paper as needed. Review your plan with your supervisor or manager, discuss any differences, and obtain their agreement with your plan. Sign and date below.

<table>
<tr><td>_____</td><td>_____</td></tr>
<tr><td>**Action Plan Originator**</td><td>**Supervisor/Manager**</td></tr>
</table>

Date: _____   Date:_____

Made in the USA
Charleston, SC
02 May 2011